Praise for *Policing Fraud*

Having known Jim Ratley for over 30 years, I'm aware that he is an incredible storyteller. And the stories in *Policing Fraud*—all true—are incredible!
—*Dr. Joseph T. Wells, CFE, CPA, Founder and Chairman of the Association of Certified Fraud Examiners*

Jim Ratley tells a fascinating story of chasing bad guys—with a gun or a calculator. If you have done either, or want to, read this book! Jim's a tough Texan who lassoed fraud!
—*John Fisher Weber, M.A., CFE, CPP, ACFE Regent Emeritus, Vice President of Risk and Compliance for DIS / District Attorney Investigator*

We become who we are meant to be from our personal history and experiences. Having also served with the Dallas Police Department, Jim's story brings back many of my own memories, both good and bad. After reading this book, I hope that you'll have a new appreciation for those who serve or have served in law enforcement and the burdens they deal with. You will also appreciate the significant contributions of my friend, Jim Ratley, and how he became the person he was meant to be.
—*Walter W. Manning, CFE, President of Investigations MD*

This is an amazing story of how Jim Ratley went from beat cop to CEO of the world's largest anti-fraud organization. Through his journey, he has taken advantage of the skills he learned at each job, improving on them as well as developing new skills as he moved onto different and more challenging opportunities. This book not only provides good insights into what it takes to be a good investigator, but also how to apply those skills in all kinds of situations. It also shows how taking the initiative to do more can lead to an extraordinary and unexpected career.
—*Nancy S. Bradford, CFE, CPA, CIA, Professional Consultant, Cuthbertson and Associates*

In *Policing Fraud: My Journey from Street Cop to Anti-Fraud Leader*, Jim Ratley's journey from Dallas street cop to an international leader in the fight against fraud unfolds like a Dickens novel. Jim has the rare ability to relate a story that is both enthralling and informative. His book transports the reader directly to Jim's elbow, and the turning of each page makes the moment more personal. For those of us interested in understanding human motivation, Jim's book continually places into the reader's mind, "And then what happened?"

    —Don Rabon, CFE, President of Successful Interviewing Techniques

Jim Ratley is the real deal—a cop's cop and a fraud investigator like few others! His rich stories speak volumes about how to live a life with accountability, integrity, and purpose. This is the book if you too want to make a difference in fighting fraud.

    —Martin T. Biegelman, CFE, Chairman of the Board for the Economic Crime
        & Cybersecurity Institute and former Director of Financial Integrity for
        Microsoft Corporation

POLICING FRAUD

MY JOURNEY FROM STREET COP TO ANTI-FRAUD LEADER

JAMES D. RATLEY

For ordering information and other products and services, please contact the Association of Certified Fraud Examiners (ACFE) Membership Department at (512) 478-9000 within the United States or visit www.acfe.com.

ISBN-13: 978-1545318232
ISBN-10: 1545318239

I dedicate this book to Gloria, my wife who makes me the luckiest man alive every day, and to Leslie, Sarah, Matt, and Nikki, for being the best kids in the world while Daddy was on the road.

CONTENTS

CONTENTS

PART ONE

INVESTIGATOR

"The quality of a person's life is in direct proportion to their commitment to excellence, regardless of their chosen field of endeavor." —Vince Lombardi

"If you're going through hell, keep going." —Sir Winston Churchill

CHAPTER 1

DUTY AND DANGER: INTERNAL AFFAIRS

I t started out like any other night in the summer of 1982. I was driving home after having a beer with some fellow officers at the Dallas Police Association Club, a downtown private bar frequented only by people on the force. As usual, I took Interstate 30 out of town, kicking my civilian Ford LTD up to 75 miles per hour on the road to Mesquite, a small city 15 miles east of Dallas. The heat had dropped from daytime's triple digits, but not enough, so I kept the windows down. As I gained speed, rapid thumps of semi-cool wind rushed in. Then a rumbling roar, surging in the darkness, gained on me from behind.

At first I thought it was a weird kind of thunder. But a glance at my rear view mirror showed a bevy of single headlights: motorcycles—lots of them. Damned Bandidos, I muttered, thinking of the numerous times I had arrested members of this notorious biker gang for all kinds of mayhem. Formed in Texas by a Viet Nam veteran who thought other outlaw crews were too tame, the Bandidos were known for mutilating people who crossed them. Our hate-hate relationship had begun earlier when, as a street patrol officer, I had hauled one after another of them into jail. Although I doubted they knew what model car I drove off-duty, I couldn't assume they didn't. If they were behind me now, my dander was up, and I welcomed another chance to tangle.

As my eyes darted again toward the mirror, I had a momentary vision of my service revolver in the bottom left drawer of my desk in Internal Affairs, where I now worked as an investigator. Because it was mostly a desk job, I didn't wear my weapon at all times. That satisfied regulations, but didn't help me now. Perhaps worse, because this was my own car, it had no police radio. Being unarmed and isolated on a dark road was not the best plan if I were indeed being tailed by vengeful misfits.

Sometimes I curse myself, and this was one of them. Instinctively, I refocused that energy on dealing with the motorized herd about to pull even with me. Although I was outnumbered, my 350-horsepower, two-ton sedan could ride steady up to 120 miles per hour, where bikes become hard to handle. I wasn't exactly comfortable with the odds, but I was ready to play them.

Yet something wasn't right. Amid the overall darkness, I could see by the headlights of the last bikes that the leader, closer behind me, wore a helmet—a stylistic no-no among the macho Bandidos. I could also make out that each bike was the same size and had identical red running lights, which again didn't tally with a gang profile. A crazy thought crossed my mind, and I quickly rejected it. An instant later, though, it proved right as the pack surrounded me. While hard to believe, it was definitely happening: About a dozen Dallas Police Department (DPD) highway patrol officers in white helmets and blue uniforms on big white Harley Davidson cruisers advanced in unison like a single organism and enveloped my LTD.

At nearly 80 miles per hour, the leader settled three feet left of my door, and shot me a long icy glare. Through my passenger window, his twin did the same. They made no pull-over gestures, so I maintained speed. It went on like that for several miles as we got farther from Dallas and into the countryside. Just me and my brother officers, flying through the empty darkness, and not another soul around.

My intuitions of revenge were partly right. Only it wasn't the Bandidos who were after me; it was DPD's motorcycle unit. Why? Because I was investigating some of its members for allegedly falsifying their overtime cards to get unearned extra pay. What were they trying to pull tonight? And how could I counter it?

The next few minutes would tell as we sped along, an island of bright lights and thundering engines in the night. The steadiness of our relative positions made it seem, though, as if we were barely moving. And while the cascade of sounds was overwhelming, the only communications between us were the looks we exchanged— the two jocks' cold and hard, mine steady and expressionless. Another tense mile raced by, and yet another. But still the jocks did nothing, letting me sweat it out. We seemed almost frozen in time as each minute dragged by.

Because motor jocks wore elite uniforms, including knee-high, spit-shined boots, and earned slightly better pay than street patrol officers, others in the department sometimes perceived them as arrogant. But the important thing, everyone agreed, was that we all were brothers in arms. So it was unthinkable that these men would do me any harm.

Yet history shows that people might do anything under the right amount of pressure and circumstances. My investigation had turned up irrefutable documentary evidence that 15 motor jocks— working simultaneously on two unrelated and separately managed assignments—had frequently reported working more than 24 hours in a single day, which in some cases doubled their pay. As we sped deeper into the darkness, I wondered what, if anything, these jocks were going to do about me and my investigation.

In front, behind, and on both sides of me, they had the upper hand. All I could do was react. But before I could think of anything to prevent them from eventually forcing me off the road, they called it quits. By some signal I didn't see, the leader apparently had commanded the entire squad to open their throttles all the way in a stupefying display of power. The resulting explosion of blue exhaust from so many big engines clouded the air, flattened the skin on my face and almost deafened me, left behind like I was standing still.

The jocks' message was clear: Lay off. I'd be lying if I said I wasn't scared. But all they accomplished by surrounding my car was to convince me that my investigation was on the right track. The week before, I had called some of them into the Internal Affairs office for questioning, and they had denied everything.

"This entry was just a mistake," one of them told me. "And so were these. It wasn't intentional."

And I said, "Well, gosh, you filled out 12 overtime cards in the last six weeks, and there're errors on ten of them. That's a lot of mistakes."

Right away, this guy answered me with an aggrieved look. "You expect perfection, don't you? Get off our backs. We're doing our best."

He actually had me thinking, "Could I be wrong on this? Could these be accidental clerical errors? These guys couldn't be so stupid as to do it on purpose and think they could keep on getting away with it."

That night on the highway, I got definitive answers to my questions. Yes, those officers were that foolish and unprincipled, and I'd hold them to account for their frauds. As their taillights vanished into the night, I made up my mind to safeguard my evidence and push ahead with the investigation, even though I had close friends in the motorcycle unit.

From my experience in Internal Affairs, I knew very well that these weren't the only officers committing time-card fraud. In another case I was working, street patrol officers had done much the same thing for a fatter paycheck. Their reasons and excuses didn't matter, but I wondered whether Internal Affairs was the right place for me. Fraud cases were the first ones in which I was unable to relate to what the suspects were accused of doing. When I worked on street patrol and someone broke into a home and stole things, I didn't approve of it but I understood the motive. Many of those petty thieves had drug problems and desperately needed whatever cash they could get from a "fence" or a pawnshop. But when I encountered police officers stealing from the city, I was stunned by their mindless dishonesty.

My job, as I saw it, was to expose people and practices that dishonored the integrity and steadfast performance of thousands of other Dallas police officers. They too had financial challenges. They too sometimes felt the sting of perhaps inadequate compensation, unfair treatment, or lack of professional recognition. They too dealt with the countless other injustices and slights—real or imagined—we all faced daily. But that didn't stop them from fulfilling the trust placed in them by their fellow officers and the people of Dallas. So I stayed with Internal Affairs and did my utmost to become a better investigator of the frauds that now formed most of my caseload.

My Word Is My Bond

When I worked in Internal Affairs, I often wondered how police officers could commit frauds that jeopardized their careers, livelihood, and ability to support a family. In some ways, it's an unanswerable question. We all are, to a large extent, mysteries to ourselves and each other. But this much I knew: Because actions matter more than intentions, there could be no justification for betraying those who rely on you. So my actions at home and on the job were going to be as good as I could make them. I was no saint, and still am not, as you'll learn in the following pages. But I try to learn from my mistakes, and when I make a commitment to my family, my friends, my colleagues, or my employer, I honor it.

It was therefore a shock and a deep disappointment to me that DPD did little about the time-card fraud that a couple dozen officers in the motorcycle and street patrol units had committed. A few of the officers involved were transferred to other units; most of the offenders, however, were reprimanded but not disciplined or penalized.

A cynic would have said the results were predictable. But you didn't have to be a starry-eyed optimist to think the department would enforce its own regulations. These requirements supposedly were equivalent to the word of God, and they spelled out everything from when to draw your weapon and how to file arrest warrants and expense reports to what meritorious citation ribbons you could wear above your badge. Although these rules numbered in the hundreds, if you didn't adhere to them, you'd be cited for noncompliance, which would negatively affect your pay, chances for promotion, duty station, assignments, working partners, and days off—in short, your entire professional life. So I followed these sensible rules and expected the department to enforce them fairly without exception.

But for the dozens of officers implicated in the time-card frauds, there was safety in numbers. Prosecuting so many of them would have severely tarnished the department's public image and was therefore politically unacceptable to the top brass. So, despite my lieutenant's and my protests, the case was hushed up and forgotten as quickly as possible. But it was clear to me—and to any crook in DPD—that the bigger the fraud, the smaller the punishment would be.

Truth, Duty, and Friendship

I arrived at Internal Affairs after spending two years in DPD's Child Abuse Unit. I had earned a new, less depressing assignment. Few investigators can deal with child abuse on a daily basis for very long, and I was no exception. Sensing that it was time for me to move on, my sergeant arranged my transfer but didn't inform me until it was time to leave. Although I had no particular interest in investigating fellow officers, I was determined to do a good job in the hope of maintaining DPD's integrity and effectiveness. Little did I realize that my first case would test my dedication.

A child abuse investigator named Gerald Prossman[1] and I had been friends when I worked with him in my old unit. Ironically, soon after I arrived in Internal Affairs, the lieutenant in charge directed me to investigate a DPD allegation that Gerald had ignored arrest warrant procedures, delaying the apprehension of a previously convicted murderer who had just been accused of sexually molesting a young girl. You couldn't have put me in a tougher position. When I worked in the Child Abuse Unit, I did everything possible to identify and apprehend whoever was responsible for this kind of offense. But because I knew that Gerald had the same goal, I was reluctant to work this case. If Gerald had somehow bent or broken the rules, he'd have to pay the price, regardless of how good his intentions might have been. So I asked my boss to take me off the case.

"Look, Lieu," I said. "Can you assign this to someone else? He's a friend of mine."

That got me nowhere fast.

"Either take this case or get out of my office," the lieutenant said. "I won't have conditional honesty here. I need officers I can trust to do an investigation even if it's of their mother."

---

[1] To protect the privacy of certain individuals, their names have been changed.

9

And he was right to say that. I was raised to believe that you're responsible for your actions. But a lot of people, including some police officers, can't deal with that. The way I saw it, if you might have done something wrong, it was appropriate and necessary for Internal Affairs to investigate. At the same time, though, I didn't want to let my friend down. I wouldn't interfere with the investigation, but I didn't want to conduct it.

Police departments manage themselves by quantitatively analyzing their operations, such as arrests and closed cases for a given period. So it's only natural for officers to perform and report their activity in ways that not only meet departmental objectives, such as incarcerating criminals, but that also benefit the officers by giving their superiors solid reasons to reward good performance.

The file on the case Gerald was accused of mishandling was a good example of these factors at work. In many child abuse cases, there is a strong suspect, which greatly reduces the need for a lengthy investigation. And Gerald quickly found *prima facie* evidence of a felony and filed a case against the suspect.

As happened most often, the child's school reported the abuse to us. The young girl had told a classmate, who told her parents, who called the school. Gerald visited the school and the child's doctor and also spoke with the girl. So he felt he knew who had assaulted her. And he was going to put that person in jail.

One of the criteria we investigators were evaluated by was the number of offenses we cleared, which we did by arresting perpetrators. Gerald therefore wrote up a report on the case, and he brought it to DPD's Legal Division for approval. Next, he walked the report over to City Court, where a judge promptly issued a warrant for the suspect's arrest. Knowing where the suspect lived, Gerald planned to go there and quickly make the arrest. Unfortunately, when Gerald got there, the suspect wasn't home.

At that point, Gerald should have brought the warrant to the Warrant Division so that they could have entered it into the system and assigned someone to find the suspect and arrest him. But Gerald didn't do that. Instead, determined to clear the case himself, he kept the warrant with the intention of returning to the suspect's home and finally making the collar and recording it on his activity report. That might have worked, but Gerald didn't follow through on his plan. He let the warrant sit in his inbox, while the dangerous suspect remained free. Tragically, while still at large, the suspect molested another child. And that's what got Gerald in trouble.

When I left the lieutenant's office, I knew I had to lay it all out to Gerald before I decided what to do. So I called him over and said, "If I turn this case away, they'll transfer me back to patrol. But your friendship means more to me than this assignment. I'm willing to do it."

And he said, "No. I trust you. I know you'll do a good investigation."

"Gerald," I replied, "I'll do anything I can to help you, but I will not lie for you."

He looked me in the eye and said, "No problem. It's fine. I turned that warrant in."

I got him to tell me exactly whom he had brought the warrant to and when.

Then I investigated. It took me about ten days. I went and talked to the person he had named, and she said that he had never turned in the warrant. I also interviewed someone else in a position to know, and he said Gerald had told him, "I'm going to hang onto this warrant until tomorrow, and then I'll go out and get the guy."

Gerald had lied to me. Still, before I submitted my report, I wanted to let him know what I had found. So I called him to my office once more.

"Here's what I'm getting ready to turn in," I said.

Gerald read the report and smiled. "I always knew you were a good investigator," he said. Then he just walked out of the office.

Unlike the time-card fraudsters, Gerald was the only officer implicated in this case. So there were no political reasons to look the other way. Gerald's punishment was a 30-day suspension and transfer back to street patrol, which is a young man's game. I did that job for seven years; you answer one call right after another. When you work your way up into an investigative position, you get to work a saner schedule—something everybody wants.

Later, there were times when I wished I had turned down that case, and just told the lieutenant to transfer me back to patrol. Gerald pretty much avoided me after that. He and I would run into each other here and there, but we never got together for lunch or a beer. Five or six years later, he died of cancer. I had liked Gerald, but my investigation of his violation and cover-up ended our friendship.

CHAPTER 2

BEFORE INTERNAL AFFAIRS:
THE YOUTH DIVISION

I never forgot how hard it had been for me to file the Internal
Affairs investigation report that incriminated Gerald Prossman. He and I had been good friends, but my first obligation
was to those who depended on the Dallas Police Department.
When it came to the Child Abuse Unit, in which Gerald and I had
worked, that meant vulnerable kids. Another child abuse investigator, Billy Hooker, took this ethical responsibility as seriously as I
did. In fact, Billy and I had founded the Child Abuse Unit before I
moved on to Internal Affairs. Two factors led up to us being chosen to establish the unit.

First, Billy and I both had been with the department for
ten years or more. During that time, we'd developed our general crime-fighting skills by putting in seven or eight years on

uniformed street patrol. Then, we'd graduated to plainclothes work in specialized investigative units, like the Vice Squad, where I had worked for four years. My next assignment was in the Youth Division, where I met Billy in late 1981. He had arrived there a year or two before me.

Billy was one cool dude, about five years older than me, and well respected for the quality of his work. I'd soon see in person how good an investigator Billy was. That and his great sense of humor appealed to me. Besides our relentless determination to put bad guys in jail, we had other things in common. Like me, he grew up in a small town near Dallas, and had children. We quickly became fast friends as well as colleagues.

Billy's experience influenced me as I developed my own investigative approach to Youth Division cases. We worked well together and frequently collaborated. But we each had our respective caseloads and mostly worked independently of each other. Even then, though, we'd exchange ideas. If I was unsure about the best way to handle a case, I'd talk it over with Billy. And, after I gained experience with juvenile perpetrators, he'd do the same with me. But the deck was stacked against us in an important respect.

At that time, Texas law prohibited the incarceration of anyone under the age of 17. You could not lock up a 16-year-old delinquent, no matter how much evidence you had of his guilt. Instead, you'd have to release him into his parents' custody with a stern warning about what would happen if he continued his criminal behavior.

My first experience with this came soon after I began working in the Youth Division. Two uniformed officers on night patrol responded to a report of a residential burglary in progress. When they arrived at the scene, they caught a 14-year-old boy running out of the house with everything he could fit into a pillow case—a jumble of prescription drugs, jewelry, and other small items.

When the patrolmen brought him downtown, the Burglary Unit said they were investigating several other home break-ins with

14

the same modus operandi. There was a good chance that this kid was the thief behind them all. So who better to investigate the case than the Burglary Unit?

But the nature of the crime was less important than that of the suspect. Because he was a minor, they brought him to me in the Youth Division. When I checked his record for prior arrests, I found four—all for burglary. If he had been an adult, he would have been in prison. Already frustrated by that realization, I began a preliminary interview.

"What's your name?"

He ignored that. "You call my momma yet?"

"No, I haven't called your momma," I answered, wondering who was interviewing whom.

"Well, you need to call her so she can come pick me up."

"What are you talking about…pick you up?" I said, my blood starting to boil.

"That's what happens. You all call her and she comes to take me home."

No way I was going to let that happen; I had another plan. "I'm sending you to the juvenile detention center; you'll spend the night there."

"I won't have to," he said. "They'll call my momma, and she'll go there to pick me up."

That was bad, but he made it worse.

"The juvenile center is better," he added. "Closer to our house."

I sat there speechless, knowing I couldn't win. So I called his mother and told her to come take him off my hands. After less than a month in the Youth Division, I was sure I didn't want to work there. While my fellow investigators and I wanted to do a good job, the "system" made that very difficult. Many of them were dispirited and near retirement, but I was young and full of fight. I didn't want any part of calling Momma. What I loved was that metallic *clink* when you locked the cell door on a crook.

The second factor that led to Billy and me founding the Child Abuse Unit was our reputation as top-notch investigators. As I said, Billy had earned that respect before I met him, and I'll explain later what a jaw-dropping experience it was when I first saw him conduct an interview.

For my part, in most months I was with the Vice Squad I had racked up the highest number of arrests that led to convictions. Because of my effectiveness, I was appointed to be a training officer, responsible for teaching new members of the squad how to enforce the law, conduct investigations, and handle themselves on Dallas's seamiest and most dangerous streets.

One of the biggest challenges a Vice Squad officer faces is keeping his nose clean while sniffing out street crime and corruption. DPD brass had reasonably concluded that limiting the length of time officers were exposed to the narcotics and prostitution underworld would minimize the opportunity for them to become corrupt. So, after two years in Vice, they'd rotate you on to another unit.

But solving this problem without creating another required a nuanced approach. While the two-year rule helped keep bribery and other ethics violations down, it sometimes needlessly took unwaveringly honest officers off the Vice beat just when their hard-won experience had made them most effective. I was one of those officers—a street-savvy professional crazy enough to like the job. So, the department took a chance on me and others who had the right blend of experience, attitude, and performance.

As my second anniversary in Vice neared, my sergeant formally requested that my tour be extended for the maximum period permissible—six months. The chief approved that extension, and three more for me in the following 18 months. I had been in Vice for four years when another of the squad's sergeants was caught taking bribes. Not surprisingly, this led to a shakeup of the entire unit. Everyone who had been there more than two years was transferred out of Vice. I wound up in the Youth Division.

Fortunately, fate stepped in, and I didn't have to wait long for a new assignment. When DPD's leadership decided they needed a stronger and more effective response to crimes against—not by—children, they zeroed in on Billy and me as the investigators best qualified to establish a unit dedicated to that important task.

Opportunity Knocks

One morning, Billy stopped by my desk in the Youth Division office.

"Rise and shine, brother. The man wants to see us."

"About what?" I asked, looking up at him as he stood before me with a facial expression I couldn't read. "C'mon, spill the beans."

"I heard they're looking to start a new unit," he replied.

My ears perked up. "Just what I wanted to hear! Let's go!"

When we got up to Sgt. Jackie Davidson's office on the second floor, he motioned for us to come in.

"Close the door," he said. "I've got an opportunity I want to discuss with you men."

We did so quickly and crowded up to Jackie's desk, eager to find out what this was all about.

"The chief has decided that the department's response to child abuse cases is too spread out," Jackie said.

Everyone in the Youth Division knew this all too well. DPD had no central intake point for youth crime or child abuse cases. In a way, this was a sign of the times, before computerization improved communication and management within large police departments across the nation. DPD's various units didn't share information about youth- and child-related crime. In fact, DPD didn't even know how many such cases it had. And that sad fact had alarmed the chief of police and spurred him into action.

"We need to set up a unit dedicated to tackling child abuse," Jackie continued. "You're two of the department's best investigators—the right people for this assignment. What do you say?"

Billy and I exchanged glances, and told Jackie yes. After a few minutes of contingency planning, the meeting was over. We shook hands with him and went back to our desks with a new sense of purpose. That day, Jackie sent the word out across DPD and to all related agencies, introducing the Child Abuse Unit and naming Billy and me as the go-to guys on crimes against children.

Little did we realize how much work would quickly come our way. Few people, if any, had anticipated the greater volume of cases Dallas's child welfare agencies would send to DPD now that it would have a central repository for such cases. Not knowing what the future held, Jackie had sought our agreement on a final stipulation before closing the deal: Whenever there weren't enough child abuse cases to keep us fully occupied, Billy and I would help the remaining Youth Division investigators process their cases. Again, we had said yes.

But that eventuality never came to pass. From day one, Billy and I were buried in child abuse cases. We each received four or five new ones every day. In a sense, this was exhilarating because we were helping solve a problem that was escalating out of control. But at the same time it was deeply depressing to see how terribly some parents and other adults mistreated children.

On-The-Job Training

When you quickly bond with a new colleague as I did with Billy in the Youth Division, you sometimes don't know as much about him as you think you do. For example, although I realized Billy was a seasoned investigator, I didn't yet understand how good he was. But that changed during the first child abuse investigation I did with him.

Soon after we founded the Child Abuse Unit, Billy and I received a report that a mother suspected her four-year-old daughter had been sexually abused. The child had suddenly become withdrawn and had begun wetting her bed, but wouldn't say more than a few worrisome words about what was bothering her. And that had prompted her mother to call the police. So we went to their home to investigate.

Among the things I did know about Billy was that as an officer on street patrol he had been involved in at least one shootout and God knows how many violent arrests. So it was with some surprise that I watched how Billy interviewed the little girl about the suspected incident. We were wearing suits, and Billy took off his jacket. Earlier, he had put his pistol in his pants pocket so the child wouldn't see it. Then slowly he walked toward her as she played with stuffed animals on the living room carpet.

"Hello, I'm Billy," he said gently with a smile. "What's your name?"

Shyly she told him, and he asked if he could sit nearby on the floor. Looking up at her mother, who nodded approval, the child quietly said he could.

And for the next ten minutes, I watched them play with the stuffed animals, saying little if anything to each other. During that time, the little girl focused her attention on a small bear, and Billy took that as his cue.

"What do you call your teddy bear?" he asked, and she told him its long, involved name. Then Billy asked her about a blue plastic alligator she hadn't paid that much attention to, and the child said it didn't have a name. Billy wanted to know if he could give it one, and she said he could if he felt like it. So for the next few minutes, he pushed the alligator here and there on the carpet, calling it by the name he had chosen.

Watching this scene unfold, I could see Billy was building rapport with the child. But would it be enough? I doubted that a tough cop could really connect with a quiet four-year-old who might have been sexually assaulted. To me, they were separated by nearly unbridgeable gaps in age, gender, and point of view that only someone with psychology or social-work skills could hope to overcome. If

19

it had been up to me, I would've just come out and asked the child to tell me what—if anything—had happened and who had done it.

But Billy knew better. By emulating her interests and demeanor Billy had become an unthreatening playmate—one who asked permission before he touched toys and didn't get too close to her. Soon they were giggling together. In no more than 20 minutes, he worked his way far enough into that child's confidence to begin asking her the questions we came to have answered.

While the effectiveness of Billy's subtle approach impressed me, I knew that his interview—so smooth and successful up to now— had to be free from distractions by me or the mother. So I gradually shepherded her toward the kitchen for a separate discussion while Billy and the little girl continued playing and occasionally talking. But I stayed in the hallway so I'd know exactly what was happening.

When Billy asked the little girl if she had any brothers or sisters and she said no, he inquired whether she lived there alone with her mother. We knew that the child's father was gone and that her mother's boyfriend lived with them, but Billy didn't put any words in that child's mouth. So when the girl said someone named John lived with them, Billy asked if that was her father. No, the child said, John is Mommy's friend. Then Billy quieted down and went back to his plastic alligator.

After a while, he asked, "Where's John now?" and the child said, "He goes away during the day, and he comes back at night." With her permission, Billy spent a few minutes examining other members of the tiny menagerie.

Then he said, "Is John a nice man?"

"No, he's not," the child replied.

Again Billy laid back for a while. Eventually he asked, "Why don't you like him?"

"Because he does things to me."

"What does he do?" Billy asked, and it was as if he had just dialed the final number in the combination of a safe. The little girl got agitated and began spelling out in childlike terms how John had repeatedly fondled her.

Thanks to Billy's insightful interview, the child's spontaneous account bore credible witness to the suspected incidents and the perpetrator's identity—all without coaching or encouragement. Amazingly, Billy had established so much trust with her that she revealed to him something she might have been afraid to tell her mother, who, after all, had brought John into their home.

The next steps were to separate the child and the mother's live-in boyfriend, have the child examined by medical and child welfare professionals, and prepare for filing sexual molestation charges against the suspect. Prosecutors and the courts would take it from there. Billy had executed his part of the process flawlessly. And he had given me my first object lesson in child abuse investigation—an impressive interview on Billy's part, especially because he, like me, had never received any training in how to handle this kind of case.

I was completely awed by what Billy had accomplished and how he had gone about it. When that little girl described what John did to her, she hadn't been speaking to a DPD investigator; she had been confiding in her new friend, a boy named Billy. I realized that from then on whenever I interviewed suspects, victims, or witnesses I'd have to do a much better job of putting myself in their shoes. If I couldn't do that, I'd never persuade them that I understood their situation and accepted how they felt about it. And if they didn't trust me on that, they wouldn't tell me what I needed to know.

Later that day, I tried to pick Billy's brain about his strategy, but it seemed he didn't exactly have one. And then I realized why: because Billy's interviewing expertise came more from his gut than his head. I wasn't even close to having those instincts yet.

Billy had given me a sterling example to emulate, and I made up my mind to become a good interviewer like he was. But I had an urgent problem; even though I needed to get better fast, there didn't seem to be a clear way to make that happen anytime soon.

CHAPTER 3

MY SKILL GAP IN THE
CHILD ABUSE UNIT

One of the first child abuse cases I handled alone involved a statutory rape allegation; 14-year-old Amber Wrenmarsh had accused her mother's boyfriend, Lamar Casanegra, of having sex with her. A medical examination confirmed that although Amber wasn't pregnant, she recently had had intercourse. In those days before DNA analysis, however, there was no physical test to determine who her partner might have been. The best way to find out was to very carefully interview her about what had supposedly happened.

So I paid the Wrenmarshes a call. With her mother beside her, I asked Amber to tell me everything she could remember about when and where the incident took place, whether Casanegra wore briefs or boxers, what color they were, if he had tattoos or scars, whether anyone else might have seen him come and go, and numerous other detailed questions. Because of her mother's close relationship with Casanegra, Amber knew him well, and there was no possibility of mistaken identity. When Amber finished, I asked her to repeat some parts of her account so that I'd be sure to understand them all and get the details right. But I had more than one reason for asking her to go over things again.

Either Casanegra really did have sex with this child or someone else did, and for whatever reason, she was pinning it on Casanegra. I therefore had to prepare for both eventualities and structure my interview accordingly. Because she might have been telling the truth, I had to burden her as little as possible with the memory of her trauma. But because she might have been lying, I had to probe for potential inconsistencies in her story that might indicate its falsity and Casanegra's innocence. I found no such conflicts in her version of events, and so I never revealed my suspicion that she was lying. Why did I doubt her? Because she told her story so calmly it struck me as implausible.

Nevertheless, because I had no proof she was lying, I had to lock up Casanegra before he got a chance to skip town, if he were so inclined. I did so despite his outraged protestations of innocence. They rang true to me, but that was just a feeling. He had no alibi or witnesses to place him elsewhere at the time of the alleged rape. So by law, I was obligated to pull him off the street immediately. Soon thereafter, the next step in the process came into play when he posted bond and went back to earning his living as a cab driver.

Meanwhile, my doubts grew about Amber's accusation. I had no factual basis for disbelieving her, but all my investigative instincts told me she was lying. Still, if I couldn't get her to admit it, my theory was just a fantasy and Casanegra would eventually find himself back in the slammer.

I've been known to sometimes say, "I feel strongly both ways." That's when—as in this case—there is no preferable course of action and the status quo is unacceptable. It's the kind of situation I can't tolerate. People were depending on me to produce well-founded results in this case. So I needed to quickly find a strategy or tactic that would enable me to tell whether Amber Wrenmarsh was lying. Eventually, I discovered where I could get help in developing that skill, and I did so enthusiastically. With the proper guidance, I would soon take my first steps toward a new way of conducting interviews. But I had no idea how powerful this technique would turn out to be.

Enlightened by a Master

After I left patrol and became an investigator, I solved more than my share of tricky cases. But I'd had trouble getting guilty suspects to confess to their crimes, no matter how much evidence I had against them. This problem persisted when I worked in the Youth Division and in the Child Abuse Unit.

So I went to my lieutenant and said, "I need training in how to conduct interviews. I'm not as good at it as I should be."

"We don't have any budget for that," he said. End of discussion, as far as he was concerned.

You'd think that such courses would be standard components in the department's basic and ongoing training programs for investigators. But such was not the case in DPD. For the most part, the department expected you to develop interviewing expertise on the job, not in the classroom.

But I couldn't—and wouldn't—let that stop me from improving my skills. So I kept my eyes open for any kind of interview training. Finally, I saw a flyer announcing the availability of exactly what I needed: a four-hour seminar by Detective Gus Rose of the Homicide Division. I had heard a little about Gus—that he was a real pro with decades of experience. But I hadn't realized that my weak point—getting people to cough up information they'd rather not share—was his specialty.

Following the assassination of President John F. Kennedy, Gus had interviewed prime suspect Lee Harvey Oswald immediately after his arrest. Oswald's murder cut short Rose's promising progress into exposing whoever was responsible for JFK's assassination. Widely regarded as one of the most effective criminal interview experts of his generation, Gus would change my life and make me a far better investigator. His class transformed my entire approach to interviewing. Blended with my own refinements to Gus's techniques, it has formed the theoretical and practical basis for all of the ACFE interview seminars I've ever taught.

I still remember Gus's formidable opening lines in his seminar. "When I interview a suspect, I tell him, 'You've got a choice: tell the truth or lie. But if you lie, I guarantee you I *will* find out, and I'll use your lie to make things worse for you. All you'll have accomplished is to deprive yourself of any goodwill the justice system might have had toward you. So think carefully before you answer. Your fate is in your own hands.'"

The rest of Gus's class provided examples of how he approached different types of suspects and the various subterfuges they'd employ to deceive an interviewer. The four hours sped by, as I filled my pad with notes on techniques I couldn't wait to try in my cases. Afterward, I peppered Gus with questions until he finally laid his hands on my back and shoved me out the door.

One of Gus's main points was that an interviewer should never accuse a suspect of lying. As he told us, "These techniques will give you the power to change the way a suspect perceives the interview."

Gus explained that a guilty suspect will initially regard the interview as a struggle he has to win by hiding the truth. If that means lying or refusing to admit the falsity of earlier lies, he'll fight off all your attempts to bully him into admitting what really happened. But if you don't come on strong, Gus said, you won't create that resistance. And you'll find it much easier to persuade the suspect that the interview is an opportunity, not a confrontation. Once you achieve that, someone who's guilty will find it hard to resist sharing his burden with you. And after he's confessed, he'll thank you for enabling him to get the whole thing off his chest.

As persuasive as Gus had been, though, his last assertion was hard to believe. I decided to put it to a test immediately, and knew just who to try it out on—even though that person wasn't a suspect.

Theory Becomes Practice

Following Amber Wrenmarsh's rape accusation against Casanegra and my interviews of them both, I had filed charges against him. And now that the date of the resulting court hearing had arrived, I'd have an opportunity to question Amber one last time. But on this occasion, I'd use a new approach, one that would give her a subtle but unmistakable chance to come clean if she'd lied before.

When I got to court, the hearing hadn't begun, but Amber had already arrived. I sat down next to her.

"How you been doing?" I asked. "Have you seen or talked to him since then?"

"No. He hasn't been around. Momma hates him."

"Yeah. Let's move over a few rows and talk about this for a minute."

She hesitated at first, but came with me when I looked back at her.

"I remember what you said. But did he do anything else that day? Something you haven't told me about?" I was just fishing, trying to get her to talk—anything that might shed more light on what happened.

She stared at the back of the bench in front of us, avoiding my gaze. But I could see her eyes widen. Then, seemingly reluctantly she said, yes, there was something else.

"Tell me," I prompted. "What was it?"

"He hit me!" she finally said.

"Really? You never told me that before. How many times did he hit you?"

"A lot!"

"Why didn't you tell anyone? It must have been terrible."

Her little shoulders sagged a bit at this point, as the courtroom began to show signs of activity and the impending procedure that would determine Casanegra's fate.

"It wasn't terrible," she said in a low voice. "It was insulting. He treated me like a child."

"What do you mean?" I persisted.

"I mean he spanked me!" she exclaimed. "I'm not a child. I'm practically a woman."

I let her words hang in the air, and gave her room to continue.

"He's an idiot. I don't know what Momma saw in him…besides his body, of course. He can get a person so mad."

She paused again. I sensed something was happening—something that hadn't occurred in any of my previous interviews. Instead of putting on the pressure, trying to force a confession, I was laying off, letting Amber speak at her own pace, as if telling the truth was natural and would make her feel better.

"Sure, he's an idiot." I said. "I could tell that the first time I met him. But do you want to take back anything you told me about him? It won't mean that you're a bad person for having said the wrong thing." Following Gus Rose's precepts, I treated Amber and her accusation separately and I took care to not accuse her of lying.

"We're about to send Lamar off to prison for a long time," I continued. "If he did what you say, he should be in jail. Don't feel bad about that. But be sure of what you told me. If he didn't do it, he does not deserve this."

The subtext of my words was that she wasn't evil, but her story—if it were phony—was bad. And if that were the case, she could make things right by recanting her false accusation. She'd still be a good person, and no lasting harm would have been done. But if she stuck to her lie, serious jail time lay ahead for a man she knew was innocent, no matter how angry she was at him. In this way, I made it easier for her to admit the truth.

"Maybe I did tell you the wrong thing," Amber replied. After a long silence, she exhaled, took a deep breath and wearily said, "Lamar didn't do it. He says my boyfriend is dangerous and told me not to see him anymore. Lamar's not my father, but he acts like he is. He and Momma aren't even married! The next time Lamar saw us together, he spanked me, and I promised myself I'd get him for that. So I went with my boyfriend one night and then I said it was Lamar."

I paused for an instant to reflect on what my new interview technique had achieved. Amber's confession would not only serve justice; it also would end the totally unnecessary anguish Casanegra—and she—had been suffering.

"That must have been really hard to tell me," I said. "But now that you've revealed the truth, you have to stand by it. I'm going to speak to some people here so that this whole misunderstanding will be cleared up and you can put all this behind you. All right?"

"All right," she answered quietly and covered her face with her hands. "I'm glad it's over."

That wasn't the kind of explicit thank-you Gus said he got from those who confessed, but it was one of the most gratifying things I had ever heard. Exhilarated, I quickly strode over to the prosecutor, and said, "Come here. You need to hear what this young lady has to say."

And Amber kept her word, telling how she had fabricated her allegation of intercourse with Casanegra. Stunned, the prosecutor repeated it all to the judge and defense attorney.

When Casanegra learned the charges against him were being dropped and that the judge was dismissing his case, he was ecstatic. His anger evaporated, and he practically sprinted out of the courthouse before the judge and prosecutor could change their minds.

What I had learned from Gus Rose is how to make interviewees feel that their previous lies or acts were understandable, and that the best way to restore order to their lives was to open up and let the truth flow out. In that way, I had made Amber actually *want* to do the right thing, and so she did.

Now that I had successfully implemented Gus's technique, I was ready to apply it to a subject somewhat more challenging than an alleged victim. Most often, I'd be up against a resistant and possibly guilty defendant. With new cases landing on my desk every day, I didn't have to wait long before I got another opportunity to apply my new skills. And in my next case, the victim weighed less than ten pounds and was near death.

CHAPTER 4

SHAKEN TO DEATH

Somewhere a phone was ringing and wouldn't stop. Gradually I realized I was in bed. Positive the call was for someone else, I pulled the covers up all the way. But an elbow from my wife, Mary Ellen, changed my opinion, and I rolled over. The orange-digit clock on my bedside table said it was 3:17. Who in the hell is that? I wondered. A filthy expression was nearly out of my mouth when a searing memory gave me an adrenaline rush and head-to-toe chill at the same time.

In my mind's eye, I saw an unconscious three-month-old child, Janeequa Mason, bathed in white light, where I had visited her two days earlier in the pediatric intensive care unit at Parkland Memorial Hospital in Dallas. She was so small that a diaper was big enough to serve as her blanket. Janeequa was brain-dead, on life support, and not expected to live. Her diagnosis was *shaken baby syndrome.* As she lay there motionless, I noticed bruises—large fingermarks, actually—on her tiny biceps.

Snapping out of that painfully intense vision, I grabbed the receiver and yelled, "Ratley!" A voice on the other end asked if I was Ratley. "Yeah, dammit! Is that Parkland?" Within five seconds I heard what I was hoping for. I lowered my voice. "I'll be there fast," I said. "Don't let him go."

Before I left Parkland earlier in the week, I had asked to be called immediately by the on-duty police officer if Janeequa's missing father, Darryl Crofter, showed up to check on her condition. DPD routinely assigned a uniformed patrolman to every eight-hour shift at Parkland, which treated many victims of violent crime. I also had asked that the duty officer detain Crofter until I rushed there to question him. He and Janeequa had been alone together at home while the child's mother—Crofter's common-law wife—was shopping. When she returned, Janeequa was unconscious. Although Crofter said the child was probably just asleep, the frightened mother brought her to the hospital, where she was immediately admitted to the ICU. Crofter didn't come along, and hadn't been seen since.

I bolted out of bed and quickly put on the trousers I had laid on a chair two nights ago in anticipation of such a call.

"Who was that?" Mary Ellen asked, barely awake.

"I gotta go," I replied without looking at her. "Emergency."

"What emergency? You can't go to work in the middle of the night!"

"The hell I can't," I said, pulling on a shirt and suit jacket while I quietly pocketed my shield and handcuffs and clipped a pistol onto my belt. I had unavoidably wakened Mary Ellen, but I didn't want to disturb our own two little daughters, Leslie and Sarah, who I hoped were still fast asleep in the next room.

"Jim, you're not on the Vice Squad anymore!" she said, fully awake now, her voice rising. "Get back in bed."

But there was no reasoning with me. I was saddled up and headed out the door.

"Sorry," I answered. "This is real important. I'll see you this afternoon. Tell the girls I love 'em." That was curt, but I didn't see the benefit of discussing my line of work at home.

It was a good thing no one was on the sidewalk when I backed out of the driveway fast. The road, too, was empty as I sped west-bound along Interstate 30 at 90 miles per hour. I covered the fifteen miles to Dallas in ten minutes flat, and then ran one red light after another until I screeched up next to an ambulance near Parkland's emergency room entrance. Fortunately, I had passed no DPD patrol or motorcycle units on the way. Explaining my haste would have consumed precious minutes. I wasn't about to let Crofter disappear into the night.

Many child abuse suspects are stable; they own their homes and won't skip town, leaving all that behind. Instead, they stay put, deny everything, and try to explain away the evidence against them. But my background check on Crofter revealed that he probably didn't own much of anything except his car and his clothes; he'd have gone on the run.

I had an important advantage, though: the fear of the unknown that Crofter and others in his situation wrestle with. I knew he'd wonder whether his daughter was near death, in which case he'd eventually be charged with manslaughter or possibly murder, as opposed to child abuse if she survived. He'd also wonder how much I knew about how she had gotten injured and how strong a case the district attorney could make against him. So I had watched and waited, hoping he'd show up to see what was going on. And it had paid off. Now that I had this lowlife, I was going to enjoy putting him behind bars.

When I got inside Parkland, I ran to the elevators, punched the Up button and looked in dismay at all the red Down arrows. After waiting a few seconds, I couldn't stand it any longer. I headed for a stairwell and bounded up it, two steps at a time.

I had a general description of Crofter and pictured him as a skuzzy, poor-postured tramp with beady eyes. I also nurtured a satisfying mental image of the startled expression he'd wear when I'd bust into the room and confront him. But when I got to the fourth floor, where the pediatric ICU was, it occurred to me that I should slow down and catch my breath before I approached him. That's the last child you'll harm, I muttered, speaking to Crofter even before I saw him.

The duty officer saw me as soon as I came out of the stairwell. "You Ratley?"

"Yeah."

"He's alone, right in here," the officer said, motioning toward a door several feet away. "I put him in this room as soon as he arrived at the nurse's station and asked for that little girl."

"Thanks," I said. "Nice work; I really appreciate it."

"You bet."

I was just about to grab the door handle, when I heard a muffled groan from inside the room.

"You said he's alone?"

"That's right."

I jerked the door open and stepped ahead in a mean frame of mind. Sitting in a plastic chair before me was a young man neatly dressed in jeans and a short-sleeved shirt, bent over with his head in his hands.

"Are you Darryl Crofter?"

"Yes," he mumbled without raising his head.

"I'm Investigator Ratley of the Dallas Police Department Child Abuse Unit. I need to ask you a few questions about your daughter, Janeequa." I read him his *Miranda* rights so that he'd know he didn't have to say anything until he had legal counsel, and that if he spoke to me now, my testimony about it would be admissible in court.

He seemed emotionally crushed—more sad than scared—and he kept talking in a weak voice. "Will she recover? I love that child. I wouldn't hurt her for the world."

33

That sounded like he meant it, which surprised me, but I didn't let it show. Ignoring his question, I silently posed one to myself: Could it be that his little girl's condition was now more important to him than his own fate? He didn't look as shiftless as I'd imagined he would, and he wasn't startled by my sudden appearance. Instead, he appeared remorseful and resigned. But all that wasn't my business; it was up to me to interview and arrest him and let the justice system do its part.

"Just tell me what happened," I said, trying to catch his eye, but he wouldn't look at me.

"I didn't do anything! I was just trying to watch the Cowboys game."

"Then how'd she get those finger-shaped bruises on her arms?"

He blanched when I said that, and turned his tearful face farther away.

"Listen," I continued. "I understand the situation; it's obvious. The sooner you level with me, the better you'll feel. And the judge will take your cooperation into account. Talk to me."

After a long silence, he said, "I didn't know it would hurt her. After I shook her, she quieted down. There didn't seem to be anything wrong."

That's all I had to hear. "I'm placing you under arrest for first-degree felony assault of your daughter, Janeequa Mason," I said. "Stand up, face the wall, and put your hands behind your back."

He did as I said. I cuffed him, opened the door and walked him to the elevator.

"We're going to Dallas City Jail," I said. "Tomorrow's your arraignment. You'll appear before a judge and be charged." I let him wonder whether he'd soon be on the hook for murder or manslaughter. Crofter remained silent, looking at the floor. I could tell he sensed his little girl wasn't going to make it. Of course, the evidence against him was mostly circumstantial, but it was powerful enough to persuade a judge and jury that he deserved a long stretch in prison.

There was no need for me to appear at the arraignment. The jail staff would take 20 to 30 defendants before a judge all at once. Those who didn't have a lawyer would each in turn be asked by the judge whether he could afford to hire an attorney. Any defendant who said no had to sign a statement to that effect. Then, if a review confirmed that assertion, within a week the court would find an attorney who would represent the defendant at no charge to him.

Meanwhile, the judge would give the defendant the option of posting bond to be released from custody until his next court appearance. The defendant then could have a bondsman pay his bail, backed by a promissory note or secured by a car or other property. But because most of my work—like the Mason case—involved serious child abuse, judges usually would set bail so high that the defendant, unable to make it, would have to stay in jail until the trial.

When Crofter and I arrived at the city jail, I helped lock him up. Crofter had looked and acted differently than I had expected. But, aside from his guilt or innocence not being something for me to judge, I still found myself trying to find a match between him and his alleged crime. My brief encounter with Crofter hadn't jibed with my expectations, which grew out of what the ER doctor told me had happened to Janeequa.

The doctor's graphic description of shaken baby syndrome churned my insides. Compared to their bodies, he said, babies' heads are big and their neck muscles aren't developed enough to support that weight. So when someone shakes a baby, its head swings back and forth. I particularly remembered him saying that this also often leaves finger-shaped bruises on the child's upper arms.

Inside the skull, the baby's brain bounces around, becoming bloody and swollen. Shaking also can damage the neck and spinal cord and break ribs. Such injuries can make the child unresponsive, interfere with its breathing, and cause convulsions. Ultimately, this

35

can result in death or blindness and mental impairment that in some cases isn't detected for several years. Sometimes, the doctor said, even if the child lives, it needs special medical attention for the rest of its life.

I already had seen plenty of child abuse in a short time, but there was something particularly tragic about this case. All the damage had happened in maybe a minute, when an ignorant parent had lost self-control. But I couldn't afford to linger over this or any other case when I had finished my part in it. There were too many others waiting on my desk in the Child Abuse Unit.

The next day, however, I couldn't help but visit little Janeequa again. And when I arrived, I found that her condition hadn't improved since my previous visit; there still was no chance she'd recover. A few days later, Janeequa passed away.

Her case was tragic, but hardly unique. One thing that amazed me while I was working on child abuse was that it crossed all socio-economic, religious, and racial boundaries; every group contained people who committed it.

In Dallas, numerous kids were doomed unless Billy and I intervened. But we seldom knew of their plight until they'd already been seriously injured. Even then, we had to act immediately. If we didn't end the abuse as soon as we learned of it, the cycle would continue and intensify. And that could result in an abused child becoming a dead child. There was no slow season in the Child Abuse Unit.

CHAPTER 5

VOLCANO INSIDE ME

J aneequa Mason's death cast a shadow over my mind, and vestiges of it haunt me to this day. While good cops do the right thing for everyone, they each tend to be especially protective of certain types of people. For me it was children, because of their innocence and vulnerability.

I've got nothing against a good, fair fight. But with their bare hands alone, adults can brutalize a youngster without breaking a sweat. And if any old makeshift weapon—even a simple household item—happens to be nearby, an adult can inflict terrifying wounds that never heal; that is, if the little victim survives.

After more than a year in the Child Abuse Unit, I'd seen the broken-limbed, bloody results of ferocious beatings that cruel, cowardly adults had inflicted on hundreds of helpless kids. Yet even with so much firsthand experience, I was, on one case, mystified by the numerous strange contusions all over the bodies of five-year-old twins, who somehow were still able to walk. It was eerie; each wound was several inches long, shaped like the tail and rounded head of a sperm cell. The two boys' scalps had taken most of the blows. While these welts were clear indications of child abuse, they weren't among the classic signs I had seen before, like the finger marks on Janeequa's tiny biceps.

"What on earth made these bruises?" I asked the ER staff at Parkland Hospital, where the boys had been transported from their school by caseworkers from Dallas's Child Protective Services office. I had gotten a call from the hospital and promptly went there to speak with the doctors and see the boys.

The doctors had never encountered any wounds just like these, however, and couldn't answer my question. But one of them answered a question I hadn't asked: In which hand did the attacker hold the weapon?

"You can see how the instrument impacted the tissue from the same side every time," he told me, pointing to a raised edge on the perimeter of each wound. "All things considered, it most likely indicates a right-handed assailant."

That wasn't much to go on, but every bit of evidence matters, so I made a special note of it.

The caseworkers, after learning from the boys' teacher that they had been injured before arriving at school, visited the mother at her home to see whether it was a safe environment for children. That turned out to be irrelevant, though, because the kids would never return. But it was a taste of things to come for their mother, Kaylee Foxroy.

The boys, Kyle and Jordan, lived in a shabby one-bedroom apartment with Foxroy and her most recent live-in boyfriend. When the caseworkers visited, she got weepy and wouldn't talk, so they left without learning who had done what to the boys. That was my job, so I wrote down her Old East Dallas address. I knew the area well from my street patrol days; it was one of the city's poorest, toughest neighborhoods.

By a combination of persistence and luck, I later found the improvised weapon used against those kids, who had brain injuries severe enough to cognitively impair them. Nothing could change that, but I vowed to find and jail whoever had done this to the boys.

Meanwhile, because I was always working three or four child abuse cases at once, I had no time to face a troubling question: How much more of this carnage could I stand before the emotional volcano inside me blew sky-high?

One thing in particular helped me keep going, day after day— the gradual improvement in my interviewing skills. If, in an earlier case, I had browbeaten Amber Wrenmarsh, she never would've recanted her false accusation of rape. Instead, I persuaded her to confess by getting her to trust me. The key was learning how to conceal my fury and disgust when a suspect described committing an ugly crime. Gus Rose, in his seminar, had emphasized the importance of establishing and maintaining a non-adversarial relationship with the suspect during an admission-seeking interview.

Be alert, Gus had advised me and the other officers attending his seminar. Your carefully cultivated rapport can quickly evaporate if you give an about-to-confess suspect the slightest reason to doubt your apparent sympathy for him and your belief in his version of how and why he committed the crime, Gus said.

I knew Gus was right. But sometimes, even when you strongly believe a theory, putting it into practice isn't easy. I learned this well in my following cases, when I struggled to maintain the trust of someone I suspected had given a child a vicious beating or worse. Throughout each interview I had to strike the right balance between firm investigative authority and apparent sympathy. At certain times it was better to come on strong, as I was used to doing. But Gus had taught me the value of being indirect and helping a resistant prime suspect develop a strong desire for my understanding and forgiveness. So, if I thought it would lead to the truth and, when appropriate, a signed confession, I found a way to choke back my anger and revulsion while encouraging the suspect to open up and tell me what really happened.

Square One

The boys had been attacked before they got to school, and the doctors had told me their injuries were at least 12 hours old, so I had good reason to suspect that either the mother or her boyfriend had delivered the beating the previous evening. That timing increased the possibility that the boyfriend could have done it after getting home from work. But I didn't jump to any conclusions; it was just as possible that the mother had beaten her boys.

To minimize the odds of her avoiding me, I didn't call ahead to say I was coming. That paid off. I drove over in an unmarked DPD sedan and parked a few doors down from her building. Foxroy's apartment was on the first floor. Its only window faced the street and overlooked ten square feet of dirt and dead grass.

A few seconds after I rang her doorbell, the window curtain moved slightly. She took a long time coming to the door, and was pale when she opened it. Kaylee Foxroy looked like a textbook illustration of someone caught between two bad options. One was obvious: facing the police. I suspected the other was facing her boyfriend's revenge if she blamed it on him.

"Hello," I said, and flashed my tin. "I'm Investigator Ratley, Dallas Police Department Child Abuse Unit. Are you Kaylee Foxroy?"

"Yeah," she said, and took a deep breath.

"I need to speak with you. May I come in?"

"All right," she answered, and led me into her sparsely furnished living room. She shoved several toy soldiers to one end of a sagging sofa, and we sat down.

"I'm here to find out what happened to Kyle and Jordan," I said.

"They're in the hospital," she replied without emotion.

"I've seen them," I said. "Have you?" To the best of my knowledge, she hadn't.

"I was just on my way over there when you rang the bell."

Her television was tuned to a soap opera. She turned it off.

I looked her in the eyes. "I want you to tell me what happened. Before we begin, I have to inform you that anything you say might be used as evidence in a court of law. Do you understand?"

"Oh, yes," she said, and looked away.

If she had any doubts about whether this was a serious matter, my reading of her *Miranda* rights dispelled them. Apparently she had given the situation some thought after stonewalling the caseworkers. Probably realizing the police wouldn't tolerate that behavior, she seemed ready to give me her version of what had happened.

"All right, then," I said. "Go ahead."

"They were misbehaving, and I had to discipline them."

"With what?"

"Uh, a belt."

I didn't buy it. If she stuck to that claim, though, I'd ask her to show me the belt. Meanwhile, I probed from another direction.

"And exactly where'd you hit them?"

"On the butt."

"How many times?"

"Five or six; I don't remember."

Obviously, she was lying, but at that point I couldn't tell why. Was it to downplay any involvement she might have had in the beating or to protect her boyfriend if he were the one who had thrashed them?

"You're not even close," I said. "Their bodies are covered with severe bruises."

"I'm telling you the truth," she insisted.

"Where was your boyfriend when all this happened?"

"He was at work," she said.

"Do you work outside the home?"

"No. I have my hands full here."

"Get your coat," I said. "I'm taking you downtown for further questioning."

"Why do you have to do that?" she cried. "I told you why I had to discipline them!"

"And I told you your answers don't match the extent of your boys' injuries. They're victims of felony child abuse, and you've admitted hitting them. That's prima facie evidence requiring me to take you into custody for further questioning. Get your coat."

As we rose from the sofa, she looked like she was about to faint. I steadied her for a moment, then waited while she got her jacket from a hallway closet. Right next to it was a small kitchen. Its red linoleum flooring was curled up at the edges, and the sink was overflowing with every dirty dish in the world. On the counter beside them lay a large wooden cooking spoon.

We left the apartment, and I brought her to the car. Neither of us spoke while I drove back downtown. My office was in the Dallas Municipal Building at 106 South Harwood Street. Jack Ruby shot Lee Harvey Oswald there.

Just Byron

Besides being the site of that notorious killing, the Municipal Building is a neoclassical landmark. Reflecting that dual nature, its stately exterior encloses five floors of gritty offices, including the Child Abuse Unit and the Dallas City Jail on the two top floors.

I pulled into its basement garage and parked a few yards from where Oswald bought it. After being arrested, he had been temporarily held in the city jail, and was being transferred to Dallas County Jail when Ruby ambushed him. We took the elevator to my office on the second floor. I motioned to a chair in front of my desk, and closed the door. Reluctantly, it seemed, she took a seat.

"What's your boyfriend's name?"

"Byron," she said tonelessly, looking at the floor.

"Byron what?"

"I don't know. Just Byron."

"Good Lord," I said with a sigh. It was clear that "Byron" wouldn't make himself available for an interview anytime soon. "You got any pictures of him?"

"Byron's not into pictures."

"Then what's he look like?"

She gave me a terse description: tall, thin, late 20s, horse-shoe-shaped "biker" mustache.

"How long's he been living with you and the boys?"

She thought for a moment. "Since New Year's."

"Does he work steady?"

"Most days."

"Where?"

"Chestnut Motel."

I knew the place—a cluster of broken-down hovels bordering I-30, which ran east-west through the heart of Dallas.

It was time to shift gears. "Wasn't you who beat those kids," I said. "You're lying. Who really did it?"

She turned away, and said nothing.

"You're looking at a long time behind bars."

She jumped up, trembling. "What do you mean? *I'm their mother!*"

"*This* is what I mean, Mother. Your sons have had the living hell beaten out of them! They both have brain damage from blunt trauma to their heads and will never fully recover."

On hearing that last part, she slumped back into the chair. She cared about her boys, but not enough. Amazingly, the morning after they were beaten, she had sent them off to school as if it were just another day. They must have staggered all the way. Maybe she just couldn't bear to look at them.

I hadn't come across this type of situation before. Foxroy had confessed to a crime, but it didn't match the one committed. As a result, I had become increasingly suspicious that it was her boyfriend who had beaten the boys. Foxroy was shielding him, I believed, and somehow I had to get her to come clean. But even if she incriminated Byron, she'd still have to answer for not reporting his abuse of her children; that too was a felony. Meanwhile, she wasn't budging from her phony story, so I stepped up the pressure.

In the Belly of the Beast

I decided to give Foxroy a tour of the lodgings she might occupy before being transferred to a long-term correctional facility if she were indicted and convicted. We took the elevator up to the city jail on the fourth floor. Its inmate population was mostly misdemeanor offenders, with a smattering of felons about to be transferred to the county jail. I led her down a drab hallway and stopped before an empty cell that reeked of antiseptic. I escorted her inside, stepped back, and slammed the door. We looked at each other through the bars.

"You're gonna be a decrepit old woman when they let you out," I said.

"I don't want to go to prison!" she wailed, tears flowing down her cheeks.

"Then you're messing with the wrong person," I replied. "I'll give you one more chance to tell me the truth. God help you if you keep lying to me."

That did it.

She leaned forward, grasped the bars and began sobbing. "I didn't hit the boys!" she screamed. "I wasn't even there!"

I opened the cell door, took her firmly by the arm, and walked back to the elevator. "Let's start over."

"I'll tell you everything," she said, gasping. "Just don't put me back in jail."

I had thoughts on that subject, but kept them to myself.

Finally, the Truth

When we got back to my office, she gave me a fuller and more truthful account of what happened. Her first important revelation was that on the evening in question she had gone grocery shopping and left the boys at home with Byron. The beating had taken place while she was gone, she said. Because she wasn't there when it happened, she didn't realize how bad it had been. But I was sure she knew even more than she was telling me, and I was determined to get her to spell it all out. I wasn't going to lead her along, though.

One of the things I learned from Gus Rose is that the information flow has got to be one way: from the suspect to the interviewer. If I had told her whatever I knew or believed and she agreed with it, I'd have no way of knowing if she had told me the truth or had just said what I wanted to hear.

In contrast, if I knew certain important facts—in this case, the severity, number, location, and unique appearance of the wounds—and compared them to her story, I could tell whether it matched the facts and detect any inconsistencies that would indicate a phony confession. That's how I knew Foxroy's original story was false and her final one true. My job was not to get a confession and clear a case; no, it was to find out what really happened. So, as we sat there in my office, I pressed her to continue.

When she got home from the store, Foxroy said, it wasn't quite dark, but the boys were already in bed.

"Byron told me he had to spank them because they were misbehaving. I asked him if they'd had supper, and he said they weren't hungry, so he'd put them to bed. I believed him."

"Did you check on them?" I asked.

"No. He said they were asleep, so I thought everything was all right."

"Well, it wasn't," I said. "How could you send them to school without medical treatment?"

45

"I didn't know they were hurt that bad."

"Not even when you saw them in the morning?" I asked, my voice rising.

She didn't answer. An awkward silence filled the room.

Finally, she asked how much longer I'd hold her.

"Never mind that now," I said. "You're going to give me a written version of everything you just told me."

I pulled out a pad and pen. "Let's get this done."

An hour later, I had her signed statement. The relieved look on her face told me she thought her ordeal was over, regardless of what shape her sons were in. Now that she had fingered the boyfriend, she expected me to turn her loose.

"When can I go home?" she asked.

"No time soon," I replied.

"What?" she said with a shocked look. "But you promised me that if I told you the truth, you'd let me go!"

"I said God help you if you kept lying. I didn't say anything about letting you go."

"So what're you going to do with me?"

"Put you back in that cell. Failure to report child abuse also is a felony, and I'm charging you with two counts of it. Upstairs. You know the way."

As we headed for the elevator, she started crying again, but I paid no attention. My mind was on her boys and Byron. I'd made progress, but had a ways to go before solving this case. Yes, I had a prime suspect, but still no idea what the hell he had used to make those awful bruises on the kids. I was determined to find out, though. And once I got my hands on Byron, I'd conduct an interview that would make him eager to tell me.

CHAPTER 6

MANHUNT

I was up before dawn the day after I arrested Kaylee Foxroy. Knowing how much had to be done quickly, I left for the office just as the sun came up. The first thing on my mind was finding Byron, and only two people could help me pick up his trail. One was Foxroy, and I'd already squeezed everything useful out of her. The other was whoever ran daily operations over at the Chestnut Motel, the small-scale slum where Foxroy said Byron worked.

I also knew, though, that before I went to question that person, I should file paperwork recommending Foxroy's prosecution. Because I had spent most of the previous day with her, I hadn't had time to finish my case report. So I dove back into it as soon as I got to my desk. Per standard DPD procedure, my report described the Foxroy household, explained everything I knew about the intentional criminal assault on the boys, and identified those who had discovered and reported it to me. I also specified the limited background I had on Byron. Along with the rest of my report, that information would document my request for a warrant when I knew more about Byron and was closer to arresting him. I supplemented my report with Foxroy's signed confession that also pegged Byron as the assailant, and enclosed individual written statements from the teacher, the ER doctor, and the Child Protective Services caseworkers. And I attached a formal written statement in which I charged Foxroy with two felonies for not reporting Byron's brutal beating of her sons.

Three hours after starting, I finished writing and assembling the report. I didn't include the written results of the hospital's medical tests on the boys. Those I sealed in an evidence envelope, marked for identification, and put them in the custody of the DPD property clerk. I then submitted the report to my sergeant. I had previously briefed him on the case, so he was able to quickly review and approve it.

Next, I hand-carried everything down the hall to DPD's legal liaison division, where each aspect of my report and filings would be carefully examined to ensure I hadn't violated Foxroy's rights in any way or otherwise run afoul of the law or DPD regulations. The liaison staff would tell me right away if they had any misgivings or questions about my report and charges. If all was well, as was virtually always the case with my paperwork after 12 years with DPD, the liaison would send the case to the Dallas County District Attorney's Office. Its prosecutors would decide whether or not the charges were warranted and, if so, whether there was enough evidence to have a decent chance of getting a conviction. Every experienced police officer worth his or her salt knows what it takes to get the D.A. to accept a case. If I had thought my charges against Foxroy wouldn't stick, I wouldn't have brought them. But with strong evidence and her voluntary written confession, I was confident the prosecutor would want to quickly take the case to the grand jury.

Now that I'd filed my paperwork, the justice system would immediately begin moving the case against Foxroy forward. First, the city jail supervisor would schedule her arraignment before a magistrate. Because Foxroy didn't have an attorney at that point, the judge would instruct her to plead not guilty with the option to change that plea once she had the benefit of legal counsel. Based on my experience in such cases, I expected the judge would set Foxroy's bond at anywhere from $20,000 to $25,000. And having seen where and how Foxroy lived, I knew she couldn't come up with that much money and that she probably had no assets a bail bondsman would accept as security. That meant she'd qualify for representation by a court-appointed public defender. It also meant that before the day was over, she'd be right back in the cell I had put her in, where she'd sweat it out until the system decided what to do with her. Her boys, meanwhile, were still in the hospital. Child Protective Services would care for them after they had healed enough to be discharged and at least some medical and psychological treatment had been set up for them.

As soon as the court assigned an attorney to represent Foxroy, he or she would want to know if the case were going to the grand jury. If, as I expected, the prosecutor had decided the case was worth pursuing, the defense attorney would ask the judge to schedule an examining trial. This proceeding was brief, but important. Its purpose was to determine whether the prosecutor was right about there being sufficient evidence to send the case to the grand jury. I could bank on spending 15 to 20 minutes on the stand, being grilled by both sides. As a result, the defense would find out what evidence I had and what I didn't have. That was routine and fine with me. My desk work was up-to-date; the wheels were in motion. It was up to the grand jury to indict Foxroy, and I hoped that would happen within a few days. Now I could begin the manhunt that I hoped would bring Byron to justice.

49

Lead Number Two

I drove over to the Chestnut Motel. Many times I'd seen it while passing by on Interstate 30: about a dozen one-bedroom shacks surrounded by chain-link fence topped with razor wire. I bet myself that they were called "cottages."

As I neared the motel's front gates, I slowed down and eye-balled the area. If Byron had beaten the boys, he would've been on the lookout for the police. So I wanted to be certain he didn't slip out of his workplace right under my nose. But no one was in sight; not a car on the street. A rusting Quonset hut across the road seemed as old as the Alamo. Silent warehouses and a few wilted pe-can trees lined the rest of the block. The only sound was the hum of highway traffic. Seemed like nothing much ever happened there. Minutes later I changed my mind.

I turned inside the open gates, and pulled up a little ways from a house trailer on cinder blocks. Outside it, a woman who looked tougher than Margaret Thatcher was sitting in a folding chair under a beach umbrella. As I got out and walked toward her, I thought I smelled rotting garbage.

The Doberman at her feet seemed asleep, but I saw his right ear twitch. Next to her was another chair. On its armrest was a small bottle that looked familiar. It was; same brand of bore cleaner I used. On the seat, a thin cloth was spread out over something the size and shape of a Colt Diamondback, little brother of the Python model I wore.

"'Morning," I said, poker-faced. "Are you the manager here?"

"Yessir. Half hour ago, I had no vacancies," she replied with a chipped-tooth smile. "But the businessman in my best cottage had to leave unexpectedly." She gave me a piercing look and glanced at my unmarked car. "I can see you're a gentleman, so no need to play games. I'll give you a good rate."

I showed her my badge, but didn't identify my unit. "I'm here on another type of business, ma'am. I hope you can help me."

The smile vanished. She stood up, and the dog let out a long, low rumble. "I got an appointment across town."

"Does a man named Byron work here?"

"I knew it!" she exclaimed. "That goddamn...!" She paused. "The trash is piling up 'cause that useless bum didn't come in *again*. What'd he do?"

"I just want to ask him a few questions. But let's make sure we're talking about the same person. What's he look like?"

"Tall, skinny jackass," she said.

"Glasses, tattoos, facial hair?"

"None of that 'cept a real dumb mustache."

"What kind?"

"Shaped like a horseshoe. Why would anyone want that on his face? Every day I told him how stupid it looked, but he wouldn't listen. You know men."

"Uh-huh. What's his last name?"

"Ya got me," she said. "Always paid him cash. Had to keep an eye on him all the time."

"Anything else you can tell me about him?"

"Now isn't that enough, officer? What am I gonna do about that trash?"

"Thank you, ma'am," I said, and turned to leave. The Doberman sprang to its feet and snarled. Avoiding eye contact, I stepped away slowly, jumped in the car and rolled up the window. Last thing I wanted to do was shoot a dog. As I made a broken U, I spotted her in my rear view, staring after me with a frown. Just the right person to run this place, I thought as I cruised through the gates.

"Hello, John Doe," I said out loud. That was what the judicial and law enforcement systems would call Byron until we learned his full name. I stomped on the gas. My pursuit of him was about to take a new turn.

Setting the Trap

I had a good physical description of my prime suspect, but his trail had petered out. Neither of my leads knew where he'd gone, and there was no one else to question. While I no longer thought there was a chance I'd track Byron down, I knew he'd eventually come out of hiding. And I'd be there to grab him when he did. Why was I so confident he'd resurface? Because I didn't think he could bear the suspense of an uncertain fate; he'd *have* to find out where he stood—just like Janeequa's father, Darryl Crofter, did.

Fear of snakes and of public speaking always rank high on lists of what really gets under people's skin. But in my experience, they dread the unknown more than anything else. I remember interviewing a twenty-one-year old murderer just after he'd been sentenced to 25 years in prison.

"That had to be pretty horrible," I said to him.

"Actually, it was the best thing I ever heard," he answered. "They told me I might get a hundred years, so I was going crazy wondering what would happen to me. Yeah, 25 years is bad, but now I know what I'm up against, and I'll find a way to deal with it."

To one extent or another, we're all preoccupied with our own needs and worries. But it would be a mistake to think that every guilty suspect or convict who fears the unknown is self-absorbed. Take Crofter for example. He risked visiting his daughter in the hospital because he wanted to know what he'd be charged with. But he also was genuinely worried about her condition; he hadn't meant to hurt her. In contrast, I strongly suspected, there was only one reason Byron would return: to find out how much Foxroy had told the police and what charges and evidence he'd face if apprehended. Yes, the duration and viciousness of the beating inflicted on those kids told me that Byron didn't care about them or their mother. All he wanted was to save his own skin. I planned to sit down with him real soon for a good, long chat.

Of course, I had yet to discover Byron's last name. But I'd obtain that once I had him in custody. Meanwhile, I could continue and intensify my pursuit of him by requesting expedited issuance of a warrant for his arrest. I called the secretary assigned to the municipal building's judicial chambers, and asked her to find a judge who could give me a warrant immediately. I explained that the violent felony Byron was charged with, plus his status as an apparent fugitive, made it imperative to bring him in without delay. I also said I needed a so-called John Doe warrant, which identifies the suspect by physical description, rather than name, and permits only the requesting officer—in this case, me—to execute the warrant and arrest the suspect.

The secretary got back to me within an hour, and I hurried over to see the judge while he was available. I brought my case report and a statement of the charges. After reading them, the judge put me under oath. I swore that the statements in my report were true and complete to the best of my knowledge. He then drew up a warrant authorizing me to arrest a person at that time known only as "Byron," who fit the physical description in my report. I thanked the judge, pocketed the warrant and headed upstairs to jail. It wasn't to see Foxroy, though.

Because I'd personally put hundreds of suspects in the city jail, I knew by name most if not all of the DPD officers assigned there. It was them I hustled to speak with once I had obtained the warrant. What I wanted was their cooperation on the tactic I had used to capture Janeequa's father. But this situation was significantly more sensitive and difficult than that had been. Crofter was an emotional mess, worried sick about his little girl, even though he was the one who had fatally injured her. It didn't take much effort to get him to stick around Parkland Hospital until I arrived to arrest him. But I was sure Byron was a selfish brute, out to save himself. That meant he'd resist any attempt to make him stay longer than he wanted, and that the officers who detained him without a warrant risked being written up for unlawful arrest. Everything would've been simple if I had known Byron's full name. If it were spelled out on a regular arrest warrant, any officer could have made the collar. But because I had to get a "John Doe," only I could execute the warrant.

Considering all those complications and impediments, I knew I was asking for a lot. But I also knew my fellow officers would be just as outraged as I was about the beating those little boys had suffered. And I counted on their willingness to bend the rules just enough to let me bring Byron in for questioning. So I laid it all out for the jailhouse officers, and they responded as I'd hoped. The deciding factor was that it was a child abuse case. Otherwise, they wouldn't have agreed to my plan.

"Sometime soon, he'll visit Foxroy to find out what she told us," I said. "When he does, I don't give a damn what time it is, hold him and call me. I'll come over right away."

I gave them my home number. They promised that if Byron showed, they'd put him and Foxroy in a visiting cell with a glass partition and intercom phone.

Now all I had to do was wait. I didn't expect it to take very long. Time and Byron's anxiety were on my side.

CHAPTER 7

ADMISSION-SEEKING
INTERVIEW

I t wasn't like me to have trouble sleeping. But that's exactly what had been happening for the last few weeks. I couldn't put my finger on just why, yet there it was. And so I was drinking milk in the kitchen when a midnight call came in from a DPD officer at the city lockup. I grabbed the phone—I hoped before it woke Mary Ellen and our little girls.

"Your boy's on time, just like you said," he told me.

"Is he in with her?" I asked.

"Yep. She just got to the visiting cell where I had him wait."

"Outstanding. Don't let him go."

"Not a chance. We're pretty busy. Might not notice right away when he's ready to leave."

My lips curled into a tight smile. "I'm on my way."

I stepped quietly into the master bedroom. Mary Ellen, still asleep, breathed softly. A peek into the girls' room showed me all was quiet there too. I quickly pulled on a shirt and slacks, pocketed a few things, and was on the road in minutes.

A thousand thoughts raced through my mind as I sped to Dallas from home in Mesquite. No doubt, Byron would raise holy hell once he realized he was being detained. But it wouldn't stop me from getting him into an interview room that night.

Before too long, the Municipal Building loomed before me against the night sky. I pulled into the basement parking area, leapt into the elevator, and punched the 4 button while donning my badge.

Upstairs, as the elevator doors opened, I could hear Byron. "You goddamn better turn me loose!" he shouted.

I stepped out of the elevator, saw the duty officer at the reception desk, and walked over to thank him.

"Glad to help," he said, as another officer stood by. Neither of them looked happy, though. They knew what I had charged Byron with. Like me, they believed child abusers belonged in the lowest circle of hell. But Byron would receive a fair trial. My job was to make sure that he'd appear in court if the grand jury indicted him.

The visiting cell was only a few yards from the front desk, but out of sight around a corner.

"Where's the prisoner?" I asked.

"Back in her own cell," the duty officer told me. "She wanted out pretty quick, and he's been making a ruckus ever since we 'forgot' to come back and let him go."

The second officer and I walked toward the sound of Byron furiously pounding on the locked wire-mesh glass door of the visitor's side of the cell. As I turned the corner, Byron and I got our first look at each other. That biker mustache didn't match the rest of him—big hat, weak chin. Not Bandido material. Suddenly he stopped yelling, and stared at my plain clothes and the badge on my neck lanyard. Then he dropped his fists. Byron didn't know my name, but he knew why I was there.

"You ain't got no right to keep me in here," he said to us indignantly. "My visit is over, and I want to leave."

"Well, as far as I'm concerned, you're free to go," the second officer said, as he unlocked the door.

"Damn right," Byron said, slowly stepping forward and looking at me out of the corner of his eye. He acted as if I were like any other officer in the jail. But it was clear I wasn't, and my presence there wasn't a good sign for him. He made a show of shrugging his shoulders, as if someone had laid hands on him. Before he could exit the cell, I blocked his path.

"I'm Investigator Ratley, Dallas Police Department Child Abuse Unit."

Byron's Adam's apple bobbed as he swallowed hard. "What's that got to do with me?"

"May I see your identification?" I asked.

"Why?" Fear had crept into his voice.

"Because I have an arrest warrant for a person fitting your description. So you need to show me some ID—right now."

Byron's eyes widened, swept past me to the other officer, and came back to my steady gaze. Then he pulled his wallet out of his right back pocket, and handed me his driver's license.

"Byron Jennway," I read from it aloud.

"That's right," he said, a trace of indignation resurfacing. "I want to be on my way."

"Can't allow that," I replied, as I pocketed his license. "You're under arrest for felony child abuse of Kyle and Jordan Foxroy. You have the right to remain silent. From this point forward, anything you say can be used as evidence against you in a court of law. You have the right to legal counsel. If you can't afford an attorney, the court will appoint one to represent you. Do you understand?"

"What's this all about?" he asked in a surprised tone.

"I just told you what it's about. Do you understand your rights as I explained them?"

"Yes, okay. What I don't understand is why you think I'd do something like that."

"You'll find out soon enough. Now face that wall, and assume the position," I said, pointing across the hallway.

The color drained from Byron's face. "But you ain't got diddly on me!" he said, backing away.

Wrong; I had almost enough. And if he were guilty, I aimed to persuade him to tell me the rest. In a flash, I locked my left hand on his right wrist, slipped behind him, and pivoted.

"You are under arrest," I repeated slowly, and waited for his arm to go slack. When it did, I released his wrist, and steered him out of the cell.

"Spread your arms and feet, grab the wall."

"You got the wrong guy, chief," Byron said hoarsely, but he complied. I checked him for weapons. Nothing.

"Hands behind your back." I yanked a pair of cuffs from my pocket and snapped them on him.

"I didn't do it!" he insisted as I led him to the elevator. "I love those boys like they was my own." He seemed to be on the verge of tears. "That's my main weakness. Too nice. People take advantage of me."

"You can tell me all about it downstairs," I said and pushed the button.

"Downstairs? What's downstairs?" he asked warily.

"An interview room," I said. "You and me are gonna talk about Kyle and Jordan."

Byron's eyes blinked rapidly, but he said nothing. Perhaps he expected a major-league whupping. But I couldn't bring myself to put him at ease on that score. Still, I'd have to quickly work myself up to an appearance of empathy. Unless I got Byron to trust me, the interview would produce little of value. But a wave of disgust was building inside me as I thought of the two boys and their dismal future.

The elevator dinged, we stepped in, and I got ready to put on my game face. It didn't mean getting tough; that was my default state. No, I'd instead have to give Byron the impression that I wanted to help him. While it wouldn't be easy, I'd have to wear that mask to get the truth in this interview. My job wasn't to decide whether a suspect was guilty. But if I felt the evidence was strong enough, I'd conduct an admission-seeking interview. This was one of those situations. So as we dropped toward the second floor, I took a deep breath and pulled that mask over my face, my voice, and my emotions. It went with the territory.

Building Rapport

Byron relaxed just a tad when we got off on the second floor, where he saw offices but no cells. I put him in front of me and told him to walk until I said stop. We had passed a few offices and a lineup room when I told him to hold up. I unlocked the door to the Child Abuse Unit interview room, flipped on the lights, and motioned for him to enter. I didn't see anyone else around right then, but often someone would be working late.

The interview room was about 10 by 30 feet and windowless with a long table and a dozen plastic chairs. When necessary, it doubled as a conference room. Its only door locked from the outside.

I took the cuffs off Byron, and told him to have a seat.

Apparently emboldened because the environment suggested questions, not a beating, he made a sour face and sat down, rubbing his wrists.

"How long will this take?" he asked.

I resisted an impulse to twist his nose off and said, "As long as necessary. I'll be back."

59

He looked around at the empty room—no phone, no pictures, no magazines; just what I wanted. I walked out, locked the door, and left him with nothing to do but wonder how much I knew.

The interview room was visible from my office, so I'd know if he tried to leave. I made a cup of coffee and put in a phone call to the DPD dispatcher's office, which was always open. Back then, before networked desktop computers were commonplace, we relied on the dispatcher to execute our online queries.

While waiting for a call back, I opened my filing cabinet, and at random pulled out a thick accordion folder. It turned out to be a case I'd closed four months ago—parents had shut their son in a closet for three days, and the neighbors heard him crying; no relation to the matter at hand.

Twenty minutes later, I got a call with the results from my queries. According to state motor vehicle records, Byron's driver's license was genuine, confirming his identity for my case file. And, per the FBI's national database of criminal records, he had no prior felony convictions and there were no other warrants for his arrest.

I stuffed two legal pads and several pens inside the accordion folder, tucked it under my arm and headed back to Byron. As I walked down the hall, I thought back to what the ER doctor who had treated the boys told me. He didn't know what they had been beaten with. But, he said, a raised edge on the same side of each wound indicated it had been inflicted by someone almost certainly right-handed.

Gus Rose's advice also echoed in my mind. "To get a suspect to confess, you have to convince him that 1) you know he did it, and 2) it's in his best interest to admit it."

Roger that. I opened the door, pulled up a chair on the same side of the table as Byron, and plunked the folder down near me but in his line of sight. I shook out a cigarette for myself, and held the pack out before him. "Smoke?"

His eyes narrowed, but he reached out his right hand to take one. We lit up.

"Here's your license back," I said, and slid it along the table to him.

He picked it up with his right hand and said, "So? You've got to charge me or let me go."

"I *have* charged you," I said, and let that sink in.

"But you got no proof," he cried. "I didn't touch those kids."

I glanced at the folder, and his eyes followed mine. It was essential that I keep the pressure on without revealing exactly how much I knew. I hoped Byron's curiosity about the evidence against him would outweigh any inclination he might have to ask for a lawyer. Many people in Byron's position have an overwhelming fear of the unknown. It compels them to keep talking with the police in an attempt to discover the evidence against them and construct alibis or denials that refute it.

But a skilled investigator can reveal practically nothing while delivering a steady stream of vague assertions that sometimes goad a guilty suspect into self-righteously explaining why he committed the very act he'd previously denied. It is, of course, the investigator's responsibility to detect a false confession, as I did with Foxroy when she tried to take the fall for Byron.

"I've got a signed statement from Kaylee, so I know what happened," I said. "Those boys have severe brain damage and will never recover. You realize what you're up against?"

"That damned bitch lied to you!" he said, his fists clenched on the table.

Although I hadn't specified what Foxroy told me, Byron assumed the worst. As it turned out, he was right. And it looked like he wanted to do to her what he'd apparently done to her sons, but this time with his bare hands. It was clear to me now that when he and Foxroy spoke an hour earlier she didn't let on she'd fingered him. No wonder she'd at first been willing to take the blame rather

61

than face Byron after implicating him. He was a real tough guy with women and children. More than ever, I felt Byron was guilty. But to be certain, I wanted and needed an unforced confession. So I stayed calm and on topic.

"Who's the jury going to believe—the boys' mother or you?" I asked.

He looked down, clearly shaken. "I dunno."

"Don't make me laugh," I said. "The jury will believe her."

By now, Byron had lowered his head in despair. "How did this happen?" he said mournfully.

That was progress. "I see it all the time." I said. "Hell, I've been close to it myself." It took a special effort not to give myself away on that exaggeration.

He looked up as if he were drowning and I'd thrown him a lifeline. "You?"

"Me. I understand how frustrated you got. I love my kids, but sometimes I spank them harder than I mean to."

"Oh, yeah!" he said in enthusiastic agreement. Then he paused, sat up straight, and spoke carefully. "I see what you mean, but I didn't touch those boys."

"That ain't gonna get it," I said. "We're not here to talk about whether you did it. I know you did it, and no one—judge or jury— is for a moment going to doubt you did it. People like you are convicted on circumstantial evidence all the time. They're going to throw the book at you if you plead not guilty."

"Why should I believe anything you're telling me?" he asked plaintively, as if he were the victim in this case.

"Because all I want is the truth," I said. "That's my job. I've talked to plenty of people about you," I continued, and patted the folder. "You seem like a decent man, and I can tell this has been preying on your mind. I understand how all of a sudden things can get out of hand. And before you even know what's happening, it's all over."

Byron looked at the folder, and put his head back down.

"I think you want to do the right thing," I said. "But you just don't know what it is, so I'll tell you straight out: Speak the truth. Because if you keep on lying to me, this will *not* end well for you. Your only hope is to explain why this happened so that people can understand it."

No denial this time; just silence.

I pressed ahead. "I know what your life is like. I've been out to the Chestnut. That old bag you work for—she's ugly enough to make a freight train take a dirt road. I can picture her chewing on your ass all day."

"She's terrible, terrible," he said. "Cusses me all the time."

"I picked up on that," I said. "I know how it is. Work is rough. You buy a 12-pack of beer on the way home. You're trying to enjoy what's left of the day, and here come the damn kids."

Those few words seemed to resonate for Byron, as if I had granted his violent rage a measure of legitimacy.

"I just had a bad day at the motel," he said in bitter resignation. "That witch was on me every time I turned around. Seemed I couldn't do nothing right for her. When I got home, Kaylee went food shopping and left the kids with me. I sat down to watch Jackie Gleason on TV, but the boys were shouting and carrying on. I went into the kitchen to get another beer, and they followed me in there, still yelling. Next thing I knew I was pounding on them with a spoon. It just happened."

Finally, the truth-telling I was hoping for…but my blood ran cold. "What kind of spoon?"

"I don't know…probably the big wooden one Kaylee uses to cook."

This time it was my head that dropped down. I ran my hand across my face to hide my frustration. I'd seen the improvised weapon in Foxroy's kitchen and not realized how its shape corresponded to the boys' wounds. Despite my growing experience in investigating child abuse, I had more to learn about the dangers children faced every day from adults in their own homes.

Byron rattled on. "That just made them carry on even worse, so I sent them to bed. All I wanted was some peace and quiet. You know what I mean?" He looked at me sheepishly, as if he had committed a mere social blunder instead of beating the boys nearly to death. I hoped he couldn't tell how badly I wanted to give him the thrashing he'd expected. But there wasn't much chance of Byron noticing that. He was wound up in his own thoughts, and all of a sudden, out of nowhere he said, "I've been going to church every night since this happened. They sing a beautiful hymn, and it goes like this."

I stared at him, stunned, thinking, "Don't you dare…"

But it was too late. He started wailing in a screeching falsetto, then dancing spasmodically…right in front of me. I wondered if I'd been teleported into a psychiatric ward.

When it finally ended, he caught his breath, sat down, and said, "I didn't mean to hurt those children."

Speechless myself, I managed only to nod in acknowledgment. I focused my attention on getting what the D.A. would need to put Byron where he wouldn't be able to abuse any more kids.

"Look," I said. "I have to appear before the grand jury and tell them what happened." I wanted to create a sense of urgency that would encourage him to talk now, before he spoke to a lawyer who'd tell him to shut his mouth immediately.

"What kind of opinion do you think they'll have of you?" I asked.

"Probably not a good one," he admitted.

"That's right. We need to let them know that you're not really a bad guy, and that this just got out of hand. I'd like to tell them your side of the story. And with your help, I can. Don't you want them to hear that?"

"Yeah," he said. "I'd like for them to know what it's like to be in my shoes."

"All right, then. Let's get to work."

It was a bizarre situation. As much as I despised this guy, I was talking to him like we were partners. But that's what was necessary, so I bit my tongue and did it.

Getting It in Writing

I pulled a pen and pad out of the accordion folder, put them on the table, and turned to face him.

"Let's go over it once more," I said. "Tell me again what happened. I'll write it down, and you can review it before you sign."

I preferred to take down a suspect's confession in my own handwriting. That way I could shape the statement so that it reflected what the suspect had told me and contained the details prosecutors needed to present the case in court.

"I give you my word," I said. "When I'm before the grand jury, I'll read to them every word in your statement."

Byron reached over, grabbed my arm, and said, "You'd do that for me?"

"Yes," I said, looking him in the eye. "I will."

And with that, we began. Here and there, as we proceeded, I intentionally misspelled a word.

When I did, I said, "I made a mistake here. Would you scratch that out and write this instead, then initial it, so people will know no one has changed your statement without your approval?"

He agreed, and we repeated that process several times throughout the confession, demonstrating his active participation in the preparation of the statement, even though most of it was in my handwriting. I also took care to include wording I always built into such documents. For example, every confession I took in my career began with the suspect stating his name and declaring that he was providing the following information to me of his own free will, without me promising him immunity or threatening him in any way.

I got more coffee, and we made good progress over the next few hours. Dawn approached, but in the windowless room, we didn't notice. For the D.A. to make a strong case, Byron's confession had to contain specific information about his beating of the boys. So, on the pretext that the grand jury needed to know *why* he had attacked them, I pressed Byron for numerous details to include in the statement. In truth, though, no one really cared why it happened. They just wanted to know who did it, and how badly the victims were injured.

When we were done composing, I made him re-read everything with me. We sat side by side, and I passed my index finger under every word as we read Byron's confession all the way to its final statement: "I have reviewed every word in this document. It is a complete and accurate account of what I did and of the circumstances in which I did it."

"Is this all true?" I asked Byron.

"Yes, it is," he replied.

"Good," I said, handing him the pen. "Sign right there."

He did, and I tucked his confession into the folder.

"After I testify, it'll be a few days before we hear back from the grand jury. Meanwhile, you've got to be someplace secure, so I'm going to have to put you in jail."

Byron took this news calmly. His future, while far from bright, seemed less tentative than it had a few hours earlier. Of course, this was largely due to the impression I had given him that his confession would help him in court. In fact, Byron was so relieved that he did what Gus Rose said people in his situation frequently do: He hugged me.

"Thank you very much for what you're doing for me," Byron said with feeling. I'll never forget his next words. "I want the good Lord to forgive me," he said, "and I want the boys to forgive me. But more than anything, I want you to forgive me."

I realized at that point the investigative power that Gus Rose had shared with me and every other officer he taught: Before a

66

guilty suspect confesses, he faces his uncertain fate alone. But by admitting his crime to the interviewer, he gains an apparent ally and a reason to hope for an outcome he can endure. This often produces a flood of emotional gratitude to the interviewer.

"I understand," was all I said to Byron. I just couldn't bring myself to forgive him then; I still haven't.

The sun was up when I brought Byron back to the city jail. Then, while the entire municipal building resumed its busy daytime rhythm, I sat down at my desk, where I worked on my case report and other matters until about three o'clock that afternoon—a 15-hour day. Next morning, I got a search warrant for Foxroy's apartment. I found that damned spoon, and secured it in an evidence bag. It was probably ten inches long. Not huge, but with it, Byron was able to ruin the lives of two five-year-old boys. I brought it to the property office, and tried to move my mind on to something else. The other cases on my desk quickly took care of that.

A few days later, when I testified before the grand jury, I did exactly what I told Byron I'd do—I read his entire confession to them.

When the jurors heard those words and reviewed Parkland's photos of the boys, Byron's complaint about not being able to watch Jackie Gleason in peace fell on unsurprisingly deaf ears. And that was what I had counted on. The grand jury reacted by indicting both Byron and Foxroy, each of whom later pleaded guilty. Byron was sentenced to 20 years in prison, and Foxroy got 12 years for not reporting the assault on her kids.

Looking back on the case after their sentencing, I saw I had approached it in the only way that had a chance of success, and it had paid off. If I had believed Foxroy's false confession and charged her with child abuse for the beating of her boys, there was a chance Byron would have testified that she didn't do it. And if I then charged Byron with the assault I couldn't get Foxroy indicted for, Byron's defense attorney would have easily been able to persuade the court that I was grasping at straws. There would've been no trial.

As a result, the boys would've gone back home with Foxroy and Byron. Of course, they would have been under the nominal supervision of Child Protective Services caseworkers. In reality, though, that agency was overwhelmed with cases, and might not have been able to visit often or at all. So the boys again would have been exposed to neglect or abuse. And if Foxroy ended her relationship with Byron because of what he'd done to her kids, he'd wind up with some other woman and do the same thing to her kids.

Moving On

With their mother and Byron serving hard time, the boys at least had a chance of getting a proper upbringing from someone else. But I don't know what happened to them. The only way I could survive such cases was to let them go. In all likelihood, the boys were either adopted by relatives or put in a foster home under state supervision. I never went back to find out. When the case was over, my lieutenant said to me, "You should be proud of what you did on behalf of those children." That meant a lot to me, and made it easier to move on and help other kids in dire need.

I had made it a priority to improve my interviewing skills, and cases like this were proof that I had achieved my goal. But a new and unexpected problem was about to confront me. It was that some of my upcoming cases involved sustained, premeditated evil, as opposed to spontaneous rage. Two of the next three child abuse cases I'll discuss will illustrate this. As with virtually every officer working such cases, the effects on me were profound.

CHAPTER 8

TIME FOR A CHANGE

After a year and a half in the Child Abuse Unit, I thought I'd seen the limits of human perversity. But that turned out to be an illusion, shattered when I investigated two similar but unrelated instances of alleged father-daughter incest. One case was mine from the beginning; the other was Billy Hooker's, and I showed him how to find the elusive suspect. Our inquiries confirmed the allegations and led to the convictions of both fathers, who received long terms in prison. The first case began when I got a call one morning from a Girl Scout leader.

"One of my scouts is pregnant," she said. When that had become apparent, the 14-year-old was transferred from her high school to a home for unwed mothers and disturbed adolescents. "I know her and her family pretty well; she wouldn't get herself into this kind of trouble," the scout leader said. "Her father seems to me like the kind of man who could force his daughter to have sex with him." The scout leader acknowledged, however, that she had no evidence to back up her claim.

I wanted to help, but there wasn't much predication for interviewing the girl. All I had to go on was the scout leader's suspicion. Most teenage pregnancies have nothing to do with incest. The scout leader could have had it in for the father for any number of reasons. Plus, I was at the same time working five other cases, each with solid proof of child abuse. So I made a note of the girl's name, those of her parents, their home phone number, and the location of her school. In a unit that consisted solely of me and Billy, it wasn't possible to investigate unsubstantiated allegations. Instead, we had to focus on the most serious charges supported by hard evidence.

Later that morning, I went to see a witness in one of my other cases. After the interview, I drove back to my office, passing through Old East Dallas. While stopped at a red light, I noticed I was at the corner of Ross Avenue, a street whose name rang a bell. Curious, I scanned my case notebook, and found that the school the scout leader had mentioned was just across the road. I hung a sharp right into the school's parking lot, and headed straight for the principal's office. Once there, I explained the reason for my visit. The principal said she'd need "special clearance" for me to talk to the girl, Samantha Fashman, who so far had refused to identify the father of the child she was expecting. But now that I was there, I was determined to interview the girl.

"We're all responsible for protecting kids," I said. "I'm sure you realize I can't postpone this interview; the suspect might abuse other children. So please get that clearance now. I'll wait right here." I sat back and hoped the principal didn't call my bluff; I really didn't have time to cool my heels in her office while all my other cases waited.

She left briefly to check with the school's chief of security, then came back and said she'd let me see the child. "The last class of the day is just ending. I'll bring her over. You can have 15 minutes with her."

"That'll work," I said. "Just introduce me, and I'll take it from there. We have to make it clear we're offering help, and not blaming her for anything at all."

A few minutes later, the principal brought the child in to me. She looked miserable and scared as hell. After being introduced, I told Samantha I was there to protect her, not punish her.

"I got a phone call from someone who thinks your father had sex with you," I said gently. "Is that true? I promise that you won't get in trouble no matter what you tell me."

In response, Samantha lowered her head and said nothing, while clutching one hand in the other. Her grip was so tight, though, that her nails dug into the skin and drew blood. Perhaps because it was now clear that the police suspected her father, she suddenly decided to speak, and the whole story came pouring out. Yes, she said, her father had forced her into having intercourse with him. I assured her that would not happen again, thanked the principal, and headed back to the office to document the interview, get a warrant, and plan how to collar Samantha's father without delay.

I also wanted to get all the information I could out of her mother, Luanne, so I called her the minute I got back to the office. I told Mrs. Fashman what Samantha had said, and asked if she wanted to come downtown or for me to visit her, but it had to be right away. She agreed to come to DPD headquarters that afternoon. At the time, I didn't know how much she knew, and I had no idea it was risky for her to leave the house without getting permission from her husband, Jerome Fashman. I was just beginning to find out how thoroughly this guy dominated his family.

When Luanne Fashman arrived at my office an hour later, she wasn't alone. A woman who looked to be in her late 20s came with her. As I expected, the younger woman was Mrs. Fashman's daughter. That was where the accuracy of my expectations ended.

Both women looked overwhelmed, and I soon found out why. It was worse than I could have imagined. They told me that Mrs. Fashman's daughter—not Mrs. Fashman—was Samantha's mother. Jerome Fashman had impregnated his own daughter, who now as an adult still lived under his physical, psychological, and financial domination. And Samantha, the child he had fathered by her, would soon give birth to yet another of his incestuous children. The commencement of a second round of abuse, along with my prompting, apparently motivated Mrs. Fashman and her daughter to speak up.

I asked why they stayed with Fashman and hadn't turned him in. They said they were deathly afraid of him, and because neither of them had a job they feared becoming homeless without his financial support. He provided nearly everything; they kept house and shopped for groceries. When they went to buy food, though, he gave them only as much money as it would cost. And he forbade them to go anywhere except to the supermarket. In this family, the father was completely in charge.

Further, the two women told me Samantha didn't know the truth about her parentage. She naturally thought Mrs. Fashman was her mother, but they couldn't bear to tell Samantha what really had happened. I asked them where Fashman worked, and they said he was a diesel mechanic at Rebuilt Motors, a truck repair shop in northwest Dallas. I knew the area well; it was right near Parkland Memorial Hospital. They also gave me a physical description of Fashman. I now had the information I needed to get a warrant authorizing me to arrest him on felony charges. I "walked" that warrant as soon as the two women left my office.

Early the next morning, I drove over to grab Fashman at his job. I brought two uniformed officers with me as backup, or cover, as we called it. The shop where he worked specialized in servicing diesel engines and tractor-trailers. A ten-foot chain link fence surrounded it, but the gate was open, so we just drove up to the front

72

of a big garage. Its ceilings were high enough to accommodate diesel cabs, which flip forward to expose the engine for maintenance. Inside the garage were half a dozen diesels, each with the cab up so that a mechanic could get under it to repair the engine.

As I paced through the building, looking for Fashman, a supervisor asked me what I was doing there. I put my badge in his face and told him who I was after. He pointed to a blue diesel cab at the far end of the shop floor. I walked down that way and saw a guy fitting Fashman's description, wedged up in the engine compartment. The variety of power tools in use around us made a hell of a racket.

"You Jerome Fashman?" I yelled.

"Yeah," he said.

"Get down here," I told him, and flashed my badge.

"What do you want?"

"You're under arrest. I'm taking you to jail."

"Can I lock my toolbox first?" he asked.

I just stared at him. An innocent suspect's first question would be, "For what?" Not this guy. That told me something right away. He had no curiosity; he knew why we were there.

"All right," I said.

He climbed down, and reached into his pocket. My hand was on my pistol the whole time. If he had pulled out a weapon, I would've made the world a better place. But he drew out only a key and locked up his tools.

"Turn around and put your hands behind your back," I said. He did, and I handcuffed him. As we walked to my car, I read him his *Miranda* rights, and confirmed he understood them. On the way to jail, he still didn't ask why he was being arrested. If he had, I'd have told him we'll talk about it downtown. But he never uttered a word.

When I got Fashman back to my office, I confronted him about his failure to ask about the charges against him. "It puzzles me that you haven't shown any interest in why you're under arrest," I said.

"Well, I figured you'd get around to telling me the charges soon enough," he replied.

"It's clear you already know about the crime committed against your daughter, Samantha," I said.

"I don't know what you're talking about," he said with a deadpan expression.

I told him I had solid evidence proving otherwise.

"But I haven't done anything," he insisted.

"Don't waste your breath," I said. "Fifteen years ago, you raped your daughter, who gave birth to your granddaughter, and now you've gotten her pregnant too."

"That's just not true," he said. "I let Samantha go to a summer camp for Boy Scouts and Girl Scouts. They all swim in the same pool; that's how she got pregnant!"

"Try that story on the judge and jury," I said. "They'll bury you so deep in the system you'll have to have sunlight piped in for the next 20 years."

Fashman never confessed, but it didn't do him any good. He finally agreed to plead guilty in exchange for a sentence no longer than the 20 years I predicted.

We didn't charge his wife; the prosecution wouldn't have succeeded. Even if we had, she would've escaped punishment simply by telling how Fashman dominated and abused the entire family. In any case, it wasn't my job to judge her. I was glad, though, that Samantha was out of her father's clutches. But while Fashman's imprisonment ended the years of sexual abuse he had inflicted on her and his other daughter, it also harmed the family in an important way. I contacted Mrs. Fashman a few months later, and found that she and her daughter were poorer than ever, surviving only by working nights at a fast-food drive-in. With minimal education, no skills, and no experience, they could look forward to decades of minimum-wage drudgery. And unless Samantha's circumstances somehow improved, a similar fate lay in store for her. I don't know what became of them all, though. I learned it was psychological-ly imperative for officers in my position to "let go" when a case ended.

Making the Most of Coincidence

Not long after I closed the Fashman case, Billy was having trouble tracking down another father who, according to solid evidence Billy obtained, had been sleeping with his daughter, a minor. This guy, knowing the police were after him, had moved out of his house, leaving his wife and the girl there alone. While there was no love lost between the father and family, they needed his income, and he had recently lost his job. So they stayed in touch while he looked for work. He'd be no use to them in jail, so whenever Billy called, the mother would say the guy was off somewhere on a job hunt.

One day, Billy griped to me about how frustrating his fruitless search had been. We had separate caseloads and mostly worked solo. But we also helped each other out by sharing information and investigative techniques. When I asked what the guy did for a liv-ing, Billy said he was a diesel mechanic. I couldn't believe my ears, but it was true. We found out later that it was indeed a coincidence: These two child abusers had never met each other, and there was no connection between them or their crimes.

I told Billy I just might be able to help him find a suspect who happened to be an unemployed diesel mechanic. He quickly accepted when I explained my plan and suggested that I call the man's wife myself. So I dialed the woman's number, and asked to speak with her husband. As usual, she said he was out looking for a job, and she didn't know when he'd return.

"Well, please tell him that Mr. Ratley from Rebuilt Motors called about his application for the diesel mechanic position I'm trying to fill," I replied. While I expected him to recognize the shop's name, I had just made up the part about him submitting an application.

"Oh, I will!" she said. "Give me your number."

Not ten minutes later, the phone rang. The suspect said he didn't remember filing an application with Rebuilt, but he was certainly familiar with the shop. I joked that we all get forgetful as we age, and emphasized that I aimed to hire someone in the next few days.

"It's almost noon," I said. "How about meeting me for lunch and a beer today? I'll tell you about the job." I named a well-known diner near the truck shop.

"That'd be great," he answered. We agreed to meet in an hour, and hung up. Billy, sitting next to me, had heard enough to be encouraged. He pulled a file photo of the suspect, and we went upstairs to invite our supervisor, Sgt. Jackie Davidson, along.

Soon the three of us were in Billy's car, parked in front of the diner. The guy showed up right on time and looked just like his photo. We got out, and Billy called the guy's name and badged him. He turned toward us with a blank look that quickly changed to one of disbelief and frustration. Billy announced the charges, then Mirandized and cuffed him.

Guilt was the last thing on this guy's mind. "Can't this wait? I gotta see Mr. Ratley in there," he said, pointing at the diner with his chin. "I been looking for work for months, and he's got a job for me. At least let me explain I'll be late for the interview!"

"I wouldn't make any plans," Billy said, and placed the guy in the back seat. We didn't know whether to laugh or cry, but it was good to break the impasse and help Billy collar a strong suspect.

Out of Control

I didn't know it at the time, but after the two incest investigations, my tour in the Child Abuse Unit was about to come to a sudden end. My last case there turned out to be one in which I saw no need to question the suspect when I arrested him. His name was Troy Bredsal, and in a fit of anger, he had brutally burned his seven-year-old daughter Emily's chest with a steam iron.

I interviewed her in the hospital, whose staff had notified DPD. As I stared in horror at the full, red imprint of the iron on her skin, the child told me that her daddy had gotten angry when she distracted him and he scorched a shirt. Her wound perfectly matched the improvised weapon's shape; there was no chance it had been inflicted accidentally. The outer layer of skin had been burned off, exposing an inner layer, which was blistered and oozing. Even with my extensive experience, I found it hard to believe someone could commit such an act. Yet it had happened, and this child's own father was indeed the culprit. The enormous scar might very well ruin her life, which had barely begun.

In a fury, I set out to find the guy. I was already fed up with the child abuse I'd seen. But this case temporarily deranged me and eliminated the last shred of my objectivity. I didn't realize the drastic change in my attitude, though. Feeling perfectly normal, I decided to circumvent the legal process because Troy Bredsal was obviously guilty. I wanted to execute him and hoped he'd violently resist arrest. That would give me legal cover after I blew him away.

I got a warrant for his arrest, and headed out for Oak Cliff, the rundown neighborhood where he and his family lived. Against regulations, I purposely went alone. Normally, on a felony arrest, I would have brought two patrol officers with me. But I didn't want any interference or witnesses that might prevent me from dealing with Bredsal in the way I felt he deserved.

When I got to his house, I knocked on the door. A big muscle-bound guy wearing a pair of sweat pants answered it. He must have outweighed me by 75 pounds. Because he was far larger than me and suspected of a violent felony, I figured I could shoot him and claim self-defense.

I showed him my badge. "You Troy Bredsal?" I was wearing a suit. My left hand was inside my jacket's left pocket with a .357 Magnum Colt Python. I had flipped off the safety, and my index finger rested on the trigger guard.

"That's right," he said. "What do you want?" He glanced at my bulging pocket.

"You're under arrest for felony child abuse of your daughter, Emily. Raise your hands and turn around!"

He did. I frisked him for weapons, found none, and reflexively reached for the cuffs in my back pocket. But halfway there my hand froze; I didn't want to restrain him. I steered him out on to the stoop and closed the door.

"Take a good look at this dump before you leave," I said. "It'll be a parking lot when you get out of the joint, and your wife won't even remember your name." I was being as disrespectful as I could, trying to egg him into jumping me so I could put a bullet in his head. I grabbed his arm, walked to the car, and opened the front passenger door. "Get in," I said. "If I have the slightest notion you're about to jump me or leap out, I'll blow you away in a heartbeat."

"I believe you will," he replied.

Gradually my rage began to subside, as did my determination to kill him. Still, I hoped he'd try something that would give me a reason. I held my pistol in my left hand under my jacket, pointed toward him on my right. I maintained that position and steered with my right hand as I drove downtown. Neither of us said a word on the way. When we got there, I photographed him as our procedures required, and then locked him up without incident.

Next I took the elevator down to my office and wrote up a detailed case report, including the photo and an account of my single-handed arrest. I knew I had violated DPD protocol in going solo on that collar and hoped I wouldn't be written up for it. But after managing to spare Bredsal's life, I was in no mood to take criticism over my handling of the case.

I brought the report up to Jackie's office and dropped it in his in-box. He signed off on it, and returned it to me later that afternoon.

"Nice work," he said. "Looks like you've got him dead to rights."

I gave him a tight smile.

"Your report didn't identify any officers who assisted in the arrest," he added.

"I went there alone."

"Why?" Jackie asked, looking at me as if he could read my thoughts.

"Because I was looking for a chance to shoot him," I said. "That girl's gonna have a scar on her chest for the rest of her life."

Jackie just nodded slightly and walked off.

Next morning when I came in, Jackie stopped by my desk.

"Tomorrow you'll report to Internal Affairs," he said.

I thought he'd written me up for going out alone to arrest Bredsal.

"Damn it, Jackie," I said. "You didn't have to do that."

"Oh, yes, I did," he replied, laughing. "You work there now."

My jaw dropped. I'd misread him, but I still didn't like the news.

"I don't want to go to Internal Affairs."

Jackie, who was significantly older than me, leaned over and looked into my eyes.

"No one can take this job very long, son," he said. "It's time for you to get out of here. We can't just override due process. I wouldn't be doing my job if I let you go on like that. You've performed well here, and you'll do the same in Internal Affairs. I'm not going to stand by and let you ruin your career and bring dishonor on the Dallas Police Department. I've got to do my job. Bredsal might deserve a lead slug between the eyes, but denying him a fair trial would make us no better than him."

"I'm not a bad man, Jackie," I replied. "But when I think of what he did to that little girl, it seems only fair that he die."

"That's not up to us," he answered. "Our job is to take him into custody. The judge and the jury decide his fate. Your inability to see that at the moment tells me you've been in this unit too long. It's time you had a new assignment."

Later I saw that Jackie had been absolutely right. It was time for a change, and Internal Affairs turned out to be one of my most rewarding assignments. In retrospect, I realized that the Bredsal case, more than any other, reflected the intensity of my experience in the Child Abuse Unit. It was the last in a series of cases that made me feel so responsible for protecting children from abusive adults.

Did I handle the Bredsal case properly? No. But after a while you can't help becoming subjective and driven by emotion. It was sobering to see how warped I, a normally rational person, could become under difficult conditions. There were times when I couldn't tell right from wrong; few people know what to do in every situation. But until the Bredsal case, I had always followed the penal code and worked within the law. I had conflicting feelings after my incest case, in which I helped a child and family by jailing the abuser, but hurt them by taking away the source of their income. Nevertheless, I had not taken it upon myself to determine guilt and mete out punishment. As Jackie said, those judgments belong to the judge and jury. He did what was necessary when he learned I'd lost touch with the fundamental principles of our criminal justice system. I've always been grateful to him for promptly doing something constructive about it.

A Better Interviewer

I've probably told you more about child abuse than you ever wanted to know. Yet, despite the pain and suffering they chronicle, the child abuse case histories I've shared with you also trace my evolution from frustrated rookie investigator to fact-finding case-closer. The key to my increased effectiveness? Becoming a better interviewer. As you've seen, I didn't develop that skill over-night. But I've always wanted to be as good as I personally could be at whatever I do. And that drove me to improve my interviewing skills. It would've taken me a lot longer to achieve my goal, though, if I hadn't met Gus Rose. I'll always be indebted to him for helping me better understand how people think and what techniques best cause them to open up and tell me what they know. Over the years, I've refined Gus's methods to suit my personal style and professional requirements.

I've also related these case histories to raise awareness that might in some small way help counter a disease that afflicts every demographic in our society. My tour of duty in the Child Abuse Unit was perhaps my most difficult assignment with DPD, and it pushed me to the brink of taking the law into my own hands. But I resisted that impulse, and, with the help of an attentive, proactive supervisor, moved on to a fresh and equally important assignment. The faces of the children I did my best to protect are with me every day, though. I expect they always will be. When I look back on the work I did on their behalf, I'm proud to have been a co-founder of DPD's Child Abuse Unit, which has grown from my two-man squad into one of largest and most progressive organizations of its kind in the nation. The children of Dallas need and deserve no less, and I'm glad I had the opportunity to provide that service.

While far from perfect, my own early years were happy and free of the abuse I'd seen heaped on so many kids in Dallas. The best way to explain what I mean is to travel back in time to when and where I grew up—Marshall, Texas, a small but lively town 150 miles east of Dallas. Turn the page, and I'll meet you there.

PART TWO

YOUNG MAN

"No one has ever drowned in sweat."
— *Lou Holtz*

CHAPTER 9

STEPPING BACK IN TIME

Anyone who knows me will tell you I'm as Texan as they come. So it'll surprise some of my friends to read here that I was born in New Mexico. My parents were native Texans, and had temporarily moved to the Land of Enchantment with my grandfather so the men could work there at an enormous construction site, the Tucumari Irrigation Project, which was funded and coordinated by the U.S. Department of the Interior. It produced a dam, reservoir, and two canals. With irrigation, land that never got much rain became suitable for cotton and other crops. Because assignments on projects of that size lasted months, even years, my mother went along when they set out in early 1949.

Daddy, a master carpenter, traveled often to find jobs. He and Momma were teenagers when they married, and she was carrying me, her first child, when they left home in East Texas. Her father, Pat Anderson, was a master plumber. The success of the

Tucumari project depended heavily on the skills of men like Daddy and Granddaddy Pat, who helped in the final stages of the construction.

That fall—on November 13, 1949—Momma gave birth to me in New Mexico. Three weeks later, the men's assignments ended, and we headed back to Marshall. We made the 700-mile trip in a 1941 Willis sedan with no heater to fend off the December cold. They said I cried all the way.

My Hometown and Family

About 25,000 people live in Marshall, which is the "seat," or governmental center, of Harrison County, but has very little industry and no big businesses. Even now, if you want to shop in a good-size store, you have to go to Longview, about 20 miles west, or Shreveport, Louisiana, about thirty miles east. Although Marshall is mostly flatland, it's in one of the most beautiful parts of Texas, surrounded by tall pine forests and gently rolling hills, speckled with red earth. For outdoorsmen, it's a paradise of good hunting and fishing. Summers are hot, with the temperature sometimes passing 100 degrees. But the winters are generally mild, with snow flurries every now and then. I remember one time we got six inches (which is a lot in Marshall), and Momma ran outside to get some and make snow cones for me and my little sisters, Debra and Patty.

My parents and all their relatives except me were born and raised in Marshall. Aside from when the men traveled to find work, no one went farther than 50 miles away. Marshall was—and still is—a small world, in which everybody knew everyone else's name and most of their personal business too.

Momma's maiden name was Patsy Pearl Anderson. Born in 1931, she's petite and trim, with black hair and blue eyes. She has always detested her middle name, and tried to leave it behind when she married after graduating from high school. But being a smart-aleck kid, I would sometimes leave a phone message for "Patsy Pearl" at the office where she worked. And that always led to a lot of teasing from her coworkers. On those occasions, she'd call back and threaten to tan my butt. So I'd wait until she cooled off, and then do it again.

I got my mischievous sense of humor from my daddy, Harry, who was born in 1929. Everyone called him Red because of his rust-colored hair. Daddy wore that nickname with pride, always driving a red truck and sporting red socks. He never finished high school and died before his time, at only 62 years of age.

I was a skinny little kid with big ears. Daddy thought I looked like a pickup with both doors open. A good wind, he said, would carry me off. My mother, who has always been more of a doer than a talker, didn't joke about my ears; she took action. When I was little, she taped them to my head. I like to think it helped some.

My earliest memory is of my third birthday, in late 1952. At that time, the Truman administration was in its last two months, and President-Elect Dwight D. Eisenhower was trying to figure out how best to deal with the Korean War, which by then had devolved into a stalemate. On a much smaller scale, I too had challenges, but Momma always helped me overcome them, as she did on that November 13.

That day, after lunch, she brought out a chocolate cake with three lit candles. "Happy Birthday, Jimmy Don," she said, smiling as she served me. To this day she calls me that. I remember her white blouse and blue skirt and how pretty she was. While I ate, Momma wheeled in my present: a red tricycle. In ecstasy, I rolled it outside, jumped on, and rode straight off the porch. Landing on my elbow sure changed my mood, and I wailed in pain. But Momma helped me up, cleaned my bruise, and pulled a sweater over my head.

"Now get back on, and ride around the yard," she said. I did, and felt better immediately. Over the next few years, I put a lot of miles on that tricycle.

We lived on West End Boulevard, on the—you guessed it—western perimeter of Marshall. Like all the other homes in that modest neighborhood, ours was a small frame house—not much more than a shack, really. But life was good. My parents and we kids were happy together.

One of our neighbors was disabled and got around on a motorized three-wheel bike with a little flatbed trailer. Trouble was, the flatbed was wooden and had begun to rot. One day, Daddy noticed that, and said he could re-do it with new pine. Daddy didn't want any money, and the neighbor gratefully accepted. When Daddy finished, that flatbed looked factory-fresh. He saw something needed doing, knew how, and just did it. My little heart swelled with pride.

Life Gets More Complicated

For most of the time I lived in Marshall, Harrison County was "dry"; you couldn't buy alcohol there. Back in the 1950s, a new liquor store opened in Longview, in "wet" Gregg County, just west of the Harrison County line. On its first day in business, dozens of cars from Marshall and other towns in Harrison County lined up outside. People could barely wait their turn to push in and buy some alcohol. After only one month, the owner made enough profit to pay off his mortgage.

"Dry" didn't just mean you couldn't buy; it also meant you could possess only so much. If you had more than a certain number of cases of beer or bottles of whiskey, the police could arrest you for bootlegging, even if you had bought the stuff in a "wet" county and had no intention of re-selling it.

For convenience, Daddy still chose to buy small amounts of liquor illegally in Marshall. And because he particularly liked my company—I was the only other male in our immediate family—he often took me with him when he went out on an errand. It wasn't long before one of those trips was a visit to the local bootlegger.

One hot Sunday morning, I heard the front screen door slam shut. Momma was in the back yard. I ran to the front window and saw Daddy in the driveway, getting into his red truck. I called to him, and he saw me.

"Come on, boy!" he shouted, so I ran out and climbed in.

"I'm riding shotgun!" I yelled.

"My shotgun man!" Daddy cried.

He didn't say where we were going, but I didn't care, as long as we went together. My excitement turned to puzzlement as Daddy drove east into a rundown part of town with few houses. Right after we passed a Pack-n-Sack grocery store, he hung a sharp left down a dirt road. Up ahead was nothing much, just a shabby-looking house, and I wondered what Daddy had in mind.

Then he downshifted and, as we slowed, he said, "Get down on the floorboard, boy!"

I stared blankly at him; this made no sense.

But he frowned, dead serious, and motioned for me to lay low.

"Can't have anyone see you coming along to the bootlegger."

I had no idea what "bootlegger" meant, but I did as he said.

Then Daddy pulled up on what sounded like gravel, and got out. I felt strange, crouched on the floorboard, facing the transmission hump. Through his open window, all I could see was Daddy's head and shoulders against the bright blue sky.

"Stay down," he said without looking at me. "I'll be right back." And he was. Clutching a paper bag, Daddy once again wore a smile. He slipped the package under his seat and acted as if nothing had changed between us. But I was ashamed because he made me hide. I wanted him to be proud of me all the time, as he usually seemed to be.

After we rode a few blocks homeward, he slapped the empty seat and said, "Where's my shotgun man?"

Silently I climbed up from the floor and took my place beside him.

"Don't be a sad sack, boy!" Daddy said, throwing me a grin.

I smiled weakly and thought of asking what all that had been about. But something in Daddy's manner told me I shouldn't.

Making Choices

For a while, Daddy got to work nearby when he and Granddaddy Pat built a house right down the street. One time, they gave me a nickel to collect their small, scattered scraps of wood. So, piece by piece, I began to accumulate a little pile. Granddaddy noticed how I went about this.

"Son," he said to me, "if you can't move more than one scrap at a time, you'll never be much use to anybody." I had received my first lecture on work habits, and it was from someone who himself set a good example.

When my mother was a child, Granddaddy Pat supported her, Grandma Nina, five other children, and himself through his work as a plumber. He was a great big bull of a man, and he always found a way to earn a living—even when times were tough. At the beginning of each construction project, he'd call his new crew together, take an inch-thick rod of black steel and bend it in two. They got the message; no one questioned his authority. For many years, Granddaddy Pat was very successful. But somehow he succumbed to alcohol and became Marshall's town drunk. Daddy, 25 years younger than Granddaddy Pat, eventually did the same thing.

The striking thing was that although alcoholism plagued both sides of our family, it did so unevenly. Daddy's father was a church-going man who didn't drink. And while Granddaddy Pat lost his fight with the bottle, my mother has never touched the stuff. Genetics no doubt play a role in determining who becomes an alcoholic, but so do the choices a person makes in life. Daddy chose not to follow his father's good example, and Momma chose not to follow her father's bad example. At this early stage of my life, Daddy's drinking was relatively under control, and I chose to idolize him.

Room to Roam

As construction began to pick up, Daddy's bigger paychecks made it possible for us to move five miles south to a brick house on Rosborough Springs Road. With three bedrooms and two baths, our latest home was a real step up for us. I thought I'd died and gone to heaven.

My ecstasy soon ended, however, when the time came for me to begin attending school. As the first-born, I didn't know anything about it. In those days, small towns like Marshall didn't have preschool or kindergarten programs. Every day, I'd just wake up, go outside, and play. Then one day Momma woke me early and got me very neatly dressed. I figured we were going to the doctor, and didn't ask any questions.

Instead, she took me to William B. Travis Elementary School, which, like many other buildings in Texas, is named after the hero of the Battle of the Alamo. Everywhere in sight were kids I didn't know. I feared something unpleasant was about to happen. When it became clear to me that Momma would leave and not take me with her, I panicked and tried to jump out the classroom window. Fortunately, we were on the first floor and I had a skilled and kindly teacher, Mrs. Pope, who wore her black hair in a little bun.

She managed to distract me with a special assignment—ringing the hand bell that announced the beginning of class. Weeping profusely, I swung that bell back and forth with Mrs. Pope urging me on. At lunchtime, she had me repeat my performance. That kept me on the right side of the window and helped me make it through my first day of school.

I felt better back at home, when I got a chance to explore my seemingly vast new stomping grounds. Although our home was barely outside the Marshall city limits, its surroundings seemed like open countryside to me. But not far from our house, behind tall stands of pine that occupied much of the neighborhood, was the Atlas Chemical Company, which mined the earth for lignite, a soft coal composed of ancient peat moss.

Sometimes Atlas's mining operations broke through to cold, underground springs. Then the water, surging up, became clearer as it passed through the charcoal-like lignite and formed deep blue ponds among the pines. Nothing could be more tempting or dangerous to a young boy. Without my parents' knowledge, I swam in those ponds, which I later found were as much as sixty feet deep.

My antics didn't end there. My mother, ever intent on improving our quality of life, got a job at Atlas, testing ore samples. Her wages made it possible to hire a part-time housekeeper. Annie, a generously proportioned, warm-hearted soul, cleaned up and took care of us kids while Momma was at work. She was like a second mother to me and my sisters.

Like many other families, we had bought our first television set. Back then, there were few programs and they all were, by today's standards, squeaky clean. Still, we kids were forbidden to watch anything other than Pinkie Lee and Howdy Doody.

One day, my sisters weren't at home and Annie was outside hanging laundry. Taking advantage, I surfed the channels and stumbled across a film starring the voluptuous Jane Russell. I watched, spellbound, as she and some guy with a mustache romped in a hayloft. I was eager to see more but realized that Annie would put a stop to this if she came in just then. So I locked the front and back doors.

Russell and her lover still hadn't come up for air when I heard the back door rattle and Annie bellow, "Mr. Jimmy Don, you better open this door right now!" But I watched on while Annie went around to the front door, found it too was locked, and promptly went ballistic.

"Mr. Jimmy Don, I'm gonna tear up your little butt!" she shouted. That did it; unlike William B. Travis, I surrendered. After I unlocked the door, Annie gave me the paddling I deserved. I accepted my punishment...without regret!

All Kinds of Lessons

My mother is strong-willed. The words *give up* do not exist for her or her children.

For years, she worked at the Atlas Chemical Company doing the same lignite sample testing men did, for a fraction of what they earned. As if that weren't bad enough, management stuck her on the night shift. But none of that stopped her. Momma took college courses and became one of the few certified professional secretaries in Texas at that time. With her commercial credential, a solid academic background, and the ability to take shorthand and burn up a keyboard at 140 words a minute, she carved out a career for herself. When Alcoa, the global aluminum producer, set up a facility in Marshall, its general manager snapped her up as his executive assistant the day she applied for the job.

Mother's hard work paid for our dance lessons, piano lessons, and membership in the Corral Club, where kids could dance and hang out under adult supervision from 7:30 to 10:00 on Friday and Saturday nights.

There we took ballroom dancing lessons from Miss Crowley, who was in her sixties and heavy-set, with an abundance of bosom. To demonstrate a waltz box step, for example, she'd have me dance with her. Problem was, though, that her breasts were level with my face. Many a time one of them poked me right in the eye, and I turned fire-engine red. The last thing a small boy wants to do is touch a girl or a woman. Of course, when my friends witnessed it, they'd rib me mercilessly for days, and I'd do the same when it was their turn. Ironically, Mrs. Sport, the Corral Club "house mom," diligently patrolled the dance floor, putting her hand between you and your partner to make sure there was no belly-to-belly contact. It never dawned on her to do that with Miss Crowley. Despite such embarrassments, the Corral Club was great fun.

Mother set high standards for behavior and achievement. Having a parent like that is a great benefit; but it can also be a trial if you're not ethically up to snuff. Initially, I wasn't; but she showed me how to get there.

Daddy used to put his loose change on the dresser. One day, I snatched two quarters and went to school, where I bought five-cent ice cream sandwiches for myself and nine other kids. We were too busy to notice that our teacher had observed this unusual purchase. She phoned my mother and told her.

Later that afternoon, I sauntered in the front door, blind to my fate. When Momma asked if I'd taken money from the dresser, I denied it. I was wearing a little Roy Rogers belt, and she told me to give it to her, so I handed it over.

"Listen good," she said afterward. "You will tell the truth and you will not steal, or I'll beat your butt seven days a week."

From that day on, I've been up to snuff and will always be grateful to my mother for setting me straight.

Summers in the Country

My sisters and I stayed at Momma's grandmother Blanche's house in the countryside near Marshall quite often, especially when it was hot. Her husband, Nat, was a barber and used to cut my hair. Their house had no indoor plumbing. You drew water from a well and used the outhouse.

Great-granddaddy Nat told us how he once had written to Sears & Roebuck, ordering some toilet paper. Sears wrote back telling him to re-order using the item number from the catalogue. Nat replied that if he had the catalogue, he wouldn't need the toilet paper. That amused us, but we amused Blanche as well.

"You city folks beat anything I've ever seen," she said. "You think you're a success when you can eat outdoors and go to the bathroom indoors. Well, you've got it backwards."

Blanche was very self-sufficient. She churned butter, and every fall, she and Nat canned vegetables they'd grown. One time, I saw a flock of blackbirds out back, and I called to Nat, who loaded the shotgun he kept at hand. Nat moved fast, and two shots boomed in quick succession. Minutes later, he brought in four birds, and Blanche roasted them for dinner.

Perhaps my most precious possession at Great-grandma Blanche's house was an old car tire that I rolled beside me everywhere I went outdoors.

One day she said, "Go out there and feed the chickens, Jimmy Don."

"All right," I said. "I'll get my tire."

On a family farm, few animals are as important as the rooster. Without him, production stops. Blanche's rooster hated me. Every time I went down the back porch steps, he'd run after me and peck at my bare little legs.

I fetched my tire and a bolo paddle that used to have a rubber cord with a ball at the end. The cord and ball had fallen off long ago; I'd use the paddle to knock small rocks through the air.

For about an hour, I had a good time rolling my tire and swatting rocks. Then I remembered I had to feed the chickens, so I headed back toward the hen house, which wasn't far from the back porch. Little did I realize that vicious rooster had all the while been under the porch waiting to ambush me. As I neared the hen house, he rushed out on the attack. I sprinted away as fast as I could, but that damned bird kept up with me, getting in some good pecks on my calves.

As I ran, my arms flailed wildly in every direction. When the rooster closed in on me, I accidentally slammed my bolo paddle hard into his head, and down he went. Minutes later, he got back on his feet, and silently stumbled away. When I told Great-grandma what had happened, she looked the bird over and got angry, but didn't skip a beat. First, she fed the chickens. Then she simply wrung the now useless rooster's neck and cooked him.

When I wasn't endangering other people's property, I found ways to put myself in jeopardy. I came across some old pieces of lumber behind Blanche and Nat's house. Among them was a salvageable pair of ten-foot-long two-by-fours that I could turn into stilts. On them I nailed foot pegs and stirrups made out of rubber strips from an old inner tube. I put the pegs up high. Once on them, I'd be a few feet off the ground. But first I'd have to find a way to mount them. I could climb like a monkey, so I leaned them against a tree, and that worked fine. Soon, I was pretty good on my stilts and walked all around on them.

One day I came to a mud hole that cried out to be crossed on stilts. So I thrust one in, and then the other. Suddenly I began to sink deeper and couldn't pull my stilts out. Worse, I'd made the stirrups so snug I couldn't get either foot loose. I was trapped and alone! As I struggled to free myself, the stilts swayed back and forth, and that's how I got out—but it wasn't pretty. Rocking one way, then the other, I fell forward and landed on hard dirt at the edge of the mud hole. My chin was bruised, and I'd had the wind knocked out of me, but I was out of that mud hole. At dinner, I said nothing of this. Some things are best kept to yourself.

Rules of the Game

After about two years, we moved back into town. There still was plenty of construction going on, so Daddy was able to find one job after another, and Momma was working at Alcoa. Our newest home was on Mark Drive in Belair, a middle-class neighborhood on Marshall's south side. It too was a brick house, and Momma

96

liked it enough to remain there for a while after we kids had grown up and moved out on our own.

I was in the third grade at William B. Travis Elementary School, which we now lived within walking distance of. The school let students go barefoot when the weather warmed. I took full advantage and shed my shoes in early spring. My feet were callused by late April, and come summer, I could run flat out on a gravel road and feel no pain.

Until then, the only sports I'd played had been informal pick-up games. But then I tried out for and made our neighborhood football team, the Belair Bears, one of eight in Marshall's Little League. Its colors were red and white, and its coach was Leroy G. Hartzel, who became one of the greatest positive influences in my life.

Coach Hartzel was a true gentleman who never used profanity around us. He and my mother had gone to school together. She remembered him as an outstanding athlete. Although he was a kind and caring man, he was tougher than woodpecker lips. When he had the team run laps around the field, he'd give us a hundred-yard start and then pass us anyway.

Coach and his wife didn't have children, but you could tell he liked kids, spending two to three hours with us every afternoon during football season. Throughout those times, Coach instilled discipline in our young minds, and taught us that we were responsible for what we did and didn't do. He also made it clear that victory belonged to whoever wanted it most. On the field, that meant those who moved fastest and hit hardest. Off the field, additional rules applied: no candy, soda, or long hair. Always wear a belt and socks, call our parents "sir" and "ma'am," and show Coach every report card.

We also received good training in the game's fundamentals. As a lineman, I was face-to-face with our opponents. Coach showed me how to position myself most advantageously at the line of scrimmage. He acknowledged it's uncomfortable to keep your shoulders down, rear end high, and feet planted firmly. But, he said, that gives you the power to spring up fast and stun your opponent with a forearm to the chin.

"Make him cross-eyed on the first play of the game," Coach said. "Let him know it's gonna be a long sixty minutes." That technique worked well for me. All through Little League and later, in high school, I hit opponents with everything I had. With such guidance from Coach Hartzel, we Bears were always near the top of the league.

While I expected my share of knocks from the opposition, I was surprised to get them from a teammate. One guy, Eugene Simmons, was a year ahead of me in school, and was already on the Bears when I joined. For some reason, he targeted me. Back then, everyone played offense and defense. Simmons and I both were guards. During practice, whenever we were on opposite sides of the line, Simmons would knock the hell out of me. One day, well into the season, he cleaned my clock, and I started bawling.

Coach grabbed me by the shoulder pads and said, "Boy, are you a sissy?"

I cried even harder.

When I got home, my Daddy called the coach. I remember Daddy being pretty mad when he first got on the phone. Gradually his tone softened, but it was clear he still wasn't pleased. After hanging up, he took me aside for a talk.

The next day at practice, as soon as Coach put me in, I found Simmons and flattened him. Every play after that, whenever I could find Simmons, I knocked him to the ground as hard as I could. It felt great.

The following week, Coach called me over.

"You're doing so much better," he said. "I'm putting you in the starting lineup for Friday night's game." I was just beside myself.

When I told Simmons, he said, "Bull. He wouldn't start a jerk like you."

I walked away thinking, "He's probably right. I must have mis-understood the coach."

Time would tell, and so would our daily newspaper, *The Marshall News Messenger*. Every day, the paperboy threw it on our lawn before breakfast. This time it never hit the ground. I was out there waiting, and caught it on the fly.

I turned to the sports page, and saw what I'd hoped for. I was indeed listed as "first string" guard for the Belair Bears. I still have that newspaper.

Daddy, a referee in our football league, was beaming. Every week, he'd be out there on the gridiron in his striped shirt, running up and down the field with us players. He took officiating seriously, and was careful not to favor my team when making calls. He also was an umpire when I played baseball.

Tears and Laughter

The confidence I developed on the playing field gave me courage in another arena as well. For some time, I'd been looking forward to my first date, and had my eye on a sweet girl named Annette McClindon. I persuaded her to come with me to the movies and see Old Yeller. Afterward, with her permission, I kissed her cheek.

All worked up, I came home and asked Daddy how old you have to be to get married.

"Well," he said, "it depends. With a good job, you might be able to get married in the fifth grade."

I could see my future, and it was thrilling: I'd be a star athlete and my beautiful wife Annette would cheer me on.

Meanwhile, football season ended, and Little League baseball season began. As it happened, the field where we played had no restrooms. So when one of us boys needed one, we were told to do our business discreetly behind a car in the parking lot. When my time came, I went to the designated area, but made the mistake of spraying the side of a car. Suddenly, I realized that someone was inside it and had seen what I'd done. Yes, of all the people in town, it was Annette McClindon. Beet-red, I turned away and tried to think of an excuse. But there was none; the evidence of my guilt was everywhere. I slinked away in shame, and didn't speak to Annette again until we were in high school.

I didn't share the news with my parents. If I had, they might have told me that while the incident was embarrassing, it also was funny. Sometimes, however, what's funny to one person isn't funny to another. Take, for example, the night when Daddy came home drunk and decided to play a practical joke on Momma, who cooked our breakfast every morning before she went to work.

It was late, and Momma had already gone to bed. Daddy's brainstorm was to hard boil every egg in the refrigerator and, without shelling them, put them back in the egg carton. In the morning, when Momma tried to break the eggs but couldn't, she shook her head, peeled the shells off, and served them boiled instead of fried. She moved on, but didn't forget. Daddy would get his comeuppance soon enough.

Because Momma grew up during the Great Depression and is therefore naturally thrifty, she sometimes has a hard time throwing things out. Daddy grew up in the same era, but it wasn't his nature to worry about running out of anything except alcohol. As my father's drinking increased, my mother did what she could to cut it down. But when she found his hidden bottles, she just couldn't bring herself to pour their contents down the drain.

Once, she found some bourbon Daddy had hidden, and she put it in a bottle that had contained vanilla extract. She then buried it in the garden, and poured watered-down coffee into the empty liquor bottle. It looked just like bourbon.

That night, we all were watching TV, and Daddy, who tended to be obvious, announced that he had to go to the bathroom and would be back soon.

100

Momma just smiled at me and said, "Watch this."

Within a minute, Daddy rushed into the living room, coughing and spitting. "She's poisoned me! She's poisoned me!" he cried.

When Momma burst out laughing, we kids did too, and Daddy saw he'd been completely suckered. But, good sport that he was, he laughed as hard as we did. Everyone knew, though, that he'd search the house. So, it was only mildly surprising when Daddy managed to find the vanilla-flavored bourbon Momma had buried. He said it tasted awful, but he was glad to have it and drank every drop.

Episodes like that were funny on the surface, but serious at their core. More and more often, Daddy would come home drunk in the afternoon and fall asleep on the living room couch. Eventually, when Momma bought herself a used car, she'd drive me and my sisters to Marshall's parade ground for some fun while he slept. Daddy was plenty peeved when he learned we were having a good time without him.

So the next time he came home drunk, he snatched the ignition coil from Momma's car. Of course, she then bought a spare coil and would remove it for safekeeping before Daddy could get to it. In the end, his childish pranks accomplished only one thing: they deepened the divide between him and the rest of us.

Finally, for a reason I can't remember, Daddy was sentenced to a short stay in Harrison County jail. His father took me there for a visit. Back then, a prisoner stayed in his cell when someone came to see him. So I actually saw my father behind bars. It was an awful shock.

After Daddy was released, he and Momma had a big fight, and she decided it would be better if they separated. So she took steps to make that happen, even though Daddy didn't agree. A judge granted the separation and issued an order giving Daddy limited visitation rights.

Meeting the Police

The court order really got Daddy's dander up. Since he couldn't overcome it, he decided to undermine it. Before the separation, you couldn't get him to mow the lawn. After the separation, he used mowing the lawn as a pretext to come back and irritate Momma. When he refused to leave, she called the police.

Two patrolmen from the Marshall Police Department came by and spoke with Momma inside while Daddy made a show of mowing in the back yard. The police could see Daddy was about six feet tall and solidly built.

One of them pulled me aside and said, "Kid, go tell your daddy he has to leave. If he doesn't, I'll have to hit him with my gun."

I was horrified. This was even worse than seeing Daddy behind bars. I didn't know what to do, and stood there.

"Go on, now," the cop told me.

So I went out to Daddy and repeated what the policeman had said.

Daddy was unimpressed. "Tell him to come on out here," he said. "I'll show him where to put his damn gun."

I shuttled back and told the police that Daddy wouldn't leave. I didn't dare repeat what he'd said.

To my amazement, the police backed down and left without helping my mother. I was relieved there'd been no violence, but far from happy with what I'd seen and heard. I didn't think it was nice for Daddy to speak that way, and I didn't think it was right for the police to use me the way they did. On top of that, they left Momma alone to deal with Daddy. My first interaction with police officers had left me with a very poor opinion of them.

Going Away

After this incident, Momma made up her mind to seek a divorce. At that time, however, society strongly disapproved of it. Still, my mother knew what she had to do. When she succeeded, I felt a sense of relief because I'd no longer have to listen to my parents screaming at each other.

When Daddy announced he was moving to Austin, I had a big decision to make. I was in the seventh grade, 13 years old. I could stay in Marshall and do the same things I'd always done, or I could try something new by leaving with Daddy. Despite his serious flaws and my resentment of them, we loved each other. I also loved my mother and sisters, but I knew they'd manage just fine on their own. So, with a mixture of anticipation and anxiety, I went to Austin with my daddy.

CHAPTER 10

TO AUSTIN WITH DADDY

N o doubt about it, I told myself the day Daddy and I set out together for Austin. This would be the biggest adventure of my young life. I didn't expect a joy ride, though; not with Daddy being the way he was.

Still, if there was any one trait I inherited from both him and Momma, it was the willingness to take a risk to achieve something worthwhile. This was particularly true of Momma, who raised three kids while making her mark as a career woman in a man's world.

Unfortunately, Daddy's achievements were clouded by the drinking that had hurt him and us so often. Back then, no one knew much about alcoholism, and today's treatment options weren't available. With Momma no longer in his life, Daddy needed someone to help keep his drinking from spiraling out of control. I realized it was one of the reasons I had gone with him to Austin.

"I'm the best no-good son of a bitch you ever met," Daddy liked to boast. That was typical of him—bragging about his faults. It mystified people. An old friend of his once told me, "Red is a very confusing person." I knew just what he meant; Daddy's words and actions sometimes didn't add up. But they didn't confuse me or the rest of our family. We understood he was ashamed of himself and too proud to admit it. I hoped a fresh start would make him happier and less self-destructive. What perils the road and an unfamiliar city might hold for us, I wasn't sure. Yet I was confident he'd back me up if I got in a jam. He was always on my side and tough as nails from years on the road.

The biggest achievement in Daddy's career was his work on a massive international undertaking in West Texas, 500 miles from Marshall. That project was a giant dam on the mighty Rio Grande, which runs between the United States and Mexico. Because it would benefit both countries, they jointly funded its construction, and named it *Amistad*—Spanish for friendship.

Hurricanes often sweep out of the Gulf of Mexico and, on occasion, way up the Rio Grande Valley, past Laredo and Eagle Pass, as far north as normally parched Del Rio, the small town nearest the remote construction site, almost 400 miles from the sea. Storm-related loss of life and property often are worst near Del Rio, where the big river, flowing from its headwaters in southwestern Colorado, is fed by two smaller but turbulent rivers, the Devils and the Pecos, that originate, respectively, in the West Texas plateau and the mountains of northern New Mexico.

From time to time a bad storm pours down a normal year's rainfall or much more in a single catastrophic day. That's what happened in 1954, when Hurricane Alice dumped 34 inches of rain on West Texas in 24 hours—nearly triple the region's *yearly* average. A wild, deadly torrent then surged across the Rio Grande flood plain, obliterating everything in its path and killing 300 people. On the Pecos and Devils Rivers, walls of water up to 90 feet high washed out railroad bridges normally 50 feet above the waters. And at Laredo, the Rio Grande crested 26 feet above the floor of the International Bridge, tearing apart its approaches.

Amistad changed all that. After its construction, the next giant tempest, Tropical Storm Charley in 1998, took twenty lives—still a disaster, but thanks to the dam, one of far smaller proportions. This time an earthen and concrete wall 254 feet (23 stories) tall and six miles long blunted the force of the floodwaters and restrained them in a 65,000-acre (101-square-mile) reservoir.

Off and on for much of the 1960s, Daddy traveled back and forth between Marshall and Del Rio. And when the Amistad project called for it, he did the same while I lived with him in Austin. Besides earning much-needed cash on the assignment, Daddy picked up new skills and knowledge. He watched the concrete crew closely, asked a lot of questions, and pitched in when the opportunity arose, learning how to use concrete on a large scale. You can't do that without being good at math, and Daddy was. He performed computations without a calculator that most people couldn't do with one. That talent served him well, and he ultimately became Amistad's concrete superintendent, managing the planning and installation of 1.8 million cubic yards of the stuff. By harnessing the fury of the Rio Grande and its tributaries, the dam brought safety and reliable hydro-electric power to hundreds of thousands of people.

As a small boy, I had listened wide-eyed as Daddy described the work he and Granddaddy Pat were doing on the Tucumari Irrigation Project when Momma gave birth to me. Clearly they had achieved something significant, helping expand New Mexico's farmland and economy. Daddy's work on Amistad made me even more proud of him, not only because the project and his role in it were bigger, but also because it saved lives. Although a career in construction didn't appeal to me, I wanted to be good at something important like he was and take justifiable pride in it.

Downs...and Ups

Our first home in Austin was a small apartment in our landlord's garage. The little money we had went for rent and as much food as we could afford, which wasn't a lot. Often, our diet consisted of pinto beans and crackers with Karo syrup poured over them.

While Daddy looked for work, I returned to the classroom, newly enrolled at Baker Junior High School, where I soon became captain of the football team and was named Best Student Athlete. Getting the award was nice, but along with it came a memorable humiliation. My wardrobe consisted of one pair of pants, two shirts, and Daddy's beat-up, hand-me-down wingtips, which were three sizes too big for me.

As soon as I heard there'd be an awards ceremony, I asked a certain cute girl if she'd let me escort her to it.

She eyed my footwear. "Are those your Daddy's?"

"That's right," I answered, blushing deeply while trying to sound proud. She just laughed and walked away. So I went to the event alone, thrilled to win the prize, but stung by her contempt.

Not long afterward, my spirits soared when what seemed like another humiliation turned out to be an unforgettable gift. Baker's football players wore traditional team jackets with the school "letter." Trouble was, Daddy and I didn't have the $13.25 necessary to buy me one. So I lied to the coach, saying I preferred to sew my letter onto a favorite sweater instead. He said he understood. A few weeks later, after practice, Coach told us the jackets were in. Beside him on the locker room floor were two large cardboard boxes containing the coveted status symbols.

One by one, he pulled them out, yelled the name embroidered on each and tossed it to the corresponding player. Figuring there wasn't one for me, I stood in the back. Then, to my astonishment, Coach held up a jacket and called out, "Jim Ratley." Stunned, I froze. But with him staring at me and waiting, I walked forward.

And that's when it hit me that Coach had bought the jacket for me. As he held it out with a smile, I felt shame not gratitude. My family doesn't need charity, I thought.

"I didn't order one," I said stiffly, not taking the jacket.

Coach's smile widened. "I know," he said. "But your daddy did."

For a moment I stood there with my mouth open. Quickly recovering, I said thanks, grabbed the jacket, and ran outside to put it on in private. "Good old Daddy," I said to myself in delight as I slowly ran my fingers over the letter and embroidery. When he got home from work, I told him how much this meant to me.

"Sure, son," Daddy said, his eyes sparkling. "A player needs a jacket, especially when he's team captain."

Later I learned he'd hocked his most needed tool—a circular saw—to get money for that jacket, which I still have. If my house ever catches fire, Daddy's gift will be the first thing I save.

In the Clutch

Sometimes during the school year, Daddy would be on the road and away overnight for several days. On those occasions, I'd maintain my routine, attending classes, playing football, and returning to the garage apartment, where I spent the nights alone. It was never a problem; I was very self-sufficient, and knew how to stay out of trouble. And when Daddy got road assignments during my summer vacation, I'd gladly go with him.

One of those was a short-term job in Brownsville at the southern tip of Texas, across the Rio Grande from Matamoros, Mexico. We made the 350-mile drive down in his red Ford pickup. At 14, I hadn't learned to drive yet, and wondered how long it would take me to master a manual "stick" transmission. I'd find out sooner than I expected.

Our stay in Brownsville was uneventful—until the last day, when Daddy wrenched his knee only hours before the job ended.

Limping, but eager to return to Austin, he wouldn't listen to my pleas that he visit a doctor. Instead, Daddy obtained his own version of emergency medicine—a fifth of Oso Negro vodka—and quickly self-administered the entire bottle. We made it to the outskirts of Brownsville without him hitting anything or attracting a police escort. From that point on, the drive would be simpler. But Daddy was fading fast, and he knew it. Suddenly he pulled onto the road shoulder, shifted into neutral, and turned toward me.

"Boy, do you know how to drive?"

"No, Daddy, I don't," I said, exasperated.

"About time you learned. I'm gonna teach you how."

I groaned, and we switched sides. Once behind the wheel, though, I was thrilled.

"All right," I said. "Where's first gear?"

I was answered with loud snoring. I looked over at Daddy; his head was back and mouth open. He looked dead, but my ears told me otherwise. I tried waking him; it was hopeless. Every time I broke through his stupor, he pushed my hand away and yelled for me to leave him alone. After twenty minutes of that, I started getting nervous. I was sure that if the police came by, they'd lock him up. Realizing I had no choice, I decided to risk stripping the Ford's transmission. Steering didn't seem hard, and I had a general idea of how to shift gears. But I didn't know which was where or how to coordinate the gas, clutch, and stick.

At first, I stalled repeatedly. But I finally got us rolling in what I guessed was second gear. Even though there wasn't much traffic, I stayed on the shoulder, doing 30 for a while. And then I tried what I thought I'd seen Daddy do when the truck got up to that speed—clutch, more gas, and pull the stick back and to the right. It worked! What a feeling!

In high gear, I pulled into traffic. As we sped along, I tried to remember as much as I could of our drive south to Brownsville. In the 1960s, highways were far less developed than they are today, and I was pretty sure Daddy had pulled up only once on our way down—at a stop sign not far from Austin. Now, behind the wheel myself, I dreaded coming to it; I just wasn't sure I could find low gear and upshift again after stopping. Meanwhile the miles zipped by.

Around sunset, it occurred to me that I might be able to run that stop sign if traffic was light. So I was mentally prepared when we got there after dark. With one dim street light and no one around, I slowed to about 30, nearly stalled, and got back up to speed without having to downshift.

All along, Daddy had been out cold. But eventually he came to, snorting and coughing. I was doing a smooth 70, steady between the lines. Daddy sat up, lit a cigarette, and said nothing. After his smoke, he asked where we were. Trying to sound casual, I told him we were about an hour from home.

"How'd we get here?"

"I drove."

"Damn. I got to cut this out. Pull in there," he said, motioning toward a gas station.

"Daddy'll take over now," I thought, nonetheless happy that nothing significant had gone wrong on my first drive; the transmission seemed unharmed. We gassed up, and he got some coffee. When we came out, I went to hand him the keys.

"Oh, no," he said, refusing to take them. "You brought us this far; you'll take us the rest of the way."

Before we got back on the road, he showed me where each gear was, and that was all the help I needed. I had won my driving spurs.

Belly Laughs

The following summer, Daddy and I went to Houston, which was much closer to us and needed plenty of workers. I was 15, but said

I was a year older to get hired as a welder's helper for Payne and Keller, a big construction firm. They paid me $6.50 an hour, which I thought was a small fortune. Meanwhile, Brown and Root, another big outfit, hired Daddy as a construction foreman.

Habitually short of cash, we could already taste the better and more plentiful food we'd soon be eating. But it wasn't coming just yet. In many construction companies, helpers don't receive their first paycheck until two weeks after they've earned it. That discourages quitting without notice, which can disrupt a project's timeline. Managers like Daddy, though, got paid after only three days on the job. It wasn't easy to work hard while still eating poorly, and those first three days passed slowly. Still, I was young and could work like a mule.

Payne and Keller assigned me to an oil refinery, where welders were running a gasoline pipeline in a six-foot-deep ditch. For obvious reasons, it was essential that the pipes wouldn't leak. So they ran six-inch pipes and encased them in eight-inchers. First, they'd lay two lengths of six and the welder would join them. Then I'd get down in the trench and grind off the slag. Next, he'd run another bead of weld around it. They'd slip an eight-inch over it, and we'd do it again. Last, they'd X-ray the welds to ensure they were good and strong. The work was hard, and it was out in the July sun. I loved every bit of it. I didn't have any illusions about it as a potential career, though. I saw how difficult it could be for Daddy to find work when the construction industry was in a down cycle. Besides, it wasn't something I'd want to do for the rest of my working life.

Every day, when we traveled between our motel and job sites, we'd pass a place called the Jet Café, which offered all the boiled shrimp you could eat for only ninety-nine cents. We had barely enough money for our room, gas, and pinto beans, so we sweated out those three days and promised ourselves we'd put the Jet out of business when Daddy got paid. And on Thursday, he did. After work, we went to the Jet and started eating shrimp; several hours later we were still wolfing them down. Finally, the manager came to our table to tell us they'd run out of boiled shrimp.

"Then get your ass back in there and boil!" Daddy said between bites. But he was just kidding, and we waddled out peaceably. I've never had shrimp that tasted that good. They were glad to get rid of us, but we weren't done with them just yet.

Friday, after work, Daddy and I looked at each other and said, "Boiled shrimp!" So we headed for the Jet one more time. When we arrived, they called the manager, who explained that the ninety-nine-cent deal was in effect only on Thursdays.

"OK. See ya then," Daddy said, and we drove off laughing. The following week, they were ready for us, though.

The manager said he was sorry but "business conditions" had forced them to discontinue the offer.

"We don't do that anymore," he said, clearly hoping he'd never see us again.

Daddy and I just smiled and went elsewhere. For the rest of his life, Daddy and I would laugh ourselves silly whenever we remembered putting the Jet Café out of the cut-rate shrimp business.

More Firsts with Daddy

After spending a few weeks in Houston and making enough money to eat and buy some cheap clothes, we were ready to head back to Austin. It was nearly September, and time for me to return to school. Daddy got an old U-Haul trailer to carry our stuff. It was junk, but all we had, and that made it worth carting home. On the highway to Austin, everything seemed normal—until Daddy looked in the side view, yelled out, and pulled onto the shoulder. Heavy smoke plumed above the left rear wheel of the trailer, where the bearings had apparently worn out, making the wheel hub red-hot.

"We got to douse that quick or the whole damned trailer'll go up in flames," Daddy cried. So we looked everywhere in the truck and where we could on the trailer. But the only liquid we found was a case of beer Daddy had made sure to pack in the back seat.

"We'll have to pour the beer on it," I said, thinking that was obvious.

"Are you crazy, boy?" Daddy yelled, looking at me as if I were a lunatic. And then he did something that made me return his look with equal fervor—he stepped up near that burning wheel, unzipped his pants, and let it flow. Stinking steam filled the air as honking drivers slowed down to watch and laugh.

"What's wrong with you?" Daddy called, turning his head toward me without losing his aim.

"Wrong with me?" I thought, dumbfounded by this spectacle and my presence in it.

"Get on up here, now!" Daddy yelled. So I joined him, incredulous and deeply ashamed. The only bright side was that our efforts actually helped. We got back in the truck and rolled along the shoulder, doing 20 for a while. Apparently the trailer wasn't going to burn up. But it didn't last. When the smoke returned, Daddy turned to me.

"Get us two beers, and drink up," he said. "We got to pee again as soon as possible."

"Can't we just pour the beer right on it?" I pleaded.

"You still haven't learned, have you?" he replied. So I pulled out two Busch Bavarians, and gave him one.

Daddy took a big gulp, and said, "You want a smoke?" I'd never yet had a cigarette or a beer, and wasn't interested in either, but I knew when I was beat.

So I sipped some warm Bavarian, and said, "Yeah, gimme one." That made two more firsts with Daddy. No…counting the wheel, it was three.

Better...and Worse

As Daddy broadened his skills to include concrete work, he made more money, and was able to buy us a nice house in South Austin. Even more important, he cut back on drinking a bit. We had plenty of food and led a somewhat normal life together.

The down side, though, was that I had to transfer to the high school nearest our new home—William B. Travis, named after the same hero as my elementary school in Marshall. But I never could get used to this place or its culture. All the boys there were ranchers' sons who chewed tobacco and drove pick-ups. They were, in fact, smaller versions of their fathers, who led the kind of life Daddy aspired to. That's why he moved us there, but it didn't suit me at all. I didn't wear cowboy boots, didn't drive a truck, and hadn't developed close relationships with other students or any of my teachers.

Daddy had always wanted to be a cowboy. And, now he had the room and money to keep two horses, which he loved to saddle up and ride. My part was getting up early to feed them before I went to school. I had no interest in riding, but one time Daddy needed me to. He'd just bought a young colt that wasn't big enough to carry him.

"Get on and see if he'll let you ride him," Daddy said. We didn't have a small saddle, so I rode bareback. I didn't expect any trouble; the colt looked docile. But as soon as I got on him, I learned that hell has no fury like an unbroken horse. He took off on a dead run, bucking all the way. I lasted maybe twenty yards before he threw me six feet in the air. I landed flat on my back and lay there groaning, the breath knocked out of me. Daddy nearly busted a gut laughing, tears coming down his face. Finally, I struggled to my feet.

Daddy strolled over with the colt, which calmed down as soon as he threw me. "Crawl back up there," he said.

I wasn't having any of it. "You and that horse can kiss my ass!" I yelled and stomped off, sore as hell in every way while Daddy laughed some more.

After that, every time I fed the colt, it looked to me like he was thinking, "I gotcha!"

Later, I met a girl who invited me to her house for dinner. When I got there, she told me she owned two horses.

"Someday soon we should go riding together," she said.

"Hmm," I replied.

Dinner was nice, but I never called her again. It wasn't just my dislike of riding; I had become chronically grumpy and began to argue with Daddy more than ever before. But my real conflict wasn't with him; it was with the culture in South Austin at that time. I just couldn't bear the idea of spending another school year there. So when the summer came, I made a difficult decision. Daddy clearly had adjusted to life without Momma, and I reasoned he'd be all right without me too. Knowing that, I chose to return to Marshall and finish my last two years of high school there.

CHAPTER 11

BACK TO MARSHALL ALONE

After living alone with Daddy, I wasn't used to discipline. He had let me go and come as I pleased. Even though I had missed Momma and my sisters, I wasn't sure I could readjust to the house rules on Mark Drive. But Daddy's parents, J.P. and Bessie, also lived in Marshall. And when I asked if I could live with them, they graciously took me in. Momma said my room was still there if I needed it, but I spent most of my time with my grandparents, who, like Daddy, let me roam at will. The location couldn't have been better. J.P. and Bessie lived within walking distance of Marshall High School and two other places where I'd wind up spending a lot of time. One was a workplace and the other, a new friend's house.

Eventually Momma married Hollis Grain, one of the finest men I've ever known. They remained married until his death, more than 30 years later. With the mental and financial stability

Hollis brought to our family, Momma no longer had to supply it single-handedly.

Hollis, who loved to hunt deer, thought I might want to give it a try. I agreed to go only because I liked him. He lent me a rifle and we headed out for the woods before dawn one November. It was 25 degrees and damp when he set me up in a tree stand before going off to his. Within ten minutes, I was shivering so bad I couldn't have hit a deer if I wanted to. About three hours later, he came back.

"I didn't see anything," he said. "Did you?"

"No," I replied, my teeth chattering. "Let's go home."

Hollis was a wonderful person, but I never went hunting again—with him or anyone else.

A Lesson and a New Friend

One of the first things I had to do upon returning to Marshall was resume my education. So I enrolled as a junior at Marshall High. Immediately, I made it onto the football team as a defensive tackle. And in the spring, I tried out for and got onto the baseball team as well, playing first base. Both coaches were all right, but neither was near as good as Leroy Hartzel. I missed his guidance on and off the field.

Meanwhile, more relationships were headed my way. While I was in Austin, Granddaddy J.P. and Grandma Bessie had become members of the First Christian Church in Marshall, and they asked if I'd go to services with them one Sunday. I didn't want to, but they were so good to me I couldn't refuse. What I learned that morning had nothing to do with religion, but a lot to do with Daddy and my future.

In his sermon, the minister told of two sisters whose father was an alcoholic. One, like her parent, had a bad drinking problem; the other never touched a drop. Asked how she got to be that way, the alcoholic said, "That's obvious; look at my father." The minister

117

paused briefly for dramatic effect. Then he told us how the teetotaler used those very same words to explain her behavior, so different from that of her sister.

"Role models—good or bad—are very important," the minister concluded. "But how *you choose* to react to them determines your path in life."

That simple story made it clear that whatever I do or don't do is my responsibility and no one else's. Coach Hartzel had told us the same thing in elementary school. But now I was older and more experienced. And hearing that message again, so clearly and briefly, planted it in my mind forever. I understood it would be hard to adhere to, but the alternative was self-deception, and that was a sure dead end.

I still wasn't particularly interested in religion, but I was open to meeting people whose company I might enjoy or learn something from. So I went to an evening meeting of the church's youth group. There I met Dan Finley, my closest friend ever. I didn't know it then, but we'd always remain in frequent contact. He's now known as Dr. Daniel L. Finley, and has long been a professor at Mississippi Gulf Coast Community College, where he teaches emergency medicine to paramedics.

When I first met Dan, he too attended Marshall High. He had good grades, was clean cut, and his house was only two blocks from my grandparents' home. We became inseparable. If you saw me, you saw Dan, and he set the good example I needed at that time. We didn't use drugs or drink, but we roamed all over, listened to a lot of music, and had a great time.

Dan and I were nuts about the Beach Boys and planned to become surfers in California as soon as we graduated from high school. Our parents didn't like the sound of that, but, at least, in their eyes, the Beach Boys weren't a threat to wholesome society. They dressed neatly, and their hair was more or less under control. That applied as well to Johnny Rivers, another of my idols. But the Beatles and groups like them were another story all together. Most adults in Marshall couldn't understand why we liked them or their music. Personally, I'd have given anything to be like Johnny Rivers, bringing thousands to their feet with "Secret Agent Man" and "Seventh Son" or like the Beach Boys, in a striped shirt and white chinos, crooning "In My Room."

As our curiosity about the world grew, Dan and I realized we needed transportation. And that, of course, required money, not only to buy cars, but also to fuel and maintain them. So I got a job as a produce clerk and "sack boy" at the Brookshire Brothers Grocery Store in central Marshall.

Wheeling and Dealing

After a few months at Brookshire's, I'd saved two hundred dollars for a car, but everything in my price range was a wreck. It was clear I needed a loan to buy something reliable and attractive. One evening at home, I mentioned this to Granddaddy J.P., who generously offered to co-sign my application. Next morning, he took me over to the Marshall National Bank and Trust Building. It being a small town, Granddaddy knew the bank president, Bush Morgan, and asked to see him. Soon we were escorted into his office and got right down to business.

"Bush," Granddaddy said, "the boy needs a car loan. I'm here to tell you that if he doesn't pay on time each month, I will."

"That's all the backing I need, Mr. Ratley," Bush said before turning to me. "Young man, I hope this sinks in. Your grandfather doesn't have to sign anything. It's enough that he's given me his word and we've shaken hands. If you're late on a payment, I know he'll make it for you. And if you grow up to be like him, people will have that level of trust in you."

I felt both humbled and proud. Granddaddy's sterling reputation was a lot to live up to, but his example has guided me every day since then.

Now that I had the money I needed, I went shopping for a suitable car. Eventually I settled on something economical and not too old—a '63 Volkswagen Beetle. It got great mileage, which turned out to be important. Gas wasn't expensive, but Dan and I did a lot of gallivanting.

Our earliest forays were to Fat City, a teenage dance club in Kilgore, 35 miles southwest of Marshall. Some good local bands, like the Bad Seeds and Mouse and the Traps, played there. For a while, we went every weekend to hear them cover songs like the Doors' "Light My Fire" and "Hanky Panky" by Tommy James and the Shondells. We never took dates with us because it was a great place to meet girls. In fact, that's where Dan met Carla Bond, to whom he and later I lost our virginity. Dan was a little older than me, and more confident. He saw her, found her attractive, and asked her to dance. She did.

The next time we went to Kilgore, Carla and Dan got together, as he recounted to me in great detail. But after a few weeks, she got tired of him, and I perceived an opportunity. The following Saturday night, I persuaded Carla to listen to the radio in my VW. That car was tiny. Soon, with some contortions, we reached the back seat and moved my plastic ice chest to the front. After a flurry of activity, we paused, and I silently reflected on my grand achievement. I'd enjoyed myself immensely and assumed I'd lifted Carla to the height of ecstasy. I reached forward to turn on the A.M. radio and out came Johnny Rivers' "Midnight Special." Pure heaven.

At least that's how I saw it—until Carla pushed up on her elbow and said, "Anything left in that cooler?"

Amazingly, she sounded bored. I stared at her in the darkness, wondering how she'd recovered her composure so quickly.

I reached forward again and discovered the ice had melted. I handed her a tepid Coke.

Taking it, she sighed, popped the tab carefully and sipped.

"You're better than Dan," she said, gazing out the window.

For me, that glass was clearly half *full* and wasn't going to get any fuller. Later I got extra mileage out of it by repeating Carla's words to my best buddy. I left out the part about her lack of enthusiasm.

"I don't care what she thinks," Dan said. "I had my fun."

"Me too," I replied, thinking how sensible Dan was.

We agreed that enjoying yourself was what really mattered, and began planning a trip to nearby Louisiana, where you could get into a real bar if you were 18. In a "wet" county in Texas, you had to be 21 to drink. We were only 16 and had no great interest in alcohol. But we were determined to be cool, and that required us to go where the grownups went.

Going East

In May 1934, a young man and woman driving down a quiet country road in Bienville Parish, Louisiana, were ambushed by six men wielding shotguns, rifles, and pistols. When the smoke from 130 fired rounds settled, the men—Texas Rangers and Louisiana police—cautiously approached the bullet- and buckshot-riddled stolen car. Inside laid the bodies of Bonnie Parker and Clyde Barrow, along with a sizeable cache of weapons and ammunition. The men, after confirming their targets were dead, drove to nearby tiny Gibsland and telephoned the news to their superiors.

Clyde hailed from Telico, an unincorporated hamlet just south of Dallas. Rowena, Parker's birthplace, was about the same size as Telico, but far out on the Great Plains, between Abilene and Odessa.

When the Barrow Gang wanted excitement, they headed east to Louisiana, where the law's arm was sometimes a little short. Right next door to Bienville Parish—*parish* is Louisiana's term for county—is Bossier Parish, whose seat, Bossier City, has long been known as an easy place to have a good time. With the Barrows' deaths, calm returned to northwest Louisiana. And by the 1960s, East Texans who went farther east did so not to rob banks but to cruise bars. Most were adults, but many were underage kids, like me and Dan, who wanted a gentle taste of adult nightlife.

Being Seen

As soon as Dan and I got our driver's licenses at age 16, we made a beeline for Bossier in his car or mine. We always worked on being cool. We never said, "We're going to Bossier." We said, "Dan and I are going east Saturday night." Neither of us liked to drink much; we just wanted to be seen. We hoped that when we got back to school on Monday, someone would say, "I heard you went east."

With the transportation problem solved, our next challenge was to obtain "proof." Our licenses said we were 16; we needed to be 18 to get into the bars in Bossier. We consulted a guy named Doug who, at 18, was our circle's elder statesman. Threatening us with death if we lost them, he forked over his license and draft card. We looked nothing like Doug and, of course, both documents had the same name and date of birth.

Neither Dan nor I had been to Bossier or attempted to get into a bar anywhere. But we were confident there'd be no problem when both of us claimed to be Doug. Without knowing it, we went forth in the grand tradition of France's General Ferdinand Foch, who said in World War I, "My center is yielding. My right is retreating. Situation excellent. I am attacking." Somehow, like Foch, we succeeded.

The following Saturday night, we jumped onto Interstate Route 20 and crossed over the Sabine River into the Bayou State. The drive from Marshall is about 35 miles. We were good boys, so it typically took us 45 minutes. On arriving in Bossier City, we got off at the Allen Street exit and headed for Herby-K's to get shrimp busters—giant filleted affairs in batter, along with French fries and frosted mugs of beer. Maybe because it was a restaurant, we didn't get proofed at Herby's. But that test would come when we headed for a bar.

The first one we went to was a dive called The Carousel.

"ID," the bouncer said when we got there.

Dan and I laid Doug's proof on him, and waited for the results.

"That'll work," the bouncer said, and waved us in.

As it turned out, getting inside was the easy part. The Carousel served so-called red beer, which had been generously supplement-ed with tomato juice. It looked awful and tasted worse. But in our quest for coolness, Dan and I drank it up and concentrated on the atmosphere, which was hokey. The Carousel got its name from the fact that the bar was on a platform that rotated on a hub, where the bartenders stood. They didn't move; you did, around and around. We soon tired of that, called it a night, and headed home to Mar-shall.

The next time we went, Dan and I stepped up our game. Our target was The Stork Club, which we'd heard had "exotic" dancers. Doug lent us his ID again, and we made special preparations. Dan and I believed that cologne helped make the man. So we chipped in on a set called "Nine Flags," which consisted of 15 little bottles, each containing one variation or another of a citrus scent. That night, I picked "Caribbean" and Dan chose "Panache." We would never go out wearing the same one. The ID worked again, and for the first time, we got to try mixed drinks instead of beer. I don't re-member what Dan had, but I ordered a dry martini. In movies, I'd seen apparently sophisticated people order one. And even though I didn't know what would be in it, I was ready to find out. My mar-tini came in an elegant glass and looked harmless, so I took a sip— and promptly gagged. It tasted as I imagined the worst industrial waste would. So I put it aside and focused on the entertainment.

A young lady in a full costume came out to dance, and mid-way through her act, took off her top. Each of her breasts was

123

technically still covered—by a small tassel that flew in a circle. Dan and I liked that, but felt we really got our money's worth when she somehow made the tassels fly in opposite directions. Once again, we went home sober and happy.

Seen Too Much

Dan and I always wanted to seem cool. But we didn't want word of our travels to spread too far. As we got older, more of our friends from high school came along when we went to Bossier. One time, Dan and I went dancing there with two girls from the church group we all belonged to. And in doing so, my buddy and I brought the wrath of God down squarely on our naïve young heads. Standing in for God on that occasion was the Reverend Jim Swenson, who oversaw the church group. He liked to keep tabs on everything its members did.

Inevitably, whispers about our visits to Bossier reached the reverend's ears, and he sprang into action. Having known Dan long before he met me, the reverend called his home first. Dan and I were hanging out there while his mother was out food shopping. We had the Beach Boys on so loud the windows were shaking. But when the stereo switched from "Surfin' Safari" to "Little Deuce Coupe," we heard the phone ringing. Annoyed, Dan stopped the music, picked up the receiver, said hello, and heard a familiar resonant voice.

"This is Reverend Swenson, Daniel."

"My mother's not home," Dan said.

"Your nighttime travels worry me, young man," the reverend replied. "But I'll give you and James Ratley a fair chance to account for yourselves."

"What do you mean?" Dan asked, in a shaky voice.

At first, I wasn't paying any mind, but I listened up when Dan's tone changed.

"Don't you play dumb with me, young man," the reverend told him. "I know what you boys been doing out in Bossier City. You're already in trouble. Come see me before it gets worse."

"With all due respect, Reverend, I don't think that's any of your business," Dan said, beginning to sweat. "We didn't go with the church group."

That got my full attention.

"Let me put it another way," the reverend told him. "If you don't come over, I'll have to discuss it with your mother."

"We're coming right now," Dan replied. He hung up, looking pale.

"What'd he say?" I asked.

"Follow me," Dan said, and I did, while he recapped the call for me. It was my turn to sweat.

Minutes later, we stood before Reverend Jim, who sat ramrod straight behind the polished desk in his tomb-like office. A grandfather clock ticked loudly amid the silence, as he looked us over from hair to sneakers.

"Y'all done violated federal law, boys," the reverend said, shaking his head mournfully.

Dan and I exchanged confused glances. "We didn't do anything!" I cried.

"You transported women across a state line for immoral purposes," the reverend said, his eyes narrowing. "That's a federal offense. You want to be on a chain gang?"

"But all we did is dance with them!" Dan said as we fidgeted nervously.

"That the truth?" the reverend asked, sounding doubtful.

"Word of honor," I assured him.

"Lucky the FBI ain't heard what you done," the reverend said.

We didn't know whether the reverend was exaggerating or just plain wrong. But too much was at stake, and we were scared. So we promised to change our ways, and left with our tails between

125

our legs. Eventually Dan and I learned that the law in question was the Mann Act, and that it prohibited transporting prostitutes across state lines, not bringing a dance partner to Bossier. Until then, though, when headed east we left our dates at home.

A Second Look

When I was in the 11th grade, I got a speeding ticket in Marshall for doing 45 in a 40. I was guilty and paid the ticket right away. That was only the second time I'd interacted with the police. The first was back when Momma called them to make Daddy go away. Instead, they threatened Daddy through me and left without helping Momma at all. That's why if I had ever had a problem with anyone, calling the Marshall police would have been the last thing I'd think of doing. I thought they were worthless, and it certainly never entered my mind to become a police officer.

In my senior year, while working at Brookshire's food store after school, I saw a young guy shoplifting a steak. I was sacking groceries up front and told the cashier I'd be right back. When I caught up with him in the parking lot, he socked me in the eye. But I hung on to him until two more sack boys came out. Together we dragged the guy and the steak to the back of the store while someone called the Marshall PD.

The officer who responded was polite, but took charge immediately.

"Don't move," he said to the shoplifter.

Then he looked at me and my black eye and said, "Tell me what happened."

After I said what I'd seen and done, the officer turned back to the young guy, who denied it all. When the other sack boys confirmed what I'd said, the officer took our names down. He then cuffed the guy, read him his rights, called into the station, and took him away.

That was my first positive contact with the police. When that officer arrived, everything was in chaos. But he quickly established order. You knew everything was going to be all right.

For the first time I thought, "If I could be that kind of cop, I might like it."

My Other Mentor

I muddled my way through high school. There were plenty of teachers, but no mentors. Granddaddy J.P. and Hollis were good men, but I needed guidance from someone who was out in the world with me. That person turned out to be the manager of Brookshire's.

Jack Frank, a big, old, heavy-set guy, was a hands-on manager who walked up and down the aisles most of the day. I thought the world of him. His goal was to make Brookshire's the best grocery store in Marshall. He taught us that if you saw a can of beans in the wrong place to put it where it belongs, regardless of your job title. And he told us that when customers ask you where an item is, you walk them over to it, point it out, and ask if there's anything else you can help them with. In sum, Jack taught me the value of the human side of commercial transactions, that people are more important than money.

"People like to know you think enough of them to remember them," he said. "Call them by name if you know it." Jack understood that simple but important fact and made sure we did too. When I graduated from high school, I resigned from Brookshire's. On my last day, he gave me $10—nearly a full day's wage—as a goodbye present.

"I didn't have time to go out and get you anything," he said. I learned a lot from Jack.

On the Road Again

Now that I had graduated and no longer participated in organized sports, I realized something important was missing from my life. I wanted to be part of a team again—one with a strong insightful leader, like Coach Hartzel or Jack Frank. Having outgrown the roles of high school athlete and sack boy, I was ready for a greater challenge, whatever it might be. And steadily building inside me was a yearning to go away as I'd done with Daddy to Austin.

That combination of factors and desires might have led some boys to join the army. But the war in Viet Nam had simultaneously escalated in scope and deteriorated in purpose. I admired everyone who served there and sacrificed so much. But I just couldn't see how that war had anything to do with defending our country. I wanted no part of it.

For Dan, the whole thing was a nonissue. All along he'd planned to continue his studies. And when he was accepted by the college he'd chosen, he became exempt from the draft. So I too applied for admission to his new school, which then was known as Southwest Texas State University, in San Marcos, midway between Austin and San Antonio.

No one else in my family had ever attended college, and Momma generously offered to pay my tuition. She believed in the power of education, and didn't want her only son going off to a futile, unnecessary war. Thanks to her, I became a business major instead of a soldier. I still yearned to do something important in life, though, and didn't really think studying balance sheets and income statements would scratch that itch. But I was truly grateful to Momma, and considered myself quite fortunate.

CHAPTER 12

FINDING MY WAY

I felt a flush of relief the September morning Dan and I headed out of Marshall on the 300-mile drive to Southwest Texas State University in San Marcos. The summer heat had eased slightly and, fresh out of high school, we were eager to begin this new phase of our lives. For the most part, though, my motives for leaving Marshall differed vastly from Dan's.

He wanted to live away from home and his parents for the first time. I'd already done that and more with Daddy in Austin, Houston, and Brownsville. Sure, he was my father, but living with him came to feel more like hanging out with an unpredictable and adventurous much older brother. I wasn't after excitement now; I just wanted a fresh start. Ever since I'd returned to Marshall and moved in with Grandpa J.P. and Grandma Bessie, Daddy had been mostly on the road, working on the Amistad Dam and other projects. But people in town hadn't forgotten his periodic hijinks, and I was eager to live somewhere I wouldn't be known as the kid whose father raised hell at times.

Of course, that had nothing to do with college itself. But Dan and I also differed in our approach to higher education. He had developed an interest in science and aimed to learn more about it in college. And, at that point, Dan was more extroverted than I was. So it was no surprise that he did well in his courses, joined a fraternity, and made friends.

When high school ended, developing skills to earn a living became our immediate challenge. So, reluctantly, we abandoned our dream of the surfer life in California. But Dan had science to turn to, while I hadn't found another interest. The studies I'd barely begun had failed to stir my imagination. Although I realized how hard Momma worked to pay my tuition, I knew I was wasting the opportunity she'd given me. I supposed there might be an occupation I'd find interesting and apply myself to, but I had no idea what it could be.

Daddy, Granddaddy Pat, and many others in my family were carpenters. I didn't know what I wanted to be, but it wasn't a carpenter. So, with no insight, plan, or interest, I chose to major in business. And it showed in my marks—straight Cs. Dispirited, I formed no close relationships with teachers or even with other students. And eventually Dan and I drifted apart, not realizing we'd resume our friendship later in life.

Three unproductive semesters passed, and I couldn't bear the thought of Momma spending another cent on my tuition. I knew it was time to move on yet again—this time on my own dime. I just didn't know how to proceed, so I decided to take a break and visit my family. Because San Marcos is much closer to Dallas than it is to Marshall, I went to see Grandma Nina, who lived in Dallas. There I also got to see Momma, who visited her mother often. I explained that because my studies weren't going well, I was determined to try something more practical as soon as I could figure it out. They immediately offered me some good advice on where to go and what to do.

They'd made their suggestion before, but I hadn't been receptive. Nina had lived and worked in Dallas for years, and was now comfortably retired, drawing a pension from the city. More than once she'd told me how grateful she was to have steady income, good benefits, and job security. Now, with college not working out for me, Grandma Nina and Momma urged me to take the upcoming City of Dallas civil service exam. I listened to them, took the test, and passed it.

Big D, Little A, Double L, A, S

Moving to Dallas with a solid plan was just what I needed. For the first time since I'd left Marshall, life seemed full of possibilities, and I was open to them. My civil service career began in an unglamorous but still desirable position as an entry-level lab technician for the City of Dallas Water Department. Unlike Momma, I didn't know anything about working in a laboratory. But neither did she when she started at Atlas Chemical, and like her, I learned. The job consisted of taking water samples at various testing stations around town. My days off were during the week but I found the work interesting, and it felt good to earn "adult" wages, even if they were only $400 a month.

After I'd been there six months, I learned there'd be another competitive examination. This one was for a position as a property clerk in the Dallas Police Department's (DPD) Quartermaster Division. The job had weekends off and paid $800 a month, double what I was making in the Water Department. So I took the test, and several weeks later, DPD called to say I'd scored well. After a brief interview, they hired me.

A Foot in the Door

An important part of my job as a DPD property clerk was to man the service desk, where officers came to order new uniforms when theirs were damaged or worn out. The quartermaster division lent each officer a temporary replacement shirt or pair of trousers until the new ones arrived three weeks later. One afternoon, an officer named Rapcliff came to the service desk. He'd received a new shirt and was returning the one he'd borrowed. Normally my supervisor was on duty, but he'd gone to lunch, and I was there alone. But because I couldn't find our record of Rapcliff's loan, I wasn't able to immediately issue him a receipt for the shirt he was returning. Somehow, this set him off.

"Are you as dumb as you look?" he said.

I let that roll right off me.

"I'm sorry, Officer. When the manager comes back from lunch, we'll find your paperwork."

But he was determined to lay into me.

"Forget it, stupid. I'll just keep the shirt for free."

Focused on his indignation, Rapcliff hadn't noticed the man standing right behind him, who had seen and heard everything. I had no idea who he was, but like few others in our workplace, he was wearing a business suit.

"Can I help you, sir?" I said to him as Rapcliff turned to leave.

"I'm Director Reed. Is Director Ganaway in?"

"He is, sir," I said. "I'll tell him you're here."

One of the first things I'd learned is that directors were senior managers, usually in charge of a division. My boss's boss, Director Pat Ganaway, headed the entire Quartermaster Division. Before I went to get Ganaway, I heard Reed call out to Rapcliff, who doubtless had heard Reed identify himself to me.

"Officer, would you stand by for a minute?" Reed said. "I'd like a word with you."

A few minutes later, I came back with Ganaway. He and Reed shook hands and bantered for a moment.

Then Reed said, "Pat, would you put up with it if someone treated a member of your staff like a dog?"

"Of course not!" Ganaway said, and you could tell he was both surprised and sincere. "What's this all about?"

"Well, one of my officers just did," Reed said, nodding at Rapcliff, who stood beside him silently fuming. "Your young man, however, was courteous and professional. I need some uniform pants, but that can wait until I finish talking to my officer." And with that, he walked off with Rapcliff, who I later learned quit soon afterward.

Ganaway then turned to me and said, "I'll have someone relieve you. When he gets here, I want to see you in my office."

I thought I was in trouble for sure. Soon my relief came, and I nervously went to see Ganaway, who waved me into his office.

"Son," he said, "I've been watching you."

Involuntarily, my shoulders crept up and tightened.

"You're a good worker. Why haven't you applied to be a police officer?"

I said I'd thought about it but never had the nerve to apply.

"Well, you should," he told me. "I can tell by the way you perform under pressure that you'd be an outstanding police officer. Are you interested?"

Happily surprised, I said, "I sure am, sir."

"Well then, come with me," he said, and took me to Personnel, where he introduced me to DPD Recruiter Sgt. Kenneth Johnson.

"Sergeant, this is Jim Ratley, my property clerk. He's interested in becoming a police officer, and I believe he'd be a fine one."

Johnson surveyed me quickly and replied, "I'll talk with him, Director. We'll see."

To me he said, "Have a seat."

Ganaway left, and I sat down, confident I had it made.

"This guy won't mess with someone the director recommended," I told myself. Wrong. To my surprise, the interview began immediately, and it was brutal. Johnson hammered me for about 30 minutes.

"Good Lord," I thought, "Rapcliff's a Barbie doll compared to this guy."

"A lot of people want to be a Dallas police officer," Johnson told me. "But only three out of every hundred are good enough. My job is to find out if you're one of them."

As suddenly as my arrogance arose, it now evaporated. I realized this was an opportunity that could change my life, and I made up my mind not to muff it.

"When's the last time you smoked marijuana?" Johnson said as if he already knew the answer.

"Never!" I truthfully replied.

"Not even in college?"

"No, sir!"

"You ever been around anyone who smoked it?"

"Yes," I said, "But..."

"But what? Yes or no?"

I told him how in the dorm at Southwest Texas State, other students sometimes came in at night stinking of something burnt that clearly wasn't tobacco.

"Were you ever with anyone while they smoked marijuana?"

"No, sir," I said. "I wasn't."

Johnson leaned forward with a sly smile.

"You'll have to answer that question again," he said. "Strapped to a polygraph machine."

"Fine," I said. "I'm telling the truth."

Later I learned that Johnson's aggressive style was standard interview procedure, designed to assess my behavior under stress. He seemed satisfied with my answers, but I wasn't sure. Next, he pulled a blank application from a folder, and began filling it out as we spoke.

After many more questions and a lot of writing, Johnson put his pen down and said, "This is just the beginning. We'll also look into your background. And when we're done, I'll know more about you than your mother does."

He wasn't exaggerating; DPD did send an investigator to Marshall. She spent the better part of a week questioning all my high school teachers and neighbors. Besides the polygraph exam, I also underwent a battery of psychological evaluations. A couple of weeks later, after clearing those hurdles, I went before an interview board. One of its three members was a lieutenant named Herndon. The first time I saw him was on the day of the interview, when he stopped by the service desk.

"I need a size 34 belt," he said.

Although we hadn't met before, we knew we'd be on opposite sides of the interview table later that day.

I said I'd check our inventory, and added with a smile, "If we don't have it in stock, Lieutenant, I'll go out and buy you one."

Herndon winked at me. "I'm a rip your ass apart this afternoon," he said.

My smile froze, and I swallowed hard as he left. I knew my background was spotless. My only remaining hurdle was the interview. To my relief, it went smoothly, and I was hired as an officer trainee and assigned to the Police Academy. My next challenge was to merit a permanent place in DPD by graduating from its academy. I was hopeful and motivated, and got what I needed. Serving the people of Dallas as a police officer turned out to be the first of the two jobs I was born to do.

Learning the Basics

During the three months I spent in the academy, my military draft status returned to "exempt," as it had been while I was in college.

135

I realized how serious an undertaking it was when the academy swore in me and my fellow recruits on our first day and issued us service revolvers, along with twelve rounds of ammunition. We immediately received weapons safety training, spent hours at the firing range, and were instructed to bring our pistols home with us—in short, to be armed at all times.

Before entering the academy, I'd never experienced anything like the structure and discipline that were essential parts of its curriculum. With every passing day, it became clearer to me that these practices and modes of behavior were the keys to effectiveness as a police officer. My role models were the academy instructors, some of whom had been on duty when President Kennedy was assassinated, perhaps the darkest day in Dallas history. I grew to admire them all.

My fellow recruits and I each spent our last week in the academy on street patrol with a field training officer (FTO), a role I'd later play for many years. Each of those five days, I reported to a police station and spent an entire shift in a squad car, partnered with an FTO. A week later, when I graduated, I felt I'd entered a profession I'd be happy to spend the rest of my life in.

I spent my first day as a full-fledged police officer on solo patrol in a squad car. It was quite an adventure, but not without its moment of humor. The duty sergeant assigned me to a beat in an area I was unfamiliar with, since I'd moved to Dallas only recently. And my first arrest was of a reckless driver I pulled over, who turned out to have stolen the truck he was driving. I called it in immediately, and other officers responded to assist. But it was my responsibility to transport the suspect to custody.

Trouble was, though—and I didn't realize it until I drove off with my prisoner—I didn't know the way back to the station. After I made several wrong turns, the suspect kindly showed me the way. It was humiliating, but at least my fellow officers weren't there to witness it.

Anchors Ashore

Upon graduation from the academy, I lost my exemption and became eligible for the draft. Soon afterward, I received notice to report to my local draft board for a physical exam, which I, of course, passed. I then walked straight over to the Navy recruiting office, and signed up as a reservist. My hitch began with six months of active duty. First the Navy sent me to its San Diego boot camp, where I spent three months in basic training. During my remaining three months of active duty, I underwent advanced training as a construction electrician at Naval Base Ventura County in Oxnard, just outside Los Angeles.

Those two assignments completed my full-time active duty obligation, and I returned to Dallas, where I served in the reserves for five-and-a-half years as a Seabee in Mobile Construction Battalion 22. For one weekend each month, I took part in readiness drills. And each summer I spent two weeks on active duty, including brief assignments in Guantanamo, Mississippi, and California. As it turned out, I never was assigned to a ship; all my Navy service was ashore. During my five-and-a-half years in the reserves, I worked full time as a police officer on street patrol.

Home Again

The last day of my six months on active duty in the Navy, I flew right back to Dallas. On the way home from the airport, I visited DPD's personnel office and got permission to return to street patrol that night. After I got home, I ironed my uniform, got a few hours' sleep, and reported to my duty station at 11:00 p.m. I would have done that job for free. It was the most fun I'd ever had in my life.

PART THREE

DALLAS POLICE OFFICER

"The trust of the innocent is the liar's most useful tool."
— *Stephen King*

CHAPTER 13

BECOMING RELIABLE

I n 1971, I set aside my light gray academy shirt and trousers and put on the proudest uniform I'd ever wear—the dark blues of a Dallas police officer. My first post was the Northeast Police Substation at 8916 Adlora Lane. Northeast was responsible for East Dallas, a down-at-the-heels sprawl of open space, rundown homes, and warehouses extending eastward to the LBJ, a belt parkway that nearly surrounds Dallas. Central Station downtown and three substations in the city's remaining quadrants housed the police department's other primary units.

From that first day on the job, I strove to earn the trust of experienced cops. Their professional abilities were time-tested and renewed daily. Mine, like every rookie's, were uncertain until proven in action. That's why many officers didn't want recent academy graduates with them on patrol. Nevertheless, hands-on guidance from veterans was the only way to build new officers' practical skills.

My field training officer was named Doyle Edwards. I spent most of my first three months on patrol in a squad car with him. Whenever my days off differed from Doyle's, I'd ride with other FTOs until he returned. As a rookie, I dealt with routine matters that didn't require an experienced officer's skills or knowledge. Most of these were tedious chores—writing up straightforward arrest reports, traffic tickets, and the like. But some were more demanding, including occasional foot chases of young suspects able to outrun officers who'd spent ten years in a squad car. My biggest challenge, however, would be facing physical danger. I'd soon find out whether I could handle everything this job would throw at me.

A Special Breed

Before I became a police officer, practically all the people I associated with were ordinary citizens living peaceful lives. But now I'd become part of what was for me a new culture, that of cops, a special breed. Many I worked with were Viet Nam War veterans. They, and every Dallas police officer I knew, were tough as nails; they had to be. In their world, fistfights and bloodshed occurred daily. This was especially true in East Dallas, where I frequently dealt with drunken cowboys and motorcycle gangs.

Throughout my DPD career, if a member of the public assaulted an officer, the cop would fight back to make the arrest. But a suspect who peaceably submitted to lawful arrest received courteous, respectful treatment from the police. None of us wanted to fight; we'd get dirty, possibly hurt. And then we'd have to write lengthy reports to the chief of police, explaining what we'd done and why. Nobody wanted to go through all that.

So, when it was necessary to take someone into custody, we did our best to talk them into coming along without resisting. It took lots of training and experience before I could handle many such situations alone. Perhaps more important, I also learned to recognize those too dangerous to manage single-handled.

Rookie Blues

I first patrolled on the night watch, which began at 11:00 or 11:30, depending on which beat you were assigned to. If all beats had rotated from day watch to evening watch to night watch at the same times, the streets would have been unpatrolled and the substation overcrowded until each watch had fully changed. So half the beats began their watches on the hour and the rest did so on the half hour.

On my first night the sergeant told me I'd be riding with Doyle. I'd never met him, so I looked around until I saw the right name tag on a shirt hanging from his locker door. I walked up, put out my hand, and said, "I'm Jim Ratley. I'll be riding with you tonight."

Doyle looked me up and down and said, "The hell you will! I'm not playing nursemaid to an ignorant rookie."

I didn't know it, but Doyle was just starting out as an FTO, and I was his first trainee. He immediately protested to the sergeant, who reminded Doyle how rookies could be helpful. I stood by, hoping this wasn't going to be as bad as it looked. Ultimately, Doyle did his duty. But he wasn't about to make it easy for me.

We walked out to a squad car just driven in by an officer coming off the evening watch. Doyle exchanged a few words with him and accepted the keys. Then he gassed up the car at one of the motor pool pumps and carefully ran through a multifaceted inspection he didn't explain. When he got behind the wheel, I hopped in, and we drove off.

Eyes on the road, Doyle called in to the dispatcher. "212 is clear. One man...well, two...I guess."

He put the mike back and said, "Don't talk to me, and keep your hands off my radio."

Chatter between dispatch and other cars came through intermittently, but nothing for us.

Then, about two a.m., another officer radioed Doyle to meet him for coffee. Doyle hung a U and asked if I wanted any. I don't drink coffee, but I said yes just to break the ice.

As we arrived, I opened my door.

"Where are you going?" Doyle said.

"I thought we were getting coffee."

"I won't be seen in public with a damned rookie!" he shot back. "Stay here. I'll bring yours out."

I sat there stunned as Doyle's buddy parked next to us and got out. Inside that car was another young officer. It was warm and both cars' windows were down. For a few minutes we sat there silently, engrossed in our thoughts.

Finally, he looked over at me and said, "Would yours let you talk?"

"No," I answered. "I can't say a thing."

We fell silent again.

Twenty minutes later, Doyle and the other officer came out laughing. Doyle got behind the wheel and wordlessly passed me my coffee, which had gone cold. I drank it anyway as we drove back to his beat. Half an hour later, we hadn't exchanged a word, and I realized I'd soon need a bathroom.

"I've got to pee," I told him.

"OK," Doyle said, but gave no indication of when he'd comply.

Nearly an hour later, I couldn't wait any longer and said so. At that point, we were on a street lined with businesses. It was the middle of the night, but there still was plenty of traffic. And yet Doyle just pulled up on the side of the road and looked at me expectantly. I stared back, wondering what he was up to.

"Well," he said. "You gotta pee or not?"

Having no choice, I got out and relieved myself, occasionally lit up by passing headlights. I zipped up and got back in, feeling like

SERVICE WITH A SMILE

I'd made no progress in life and was back on the road with Daddy. Eventually our watch ended, and I returned home.

My wife asked how it went.

"I don't know if I can handle this," I said.

Service with a Smile

The next night, Doyle was off and I rode with another FTO, who favored a different shop for his coffee break. Dobb's House was in a particularly bad part of East Dallas, so I was looking over my shoulder when we parked outside it. Inside, however, was the real hazard—a waitress named Dorothy. She and the FTO had a thing going on. While he knew she found virtually all cops attractive, he'd overestimated his own personal charms and unwisely let me come inside.

Dorothy's nose opened the minute she saw me. "Hi, baby," she said, sizing me up and ignoring the FTO.

I smiled and said nothing.

The FTO made like he didn't notice and ordered two black coffees. Dorothy brought them over, her eyes fixed on me. I began to blush a little, which seemed to charm her no end. Then I gagged on the coffee, which was just awful.

"Excuse me, ma'am," I said. "Could I have some cream?"

Dorothy, wearing a low-cut top, leaned up real close and purred, "Whichever one you want, sweetheart. Both if you like."

My jaw dropped. "God!" I thought. "I can't believe this." I looked at the FTO, who was glaring at Dorothy.

"Let's go," he said, and stood up.

I followed, but not before Dorothy blew me a kiss and sashayed off. The rest of the night passed uneventfully, but I made a mental note to stay away from Dobb's.

Not the Academy

Two nights later, Doyle was back at work, and I resumed riding with him. He didn't have to tell me to keep quiet and not touch his radio; I knew the drill. Unlike the previous nights, this one got busy real quick when the radio crackled with a call for our beat.

"Respond to a disturbance," the dispatcher said. "Painted Duck, 3600 block, Samuell Boulevard."

I'd heard about that street, a long, straight drag with cowboy bars on both sides. Though the Painted Duck was new to me, Doyle seemed to know it well. It was a dive like all the others we passed on the way there. Doyle pulled up near a pickup truck right outside the bar. The driver's door was open, and a big beefy man was sitting there calmly drinking beer. His shirt was torn, his lower lip puffed and a little bloody. I wondered if he was the one who'd called the police.

Just then, a man wearing a white apron came out and yelled at us. "That's him. Beat up three people. Won't leave."

I looked at the big guy; he seemed unconcerned.

Doyle turned over to me and said, "Rookie, get him outta that truck and put him under arrest."

I didn't like the look of this; the guy had five or six inches and at least fifty pounds on me. But I set out to do this just the way the academy had trained me.

That early in my career, things I didn't know numbered in the millions. Among the important ones was the need for a swagger. Because all experienced cops have developed one, they can detect each other without seeing a uniform, badge, or gun. A direct gaze enhances the effect. Officers tend to lock eyes with a person and stride confidently toward him. Brawlers and other frequent offenders can tell from the presence or absence of a swagger how experienced a cop they're up against. I knew none of this as I approached the suspect.

"Sir," I said, "would you please step out of the truck?"

"Fuck *you*," the guy sneered.

"No, sir," I told him. "Get out of the truck."

Again, he cursed me.

Stymied, I looked back at Doyle, who rolled his eyes, and said, "Goddam it, rookie. Drag his ass outta there."

I tried another approach. "Get out of the truck or I'm going to have to drag you," I said.

He snorted. "Start dragging, asshole."

Soon as I reached up to grab the guy, he rattled my molars with a right hook and kept pounding me. The fight was on, and I was losing bad, barely able to fend off half his punches. Meanwhile, another squad car drove up. When that cop got out, he joined Doyle leaning against his car, watching this guy thrash me. Everything seemed like it was happening in slow motion. My jaw ached, I tasted blood, and my new hat was top down in the dirt. Just then the big guy seemed to tire, easing up just enough for me to grab my pistol and jam it under his chin.

"Hit me again, I'll blow your head off!" I yelled.

He stepped back.

I heard Doyle say, "It's time," and the other cop casually agree. They slammed the big guy to the ground, cuffed him, and stuffed him into the back of Doyle's squad car. "You ever touch a Dallas police officer again," they told him, "you'll go to the hospital before jail."

As I walked toward the car, dusting off my hat and straightening my shirt, Doyle pitched me the keys.

"Your turn to drive, partner," he said and got in the back seat with our prisoner.

I was hurting but felt wonderful. Doyle now knew he could count on me. Sometimes a reliable partner is the only thing between a cop and certain death.

At home, I told my wife I had a new attitude about the job. "I want to do this for the rest of my life," I said.

On the Team

As word spread of my active participation in the arrest at the Painted Duck, I got to know many officers, especially in the station's locker room, where patrolmen, detectives, and members of other units rubbed shoulders daily. Taking a cue from my name tag, most called me "J.D."

One night, a crusty old cop told me, "In here, we do two things to relax: play dominoes and drink coffee." I never did get used to drinking coffee, but I enjoyed dominoes.

Everyone rotated watches. We'd spend 30 days each on nights, then days, then evenings, and so on. I'd been there awhile when the department changed over to fixed watches. You'd choose one and, if you had enough seniority, work it continually. By then, I had enough time on the job to get the day watch. But interesting work was really important to me, so I chose the night watch. That's when most murders, commercial burglaries, and other serious crimes were committed. For five to six years, I worked nights and loved every minute of it. I even came in an hour early to play dominoes and get ready for patrol.

Each patrol area or *beat* was known by its three-digit identifier. One or more officers covered every beat for each watch, usually alone in a squad car to stay within the department's tight salary budget. The beat I spent the most time on was number 144, which covered Samuell Boulevard and its cowboy bars, where I'd gotten my baptism of fire with Doyle.

At the start of every watch, I and thirty other officers assembled in an indoor formation known as a *detail*. It took place in a 40-by-50-foot room where a sergeant or lieutenant would address officers about to go on patrol. Most often, I went on duty at 11:00 p.m., and that's when my detail commenced. And, by God, you had to be punctual. Thirty seconds late was as bad as two days late. The sergeant would walk in briskly and call us to attention. I always made it on time.

Anyone who didn't or who failed to perform their duty in any other way heard about it right there in front of everyone. The sergeant then filled us in on recent crime trends and advised us on how to handle them. Then he'd read off the entire list of beats and who was assigned to them for that watch. Usually, the detail lasted ten to fifteen minutes and ended with the sergeant calling out, "Hit the street, folks. Be careful out there."

Officers rolling in from patrol on the watch before us would park their squad cars in a driveway we called Relief Alley. Each officer had to stay with his car until the next watch relieved him. When I was on patrol, I'd top off the gas tank and check the car's police equipment and general condition. Then I'd look to see whether a prisoner had left behind drugs, weapons, or other contraband. That done, I'd drive to my beat. This was known as *clearing the station*.

I'd radio the dispatcher, "144 is cleared. One man en route," meaning I was alone and on my way.

Out on my beat, I'd spend the first part of the night looking out for fights and eyeballing people as they left bars; I wanted to see whether any drunks were about to attempt driving. Often I'd find someone passed out behind the wheel, sometimes with the engine on. I didn't want to take him to jail; that would take up time when someone else might urgently need my help. So I'd just reach in, grab the keys, and throw them as far away as I could. Then I'd call other officers nearby and ask them to drive by also and make sure the drunk was all right. For the rest of the night, I'd drive slowly behind stores and businesses, looking for anyone trying a break-in. If I arrested someone, I'd take him back to the station, which had four holding cells. Every two hours, a van would pick up prisoners and transport them downtown to the city jail at 106 South Harwood.

A Bright Officer

On patrol one night, I pulled up where radio reports said other officers had cornered two burglars inside a huge warehouse after they'd tripped a silent alarm. One of the two came out a side door and slipped into his getaway car in the darkness. But several officers saw him and pounced. The crook wouldn't give us any hint on where his partner might be hiding inside, so we tried to stay out of sight while figuring out how to locate him in there.

Luckily, one of us had a brilliant idea. Forcing the prisoner to take off his shirt, the cop put it on and got behind the wheel of the burglars' car. Then he slowly circled the block. The first pass ended with no reaction from the warehouse. But when the getaway car came to a stop sign near the door the first guy had used, the second crook ran out and jumped in, only to meet a smiling cop pointing a pistol at him.

"Not who you thought I'd be, am I?" the officer asked the crestfallen burglar as the rest of us emerged from the shadows and helped complete the arrest.

Born Under a Bad Sign

Every team—no matter how good—has a less-than-stellar player. Ours was an officer nicknamed "Trigger." He had a part-time second job, guarding a shopping center at night. One time, around three a.m., its alarm sounded and Trigger went to investigate. Pistol in one hand, flashlight in the other, he turned a corner in a store aisle and thought he saw somebody where no one had any business being at that hour. Trigger cranked off three rounds before realizing he'd shot a full-length mirror. The nickname arrived right after the report came out.

At first, some officers withheld their scorn. Could've happened to anyone, they correctly reasoned. But everyone piled on when

Trigger got his thumb stuck in a shotgun barrel and awkwardly sped to the station for help midway through the night watch. In what must have been a first-of-its-kind procedure, the sergeant on duty separated Trigger and the shotgun by squirting WD-40 down its barrel. I kind of sympathized. Poor old Trigger had been born under a bad sign, I thought. How different from me he seemed to be; I felt more like the quick-thinking cop at the warehouse.

Still Lots to Learn

As I gained experience, I became sure of my judgment and opinions. That led me on one occasion to offer a distressed burglary victim what I felt was a helpful comment. Someone had broken into the elderly lady's shabby three-room row house and taken several decorative glass fruit jars and a few pots and pans. She was really upset about it, and broke down in tears.

"It could be worse, ma'am," I said, trying to comfort her. "You're lucky; all you lost was some junk."

She looked up at me, tears on her cheeks. "You might call it junk, officer, but it's practically all I have."

That chilled me to the bone. I wanted to crawl down the deepest hole on earth; maybe that would hide my shame. I apologized and promised to write up a report, even though I knew the burglary squad would never be able to recover her things. It was the only way I could think of to make up for my blind insensitivity. The sting of that experience persisted, drilling into my mind how important it was to appreciate the public's daily struggles. When people suffer a loss bad enough for them to call the police, it's a big event in their lives. And if a cop treats it as anything less serious or important than that, those people won't dislike just that officer, they'll dislike the entire police department. From that point on, I never discounted people's losses and emotions when they called us for help.

151

Back at the station, I brought the sergeant my report on the burglary.

"I'm thinking of buying some jars and pans to replace the ones she lost," I told him.

"You can't solve all the world's problems, son," he told me. "You'll answer a lot more calls like that. Just let people know these things matter to us and that we do all we can about them."

Every time I drove past that house on patrol, I thought about the lady inside.

The Good Book

Nothing was worse than having to respond to a crime in progress at a location you weren't familiar with. This was long before squad cars had electronic maps and GPS. What we had, though, was a black leather-bound book with maps of every street in Dallas. The publisher was a firm named Mapsco.

On larger beats, you sometimes knew a street by sight, but under pressure you might forget its name. The stress was particularly intense when someone's life was at stake in, for example, a domestic disturbance where the husband had a gun. From time to time, the Mapsco book helped us find a location barely fast enough to prevent a killing.

That wasn't all it was good for. The Mapsco street guide looked a lot like a small bible. In many places, that wouldn't mean much. But back then in certain parts of Dallas, a fair proportion of people couldn't read. So it was only a matter of time before a cop used the Mapsco to perform an "official" ceremony that settled a dispute. For example, on a disturbance call, you'd always ask the couple if they were "paper married" or just "staying together." Often they'd say the former. If you asked why they didn't get a divorce, split their possessions, and go their separate ways, many would say they couldn't afford the court cost. Hearing that, some officers had

152

the couple place their hands on the Mapsco while the cop recited a few fancy words before declaring them divorced. Dispute settled; peace restored.

By a similar process, some officers removed hexes from people who were sure an enemy had placed one on them. This too produced good results. But one cop took it too far when he not only "divorced" a couple with four kids, but also ordered the husband to pay child support. Several months later, the guy lost one of his two part-time jobs and couldn't pay his "ex-wife" the whole amount. When she threatened to file charges, the husband decided to explain his situation to the local justice of the peace.

"That police saved me money by doing our divorce for free. But did he have to set my child support payments so high?" he asked. "I'm having trouble feeding myself right now."

The judge couldn't believe his ears. But the man was earnest and his request was reasonable, so the judge amended the police officer's "order" by lowering the payments. He then called the station and told the officer, "Your divorce-granting days are over. If I hear anything like this again, I'll throw you in jail." No one griped about it. After all, the Mapsco was doing plenty good simply as an atlas.

A Matter of Minutes

Some stores, like 7-Eleven and other convenience marts, never close. So when I patrolled the business district at night, I'd be on the lookout for stickups as well as burglaries. Convenience store windows are mostly covered with ads, but the managers always leave a clear view of the cashier's station. When I coasted through the store parking lot, I'd be able to see whether the cashier was at the register. If he was, we'd wave at each other. If not, he probably was in the supply closet or restroom, and I'd wait until he came back. If he still didn't show, I'd go inside for a look-see.

Late one night, passing by a little 24-hour gas and coffee joint, I waved at the clerk, who smiled and gave me the thumbs up. I kept going, drove up the street until I had to turn, and circled back past the gas station. No more than five minutes had gone by since I'd been there, so I wasn't expecting anything to have happened. Still, when I didn't see the clerk this time, I stuck to my routine and waited for him to show. I was in no rush; the radio was quiet. Several minutes went by, and still no sign of him. I wanted to move on to other parts of my beat, so I cut to the chase and went inside, figuring I'd at least get a Coke. I heard a Top 40 station as I pulled open the door.

Nobody in sight.

"Hello?" I called out. No answer. My hand automatically slid down to my pistol, resting on it as I walked farther in for a better view. I could see the cash register was open. I drew my pistol, stepped behind the counter, and saw the cashier on the floor, face up in a pool of blood. I felt for a pulse but didn't find one. No bills in the register drawer. I switched off the Top 40 and from where I was, glanced around the store, but heard and saw nothing unusual. I hurried out to the car, called for backup and an ambulance, and eyeballed the store's rear door from the outside. Closed; nothing there. I waited for the others to arrive and reflected on how suddenly life can end. Minutes earlier, that kid was smiling.

Only When Necessary

After a while, I developed a good sense of when I might need help from other officers when patrolling solo. But I was careful about how I asked for it.

Every now and then, I'd put my roof light on to stop a car that was weaving or had a broken taillight or something else of that nature. Then, before getting out to approach the car, I'd notice something that made me especially cautious. It might not be anything in particular, just a feeling that it wouldn't be wise to do this alone. Perhaps the people inside were moving frantically, as if hiding something or preparing for an altercation.

So, to play it safe, I'd call in and say what beat I was on and what I was doing: "144 on traffic."

The dispatcher would say, "Go ahead, 144."

I'd identify the location, car, and its license number. "I'm on 4900 block of Ross. A green Chevrolet four-door, Texas, 15 Ross Henry William 368. Two occupants. A lot of movement in there. Can you get me a cover headed this way right now?"

Although I wouldn't say it was an emergency—the official term was "assist officer"—I'd speak faster in a tone that clearly communicated my need for immediate backup. Why so cautious? Because "assist officer" explicitly means it is an emergency in which the requesting officer and perhaps others are in mortal danger.

In response to such a call, every officer within miles would rush to the scene. Back then, GPS wasn't available to help dispatchers track the location of squad cars and coordinate their simultaneous approach to a crime scene.

On several occasions, two squad cars speeding toward the scene, lights flashing and siren screaming, couldn't hear each other approach, and collided. Some responding officers were killed, and those who'd requested emergency help had to wait longer. With that in mind, I found ways to get the help I needed without ever making an "assist officer" call.

That didn't mean they weren't sometimes justified. One night, I was on patrol alone when a civilian broadcast a call on the police radio frequency.

"A cop's getting his ass whipped at the White Tail Lounge," the guy said and signed off. I knew the place—a topless joint on the corner of Columbia and Fitzhugh Avenues.

Before dispatch could ask, I called in.

"144 is two blocks away, en route."

155

"Copy 144," the dispatcher said. "All units, assist officer at 4900 Columbia."

Seconds later, I pulled up outside. "144, code 6," I said, reporting I'd arrived at the scene. I didn't know what to expect, and took my Kel-Lite flashlight with me. Made especially for police officers, it was a steel pipe containing batteries and a bulb. I yanked open the barroom door and plunged into a haze of cigarette smoke pierced by red strobe lights. The music was deafening, but as far as I could tell, there was no disturbance.

A crowd of drunks ogled a tired dancer trying to keep up with Wilson Pickett's *Funky Broadway*. Just as I was about to discount the call as a prank, I noticed a man on the other side of the runway, bent over and apparently punching someone laid out on the floor. When I pushed through the crowd, I saw that the guy was pummeling a cop; no one was interfering. The attacker was too busy to notice me, and I knew just what to do. I grabbed the Kel-Lite with both hands and waited. Next time the guy's elbow came up, I smashed it. He went down yelling, and I cuffed him.

This work was dangerous, especially when you patrolled alone. An "assist officer" call, when made judiciously, could save a cop's life.

Tools of the Trade

Like other patrolmen, I kept my uniform in the locker room, but not my pistol. We wore our guns everywhere, cleaned them at home, and arrived at the station armed and ready.

DPD provided us top of the line equipment. We could choose a Smith & Wesson or a Colt. I didn't like automatics; back then, they jammed. That never happened with revolvers, which I preferred. We called them *wheel guns*. For my first two years, I carried a .357 Magnum Colt Python. Then Dirty Harry came out, and I couldn't sleep until I bought a Smith & Wesson model 29 .44

magnum with a five-and-a-half-inch barrel. I carried extra ammunition in round clips called *speed loaders* that enabled me to reload in two seconds. The department permitted us to carry a second pistol if we wanted to, and I did. Mine was a Colt .38. I shaved off the hammerhead for a more comfortable fit, loose in my back pocket.

I also had a nice Buck brand pocket knife, which came in handy one night when I got in a fistfight. The guy knocked me down and jumped right onto me. With him on top of me, I couldn't get to my pistol. But I managed to pull my knife out, snap it open, and put the blade point on his throat.

"Get back or I'll rip you open," I yelled. He scrambled right off me.

"Don't cut me!" he said.

I would have. If you warn a suspect you're about to use force, you have to be prepared to follow through.

When I pointed a gun at someone, I wanted him to think I was just looking for any excuse to kill him. I didn't want to use force, but I had to sound as if I was about to. Many a suspect won't desist from an assault unless he's pretty sure you *will* pull the trigger.

Handle with Care

I never really knew what any particular suspect would do to avoid going to jail, even if it was just overnight. Some would fight me, some would run, some would submit peacefully. One reason it was so hard to predict their behavior was that they themselves often didn't know what they'd do. Once I'd told someone he was under arrest, I had to handcuff him immediately. Although it was safer to wait for backup before making an arrest, you didn't always have that luxury—the person might attack you or try to run off before other officers arrived. So this was something I had to learn to do alone when necessary.

First, I'd grab his right hand, pull it behind him, and snap one cuff on. The sound and feeling of that first cuff clicking closed on his wrist would sometimes spur a person into resistance. If somehow he got that first hand out of my grasp, he could swing those cuffs at me like a weapon. Officers have gotten hurt after taking too long to get that second cuff on a suspect. You have to move fast, and I did.

I'm left-handed, and did practically everything with my right hand. Generally, my left was either empty or holding my gun. Of course, I didn't always have my pistol out. But I always kept my gun hand free. If carrying my Kel-Lite, I used my right hand. Then, if I had to cuff someone, I put the light in my back pocket so that my gun hand would stay ready.

If it wasn't feasible to wait for backup before telling a suspect he was under arrest, I had to be ready for a flight or a fight. So I'd speak calmly but firmly and pay close attention to his eye and body movements. Like Yogi Berra said, "You can observe a lot just by watching." I learned what to look for in a person's eyes, mouth, and overall physical behavior to tell whether he was angry or indifferent and whether he was actively engaged in speaking with me or distracted and looking for an escape route. If we were near a wall, I'd move up close and steer him backward until he was against it. If he wanted to run, he'd have to go through me.

Almost all the time, someone about to run would telegraph it. He'd look to the left, then the right, but not straight ahead at me; I'd know what he was thinking of doing. And I'd move directly into his line of sight, so he'd see that I knew. Usually that wordless little dance persuaded a suspect to stay put because there was no chance of escape.

Other times, though, the suspect wasn't thinking about escaping. Instead, eager to fight, he'd look me right in the eye. He might also clench his fists, purse his lips, and have a visibly throbbing artery in his temple. To reduce the tension between us, I'd look away.

And if I were alone and had to arrest the person, I'd immediately call for backup. Then, to distract the suspect until another officer arrived, I'd carry on talking as if nothing were amiss. When my backup got there, I'd then tell the suspect he was under arrest. At that point, if he resisted, the second officer and I could overpower him.

But sometimes I had to make the arrest and transport the prisoner before help arrived. In that case, I'd put the prisoner in the front passenger seat with his hands cuffed behind him and then fasten the seatbelt over him.

I'd take that extra precaution for two reasons, one being the prisoner's safety. My other reason was that some prisoners are limber enough to slide the handcuffs from behind them to in front of them, gaining enough freedom to assault you. The seat belt prevents them from doing that. And if another officer joined me in my squad car, he'd sit behind me with the prisoner in the right rear seat; from there he wouldn't be able to kick me in the head. It'll happen eventually if you put prisoners in the left rear seat.

Help Me Make It Through the Night

Sometimes on patrol, you'd get a "meet the complainant" call from the dispatcher. This strangely labeled category of calls was a catch-all for situations that were unclear or so unusual they defied the brief descriptions typical in radio communications.

I got one of these on an otherwise uneventful night, and when I heard the address, I grimaced. The man who lived there was forever beating his wife. She'd call us, a couple cops would come over, threaten him with jail, and he'd go to bed. Each time, the wife would refuse to press charges. Like many women in her position, she and the kids needed the husband to earn money, not rot in jail while they starved and shivered. I called the dispatcher to tell him the history.

"144 en route," I said. "That'll be a family, signal 6," meaning a domestic disturbance. "Start me a cover."

"Copy, 144," the dispatcher replied, and put out a call asking anyone nearby to back me up.

This night, however, was different. When I got there, the wife was screaming with blood flowing from her badly broken nose. Adding to the commotion, their six small kids were running around yelling. I went up to the husband, who was drunk again and looked like he was going to knock me down and have another go at his wife.

I told him to turn around and put his hands behind his back. "You're going to jail," I said.

"The hell I am," he replied, and took a swing at me.

I ducked most of its force, but he jumped on me and we wound up on the floor. I got my cuffs out and was about to put them on him, when someone whacked me on the back of the head. I looked around and saw it was the wife, hitting me with a broom. I was angry, but not surprised. It's a cliché among police officers that a beaten wife often defends her abusive breadwinner from the very cops she called to protect her.

Meanwhile, the drunken husband was running out of gas, and I managed to stand up and grab the broom. But the guy pulled me down again, and that's when the kids jumped on me, hitting me in the head with their little hands and biting my legs. It was hell with a small h: painful, dangerous, and ridiculous, all at the same time.

This is what my backup officer saw when he rushed in the door. Unable to stop laughing, he let the circus run on for another minute before pulling the guy off me and helping me subdue him. We brought the kids to Child Protective Services and the parents to jail.

Before returning to patrol, we paused to speak with an officer on duty at the jail. He told us Willie Nelson had just been arrested for drunk and disorderly and was cooling off in a holding cell.

"Get out!" I said.

"See for yourself."

We walked back to the cells.

The country legend was lying on a bunk, a disgusted look on his face.

"Hey, Willie!" the cop called. "How about a couple of bars of 'Help Me Make It Through the Night'?"

Willie rolled over toward the wall. "Up your ass," he said.

Would-Be Marriage Counselor

In one domestic disturbance I responded to, the husband was the complainant. We'd see this every now and then. In this case, the husband was in his sixties and the wife was thirty-something. He'd gotten her angry and she'd badly beaten his little bald head with one of her shoes. When I got there, he told me she was in the bedroom. It was the gaudiest thing I'd ever seen. Everything was pink—the walls, the bedspread; so was her housecoat, even the shoe she'd hit him with.

"Why're you hitting him, darling?" I asked her.

"We don't have enough food, and he buys trash like this," she said, tossing a cheap paperback my way. Its cover sported a photo of an attractive woman. The title was, *How to Make a Bed.*

"Give me a minute," I said and left the room.

Long story short, he was about to go into the hospital for surgery and had bought the book to read while he recuperated. She knew this, but said the real problem was that he had his nose in that book instead of paying attention to her. I told her he needed something to read while he recovered, and that I'd overlook her assault if she promised not to hit him again.

"Besides," I added. "Did it ever occur to you that a few peaceful minutes with that book might change his mood? It could bring you closer together."

She looked at me. "You think so?"

"I can almost guarantee it."

She said all right, but I could tell the peace wouldn't last if he didn't perform. Still, confident I was about to broker a major reconciliation, I shuttled back out to the husband.

"Here's the deal," I said. "She won't hit you anymore. In return, she expects some affection."

"What do you mean?"

"What do you think I mean?" I replied, exasperated.

"I ain't doing it," he said.

"Yes, you will, by God," I told him. "It's the only thing that'll keep you from getting beat up again. Now go on over there and give that girl some kissing and hugging."

"I'll take my chances," he said. "You want someone to kiss her, do it yourself. I ain't pressing charges."

I could see it was hopeless, and walked out of there thinking, "There goes my career as a marriage counselor."

Equal Under the Law

As a member of the review board, Lieutenant Herndon had made me sweat when I applied to attend the police academy. He'd known that my boss, Director Ganaway, had sponsored my application. So maybe Herndon wanted to let me know such decisions should be made on the basis of merit, not connections. That's how he evaluated my application and why he approved it. It made an indelible impression on me; I looked up to him.

I'd been a patrolman for a few years now, and was doing well in East Dallas. Knox-Henderson is one of its neighborhoods. Someone there, at a bar at Greeneville and Bell Avenues, called in about a fight in progress. Dispatch asked me if I could respond, and I said I would. I found a kid in his twenties beating the hell out of a guy old enough to be his grandfather. When I pulled the young guy up, he turned around and punched me—a big mistake. I put him on the floor, cuffed him, and brought him to jail.

Lieutenant Herndon happened to be on duty there, but I didn't see him when I came in. I put the prisoner in a cell and began writing up his arrest. I'd temporarily taken his ID for my report and saw that his last name was Herndon. I thought nothing of it, figuring it was a coincidence.

A few minutes later, the lieutenant came by and asked what the charges were.

I rattled them off—disorderly conduct, resisting arrest, assaulting an officer...

The lieutenant just said, "All right," and walked off.

I went back to the report, and suddenly realized the two of them might be related. I caught up with the lieutenant, and asked if he knew the prisoner.

"Yeah," he said. "He's my son."

"I had no idea," I said.

"He violated the law and should be in jail," Herndon replied.

Now that was consistency. The man didn't believe in conditional justice—for anyone. Herndon nodded to me, and went back to his office. He was a great model to emulate.

Fin Del Camino

Driving on patrol at night, you see a lot of speeding drivers. At the time, departmental policy was to catch them at whatever speed it took, even if they hadn't committed an additional serious crime, such as robbery or assault.

Anytime I got into a chase, the first thing I'd do is get on the radio and call in as many officers as possible. I'd also call in to see if our helicopter was up; it had a powerful spotlight. On some chases, we'd fly down streets at 100 miles an hour. Our Plymouth Fury squad cars had 440-cubic-inch "hemi-head" engines and could do 150 miles an hour. You weren't going to outrun us.

But a guy in a Chevy El Camino tried to, and almost got away. We saw him doing 70 on Reiger Avenue, where the speed limit was 30. That night I was riding with another officer, Jim Halverson. He was behind the wheel, and we whipped in behind the speeder and turned on our flashing red light. The speeder tried to take a turn at 100 miles an hour, and almost made it. He sideswiped three newspaper vending machines, sent a small fortune in dimes flying every which way, and came to rest against a tree. Our adrenalin was pumping like mad, and that takes a while to wear off. Jim pulled up in front of the El Camino. Then he got out and grabbed the young driver by the collar and began yelling at him for his recklessness.

I came over, said, "Easy, Jim," and he backed off. No sooner did he do that than the driver staggered me with a solid punch. I gave him as good as I'd gotten, and Jim broke it up. It was another lesson to never relax your guard.

The Golden Rule

One time, driving through the business district on my beat, I noticed a car behind a big auto repair shop. It hadn't been there when I'd passed by earlier that night. A guy was asleep in the back seat— George Brantway, someone I'd known in high school and hadn't seen in years. More of an acquaintance than a friend. He was down on his luck and had driven from Austin to Dallas in search of work as a mechanic. Flat broke, he couldn't afford a motel, and was waiting for the repair shop to open so he could apply for a job. I asked for his driver's license and, following procedure, called in to check on him. As it turned out, Austin had three felony warrants for him on burglary charges. I walked back to George's car and told him what I'd found. He admitted it all.

"I hoped you'd turn your head," he said.

"I don't do that, George. I've gotta take you in," I told him. "I hope this will be an uneventful ride for us."

"It will be. I won't give you any trouble."

"All right," I said, pulling out my cuffs where he could see them. "I'm gonna put these on you. That's our policy. It's not because I don't trust you." If he planned to put up a fight, it would've been right then; but he didn't. On the way down, he asked for a smoke, and I gave him one. Then I stopped in a 7-Eleven and bought him three packs. We talked calmly all the way to the lockup. When we got there, I turned him over to jail staff and cited the Austin warrants. I also told the guards how George was an old acquaintance and hadn't resisted arrest.

"Make sure he gets a call to a lawyer," I said. I hated to bring George to jail, especially at such a low point in his life. But if you have to go inside, it's a little bit easier if someone you know and trust brings you there.

CHAPTER 14

SEASONED VETERAN

I'd been on the job for a few years now, and had seen a lot of human suffering. Realizing how fortunate I was compared to many others, I'd become more empathetic. And along the way, I'd mastered the job well enough to teach someone else how to do it. So I volunteered to add the duties of a field training officer to my primary responsibilities. As a result, I often had a rookie riding with me. I'd get each one straight out of the academy, and coach him for three months. All I really knew was that he'd had some instruction and needed more. What I didn't know was whether he had backbone.

One night I had some trouble arresting a guy who must've been the Jolly Green Giant's big brother. Unfortunately, my rookie froze and just stood there while I fought the guy alone and eventually subdued him. Before that boy's three months were up, I made sure he learned how to handle himself and back up his partner.

How'd I teach him? The same way Doyle taught me—through experience. Once you'd learned a skill the hands-on way, you could apply it swiftly and automatically, gaining a split-second advantage that could save your life or someone else's.

FTOs even helped train recruits before they left the academy. In realistic role-playing exercises, those closest to graduation would wear their uniforms and "play" actual police officers. As a safety precaution, we'd have them load their pistols with blanks. Also participating were trainees at an earlier stage in the academy program. They wore civilian clothes and in some way acted out a "criminal" role. Individuals from the two groups would pair off for exercises modeled after the more difficult situations officers encountered on patrol. This tested and sharpened the near-grads' skills before they hit the streets for real. We FTOs would observe from up close, and interrupt as necessary to correct faults and improve performance.

On one occasion, I was facing a "criminal" trainee who tried something I'd never seen in these exercises; he suddenly grabbed at the pistol of the uniformed trainee next to me. Without thinking, I knocked him down.

Immediately I helped him up and sincerely apologized. "I'm sorry. I didn't intend to do that; it was automatic."

Far from being resentful, the rookie was impressed. "Damn!" he said. "That was fast." He and the near-grad who'd almost lost his pistol knew they'd have to be ready for anything.

UFO

Shadyside Lane is an itty-bitty street in East Dallas, not even two blocks long. With a name like that, you might reasonably think it peaceful. It is now, but it wasn't in the 1970s when I was on street patrol. The main attraction on Shadyside was a rough-crowd bar named Charlie's Good Time Parlor. The owner, Charlie Banno, was in tight with the Dixie Mafia. Although headquartered in Mississippi, its members operated throughout the South. With its link to organized crime, Charlie's was the kind of place we kept an eye on.

One summer night my rookie was out sick, and I was on patrol alone. Shadyside was on my beat, and as I cruised past Charlie's I noticed a skinny young guy staggering across the road, blind drunk. I pulled over, walked up, and suggested he get some coffee in an all-night shop on the corner.

"But I'm fine," he said, swaying.

"Where you parked?" I ventured, getting to the most important issue—whether he had a car.

"'round the corner. I'll go slow. Promise."

"That's not good enough," I said. "I need to see your license."

He fumbled in a pocket, handed it to me, and I read the name.

"All right...George," I said. "Give me your car keys and go get some coffee. You're not driving anywhere tonight. The last bus is gone, so you'll have to get home some other way. Pick up your keys and license at the police station in the morning." I was doing my best not to lock up George for the night, but he was determined to drive home. That left me no choice, so I told him he was under arrest for being drunk and disorderly. He complained but didn't resist when I cuffed him, put him in the squad car's front seat, and clicked the belt over him. Seemed like it was all over but the paperwork. And that's when the trouble started.

"Hey, you goddam son of a bitch!" someone with a deep voice yelled from behind me. "What the hell you doing with my buddy?"

All in one motion, I slammed the door and turned around. Walking fast toward me with a mean look on his face was a guy the size of an industrial refrigerator.

"Stay back," I said. But he wasn't having any of it, and kept yelling at me. I could see he too was drunk but still able to do a lot of damage. I went over to the driver's side, flipped the all-door lock, and snatched up the radio microphone. "144. Shadyside and East Grand," I said. "Send me a cover." My tone made it clear the need was urgent.

Dispatch acknowledged, paused a minute, and said, "146 is en route. Five blocks." I was glad to hear that.

The big guy, finding the passenger door locked, shouted at me, "Get them goddam handcuffs off him. You ain't putting my friend in jail."

"Oh, yes, I am," I said to myself, "and you're going with him." I knew he could beat me like a dog, so for now all I did is talk calmly to him. But he came around to the front of the squad car, determined to get past me and free his friend. Before he could, I got back on the radio and called my cover, Roy Westard. "144 to 146—where you at?"

He answered right away. "Two blocks."

"Get on down here," I said. "I need you." I had a plan, but realized that if Roy didn't show soon, it might earn me a royal ass-whipping. Just as I put back the mike, I heard the distant roar of a Plymouth engine. Roy was flooring it. I walked toward the big guy, stopped a foot in front of him, and looked wide-eyed at the sky. "Good Lord, what is that?" I said.

When he turned to see, I swung from the ground up, really getting my legs into it, and planted a solid left on his chin. He went down like a giant redwood. I rolled him over, hoping he wouldn't get up before Roy arrived. The guy was still conscious but dazed, and I managed to get one cuff on him. Then I heard tires squeal to a stop and Roy's door slam. Together we got that second cuff on, and I took a deep breath before we hauled them both in for D&D. Over the years, I arrested hundreds of people like that, many of them even more dangerous. Guns and muscle aren't the whole answer; sometimes you have to outsmart them.

Rules of the Road

How the public sees you and how you see yourself greatly influence your effectiveness as a police officer. If you don't look the part, neither you nor anyone else will fully believe in your ability or dedication. While every Dallas cop understood this, many chafed under the requirement to wear a uniform hat at all times except in a squad car or during a hot spell. In addition, your hair couldn't touch your ears, and if you had a mustache, it couldn't extend beyond your lips. There was no sense in arguing whether these rules improved our image; you simply had to obey them. However, some officers resisted by cultivating Elvis-style hairdos and mustaches that barely satisfied the regs. Known as "hair gods," they were the most frequent violators of the hat rule. Perhaps their style impressed some people; if so, I couldn't imagine why. But our sergeant hated it, and constantly harassed anyone who bent or broke the dress code. I followed my own path, keeping my hair trimmed and wearing my hat when necessary.

Late one winter night, a motorcycle blurred past me at an intersection. I turned, stomped on the gas pedal, and flipped on my flashing lights. After calling in his description and direction, I tried to keep the speeding biker in sight. Adrenalin focused me on the pursuit as time passed somewhere in the background. No other cars joined me, and for what might have been ten minutes I chased him all over East Dallas. At one point, he surprised me with a sudden turn, and I jumped the curb and plowed into someone's front yard. Steering against a skid, I gained traction, missed the house by six inches, and left deep ruts in the lawn. I gunned the Fury, ka-thumped off the curb—front wheels, then back, and began closing the gap. When he took another fast turn, I cursed and punched the dashboard. But my luck held as he lost control and crashed into some bushes, shaken but apparently unharmed. My heart pounded in my ears as I leapt out and grabbed him by the collar.

When you're cool, the sun shines
all the time: me and Daddy.

At my third birthday party: After this
photo was taken, I rode that tricycle right
off the porch and nearly killed myself.

My first job in law enforcement:
guarding the backyard

The Ratley family all dressed up, 1954

My senior picture, Marshall High School, 1969

My early days in the U.S. Navy

A fine haircut, courtesy of the U.S. Navy

Dallas Police Department, Recruit Class 115, 1971

My early days in the Dallas Police
Department, back when I was so young
my mom had to buy my bullets

My first and only job as a model

Me with my brand-new Plymouth squad car, circa 1973

Just like Samson, I got my strength from my hair. I was working undercover for the Dallas Police Department.

Spider Dan was arrested for climbing the outside of the Southland Life Building, one of Dallas's biggest high rises.

As the country song says, "There goes my reason for living,"
with Leslie and Sarah, 1977

In the early days of the ACFE, my family and I had portraits done at Olan Mills.

The most enjoyable part of the best job in the world is interacting
with ACFE members and seminar attendees.

A serious face for a serious job

Opening the *27th Annual Global Fraud Conference* in 2016; I've been fortunate enough to attend every one of the ACFE's conferences.

I'm getting ready to record a video, which is a big change from when the ACFE started. I've been told I have a face for radio.

I'm very blessed to have been able to interact with the wonderful people of the Beijing, China Chapter of the ACFE.

Me at the Great Wall of China

Me with all my grandchildren: life doesn't get much better.

I always had the prettiest mother of anyone in
my elementary school class, and I still do.

Delivering food and medical supplies to Louisiana the day after Hurricane Katrina; I've never been so proud to be a pilot.

I've got the best co-pilot in the world. Gloria and I really enjoy our trips in the airplane.

I paid little attention when another squad car pulled up. Turned out it was the sergeant, and he didn't look happy. It occurred to me he might have been behind me for some of the chase. I expected hell about that lawn and perhaps about the way I was holding the biker.

Instead the sergeant walked up, fists on his hips, and said, "It ain't summertime, bubba! Where's your hat?"

Alone in the World

Whatever complaints I might have had about certain folks, others brought out the best in me. A particularly sobering situation was that of an elderly woman whose husband had just suffered a fatal heart attack while away on a hunting trip. For some reason she wasn't answering the phone at home when her husband's hunting partner had repeatedly called throughout the day. Finally, after midnight, he asked us to check on her and, if possible, tell her what had happened. Dispatch filled me in, and I drove to her home through steadily falling snow.

She took it hard when I broke the news, and I knew I couldn't leave her there alone. I asked whether there was a friend or relative who could come and stay with her. There wasn't. She and her husband had outlived their children and everyone else in the family. Racking my brain for a way to help, I noticed an address book near her phone. I opened it and saw a woman's name on the first page. Turned out it was a friend she hadn't seen in years.

I tried the number, got through, and explained.

"Son, I'm an old woman," the friend replied. "I can't drive in this snow."

"If you're willing, I'll come pick you up," I said. She graciously agreed, I brought her over and the two ladies hugged and sat down together. It was a start. Then, with the widow's permission, I called the family's funeral home, told them who I was, and the situation.

They took it from there, and I went back on patrol. So many times I'd come across people with no next of kin. My eyes were on the road, but all I could think about was my own family.

Some people had it even worse, living alone on the street. Columbus Hardin was the most memorable one on my beat. We'd watch over him, especially in winter. Columbus suffered from severe alcoholism and claimed to be the great-great-grandson of outlaw John Wesley Hardin. Maybe he was; maybe he wasn't. But he himself had been famous. Once a top-ranked contractor, Columbus built some of the most beautiful homes in Dallas's elegant Swiss Avenue historic district.

On cold nights, some of us officers would buy him a bottle of Mad Dog 20/20 rotgut wine. Then we'd get him settled some place on the street where he could drink it undisturbed. Soon afterward, we'd bring him to jail on a D&D charge, so he could sleep in safety and relative comfort. That was fine with Columbus, and we were happy to do it. He even received his Social Security check at the lockup. Unusual arrangements, to be sure, but they worked.

Preparation and Ethics

Road chases, fistfights, and the variety of other challenges patrolmen encounter made preparation essential. In addition to having the right training and experience, we also needed proper equipment. Some of it—at least one pistol and a Kel-Lite—you carried; the rest you kept in the squad car. But over the course of three shifts, up to six officers had daily access to the shared items in each car.

The most important of these tools was a Remington model 870 single-barrel, pump-action shotgun. You didn't need that weapon often, but when you did it was unbeatable. Naturally, it had to be easily available and ready to use. The pre-patrol checklist we followed ensured that it was. After I made the cut with Doyle, my FTO, he walked me through the checklist, and I did the same with my rookies. Once I'd ensured the car was clean, serviceable, and fully fueled, I'd quickly pull out of Relief Alley to make way for the cars behind me.

As soon as I left the station, I'd pull over to the side of the road, get out the shotgun, and unload it. Standard procedure called for four rounds in the magazine, none in the chamber. I'd "jack" the pump a couple of times to make sure it was empty. With the slide forward, I'd pull the trigger and listen for the click that showed it was unloaded. Then I'd put the shells back in the magazine and leave the safety in the off position. All I had to do was jack a round in the chamber, and that shotgun would be hot— ready to shoot. A clip held it vertically in front of the dash at the middle of the front seat, secured by a quick-release lock. That's all there was to getting the shotgun ready and pulling it out for use. It was much harder, however, to know when *not* to use such a powerful weapon.

Sometimes the very first responders to a fire are police officers. On one occasion, Sgt. Don Flueshay, an officer I sometimes worked with and greatly admired, arrived at a house that was completely ablaze, its residents trapped inside. As soon as he rushed in, a gas explosion blew him through a wall and out into the street. Injured, Flueshay nevertheless ran right back in and pulled the people to safety. DPD awarded him its Medal of Valor for saving several lives.

While answering other calls with him, I observed how quickly he'd take control of a situation and deal with it in the best way possible. In addition to being brave, Flueshay was effective because he was humble and ethical. He did the right thing no matter what the circumstances were. And that's why Flueshay knew when not to use a shotgun.

Responding to a nighttime report of a business burglary in progress, he and another officer silently entered the building and heard frantic movements in the darkness. Flueshay carried the Remington, loaded and ready to fire; his partner had a pistol and Kel-Lite. "Drop your weapons and come out with your hands up high," Flueshay called, not knowing how many intruders there were. Whoever was in there kept mum, but a few seconds later the Kel-Lite's beam picked out a tall man flattened against the wall, a shiny metal object in one hand.

At that point, it would've been perfectly legal for Flueshay to open fire. But he saw that the burglar was holding a hammer, not a gun. And so Flueshay screamed, "Drop that hammer or I'll blow your damn head off."

The burglar, seeing what he was up against, did as he was told. When cuffed and questioned, he said he was working alone and that his name was Richard Speck. Speck went to prison, but his name didn't mean much to anyone back then. After a year out of jail, Speck moved to Chicago, where he became world-famous for brutally murdering eight student nurses in a darkened dormitory.

Looking back on it, Flueshay told me he'd often thought about how killing Speck would've saved eight lives. "I was already putting pressure on the trigger when I saw that the thing he was holding was a hammer," he said. "We weren't that close to him; no one was in mortal danger. So the only right thing to do was give him a chance to drop it." That's the kind of police officer—the kind of person—Don Flueshay was.

Not for Sale

When Daddy wasn't on the road, working on the Amistad Dam or some other big project, he'd sometimes spend a few days in Dallas. No one was more proud of me, and he got a big kick out of coming along on patrol as a civilian observer every now and then. Some people abused this DPD program, in which anyone could participate. One mother even parked her teenaged son with us as an observer every time she played bridge. To cut back on such excess, DPD later limited how many times a person could ride with us.

One night, Daddy was with me as I spotted a small foreign car moving along very slowly. The driver might have been drunk, so I got behind him and flipped on my flashing lights. When he wouldn't stop, I stayed with him until he pulled into a residential driveway. After telling Daddy to stay put, I got out to speak with the driver, a middle-aged man who looked like he'd had one drink too many. When I asked for his license, he said he didn't have to give it to me.

"I'm on my own property."

"Don't play that game," I said. "Break it out."

"I don't have to do anything," he said, bleary-eyed. "This is my home."

I told him that if he showed me his license and promised to go to bed, I'd leave it at that. "It's that or jail," I said. "Now, give me your license."

When he took out his wallet, though, he tilted it toward me, revealing a thick wad of cash. "That's what you want, boy, ain't it?" he said.

"No," I said, and took hold of his arm. "I want you where you belong—in jail."

He backed off right away. "I'm sorry. I'm sorry. I shouldn't a said that."

"You are so right." I didn't let go.

"How 'bout I just go inside like you said?"

"That's no longer an option. Turn around, put your hands behind your back." I cuffed him and belted him into the squad car's front passenger seat after getting Daddy to move to the back.

When he saw Daddy he said, "Who's that?"

I told him it was the judge, and he tried again.

"Judge, I'm real sorry. There's a thousand dollars in my wallet.

Y'all can have it if you turn me loose."

"Officer?" Daddy said.

I glared at him in the rearview. "Don't even think about it," I replied, and headed for jail.

Although I knew Daddy was a lost cause, I was furious that this driver thought he could buy me off. He tried getting out of DWI, a misdemeanor, and wound up with bribery of a public official, a felony. He wasn't the first to pull that stunt with me. I put every one of them behind bars.

Annie Oakley

In the academy, they teach you how to approach a car after you've made its driver stop.

After pulling someone over, I'd line up my hood ornament right behind the other car's left tail light. That way, my car protected me from being hit by passing traffic. If I asked a driver to get out, I'd make him move to the passenger side of the car, away from traffic and not in between the cars in case mine got rear-ended. Also, if he fought me, we wouldn't be at risk of getting run over by a passing car.

Even if someone in the car had a gun, an officer who approached properly had a good chance of living through it. As I walked toward the driver's window, I'd scan the back seat with my Kel-Lite to see who might be there, holding what. Texas law permits windows to be tinted, but not so dark they block a flashlight.

Kel-Lite in my right hand and gun hand free, I'd stop by the left rear window so that the driver had to look over his shoulder to see me. Righty or lefty, he'd have a hard time getting off a good shot at me. I pulled over plenty of people who had guns and would've shot me if I'd given them the opportunity. The worst ones were when you'd stop a car for what seemed like a routine stop, but turned out to involve a loaded gun. Although most of the time I was alone, I was calm during those stops. While they were happening I wasn't scared, but I sometimes got the shakes afterward.

Because the foreign car owner hadn't been driving wildly and was safely parked in his driveway, I'd have let him off with a warning if he hadn't tried to bribe me. But that was an exception. I was riding with another officer on a summer night when I saw a car swerve repeatedly. After calling in the plate number, description, and location, I put on the roof lights and made the stop. As my partner and I approached—me on the left, him on the right—we saw the driver was alone.

"Gun!" he suddenly yelled, and we both drew our pistols and assumed defensive positions. When the driver didn't budge an inch, we moved closer, and I saw the pistol, lying on the passenger seat. Drunk, she picked it up so slowly I was able to snatch it right out of her hand. Still, that was no reason to lower my guard. I put the safety on her gun, shoved it in my belt, and asked for her license.

"It's in the glove box," she said.

"Then get it out." I holstered my pistol, but kept my hand on it and trained my Kel-Lite on her. Soon as she opened the glove box, she pulled out another gun, but—lucky for her—slowly and not in a threatening manner. If she had drawn it on me, I'd have shot her. Instead, I simply took this gun too without any resistance from her.

"All right, Annie Oakley," I said. "Get out of the car."

Barely able to stand because she was so intoxicated, she didn't resist as we cuffed and secured her in the squad car. Before we brought her to jail, though, we followed a special procedure designed to ensure the direct and immediate transport of a female prisoner. I picked up the mike and said, "144 at 6700 block of Swiss Avenue. En route to Central with one female 30. DWI and unlawful weapons possession. Time 03:35, mileage 116,245."

"Copy, 144," dispatch replied, and repeated what I'd said; *30* was code for prisoner.

When we arrived at Central, I called dispatch once more, reporting we'd arrived, as well as the time and mileage. Again, the dispatcher repeated what I'd said. Always rolling, DPD's tape recorders preserved every transmission for future reference as necessary.

Rollin' Stolen

Before each shift went out on patrol, the sergeant would hand out what everyone called the "hot sheet," a list of stolen cars sorted by license plate number. To have it available for easy reference on the road, I'd fold it in a certain way and position it to hang from the dashboard air conditioning vent. If I saw a car that looked suspicious or whose license number or description rang a bell, I'd check the hot sheet.

Of course, identifying a moving stolen car was easier than stopping it. If its driver took off, we'd chase them. I never encountered a car thief who ran and then stopped voluntarily. They'd never think, "Oh, I messed up. I should stop." Instead, they fought it all the way until they crashed, ran out of gas, or got a flat. Sometimes, not even that stopped them. I've chased people who had two blowouts and kept going on bare rims, sparks flying everywhere.

The first step, though, was to confirm that the spotted car's license and description definitely matched that of one that had been stolen. On a particular occasion, I made such a call. "144," I said. "Possible rollin' stolen. Edward Lincoln Victor 343. Eastbound, Peady Street, 2200 block." No one wanted to chase the wrong car because of an error on the hot sheet. Dispatch told me it was indeed the right car, so I flipped on my roof light and asked for a cover. I wasn't about to stop the car by myself; its occupants might have been armed.

Dispatch then broadcasted, "144 in pursuit of an occupied stolen vehicle," and stated my location and direction. The closest squad car called in to say where it was and take the assignment.

190

By now, the suspect had nailed it and was flying down the road, which was a straightaway. My speedometer showed 105 mph, and I sensed the chase would speed up as I closed in. At that speed, it helps to have both hands on the steering wheel. So I called the cover car and said, "I'll drive; you broadcast."

"10-4. I'll broadcast," he replied.

Now I could focus on the chase and really unleash the Fury's powerful engine. Seeing I was getting closer, the suspect sped even faster to shake me off. But he lost control and spun out, coming to rest against a curb so high he couldn't get his door open. Desperately, he scrambled across the console and pushed open the passenger door.

But I was already there and put a .44 Magnum in his face just as the cover car pulled up. The arrest foiled not only this theft, but many others as well. When we frisked the thief, he had more than 100 ignition keys stolen from a big East Dallas car dealership.

No Contest

Some situations exceeded the capabilities of even the most experienced patrolmen. In Old East Dallas, a Sears & Roebuck department store occupied a big, triangular parcel of land bounded by Ross, Greeneville, and North Henderson Avenues. It was near but not on my beat, and had been burglarized more times than I could count. So if I happened to drive past it, I'd look for anything that seemed out of place.

Three o'clock one night, the squad car on that beat reported a burglary in progress at Sears. I went over to offer any help I could. Because the store was so big, trying to locate the burglars inside was too difficult and risky, so we called in our K-9 unit, which I hadn't yet seen in action. Our sergeant used a bullhorn to tell the suspects they had two minutes to come out before we'd send a pair of German Shepherds in after them. The burglars, who we now could tell were in the auto parts section, just cursed us and said bring it on. Both Shepherds were big but nimble.

"Won't those guys just shoot the dogs?" I asked their handler, A.G. Thompson.

He laughed at the idea. "Naw," A.G. said. "My boys will be all over them before they know what's happening." And with that he unleashed the dogs and said, "Get 'em!"

Maybe ten seconds after the two Shepherds flew down an aisle of tires and antifreeze, terrible screams of agony rang out. It sounded like Slim Whitman, the yodeling cowboy, getting all his teeth yanked at once. We brought the burglars to the hospital for emergency treatment before locking them up.

Family Feuds

On a typical night, I'd answer five to ten calls of all kinds. I saw wives whose husbands had killed them, and husbands killed by their wives. Sometimes the fight was between blood relatives, and was most tragic when they were parent and child. One fine older man on my beat had the misfortune of being father to a son who'd become an addict. Every month when the man's Social Security check arrived, his son would come to steal it. There'd be a struggle, the son would beat his father and get away with the check before I'd arrive in response to the father's 911 call. When we caught up with the son, we'd put him in jail, but by then he'd have spent the check's meager proceeds on drugs. Finally, the father reached his breaking point.

Dispatch reported a shooting on my beat, and, recognizing the address, I sped there expecting to see the man dead at his son's hands. Instead, I found the son nearly cut in half by a blast from his father's shotgun when the boy again beat and robbed him.

The father was in tears, his shotgun leaning against a chair. "I just couldn't stand it anymore," he told me.

Your mind adjusts to repeated exposure to situations like that. It preserves your sanity by reducing your sensitivity; you become calloused. One time, I had a rookie with me when I answered a stabbing call. We had just stopped by a 7-Eleven for Cokes and candy bars. The stabbing turned out to be something else that still resulted in a lot of spilled blood. In another fight between a father and son, the son had knocked his father through a plate glass window, lacerating the man's throat. You have no sense of how much blood the human body holds until you see up close how much a person can lose from a bad wound. The floor was covered in blood. We called paramedics, who arrived quickly and hurried to control the victim's bleeding.

The rookie and I were standing close by when it occurred to me that my Coke was getting warm. I went back to the squad car, got the two sodas and candy bars, and returned. When I tried to hand the rookie his, I noticed he was pale. He looked at what I'd brought, ran outside, and vomited in the street. So I put his stuff back in the car and went inside again, chewing and drinking all the way. After the ambulance left, I got behind the wheel and looked over at the rookie.

"How you doing, son?" I said solicitously.

He was pretty upset. "How the hell can you eat with all that blood?"

Of course he had a point, but I'd passed it years before as a rookie. If not, I would've found another line of work. He was at the same crossroads now, and there was no single path for everyone to follow.

I told him like it was. "It's not my blood. And I'm sorry that man got hurt, but I can't feel for every victim. There're just too many of them."

Proud to Be of Service

Rookies know they have a lot to learn, but they don't realize how much. Even experienced cops are often surprised by unusual events and situations. No one knows, for example, what to expect when dispatch sends out a signal 58, "Meet the complainant." So when one of those came over the radio for my beat, I knew it could be about any of a thousand different things unless I recognized the address as that of a repeat offender or victim.

A signal 58 came in one afternoon when I was, for a brief period, working the day watch. With me was a rookie named John White, making his way through his first day on the job. This caller turned out to be a lady in her eighties.

"Come in, boys," she said, holding the screen door open for us. "I want to talk to you." We walked into the living room; nothing seemed amiss. "I'm thinking about rearranging my furniture."

Out of the corner of my eye, I saw the rookie look at me in puzzlement. I ignored him. "Are you, now? How can we help?"

"Well," she said, "I wonder if the sofa would look better over here and that big chair close by the window."

I grabbed one end of the sofa and nodded to the rookie. By now, his confusion had become full-blown disbelief. Five minutes later we were done and stood back to consider the new arrangement. When I asked which one was her favorite place to sit, she said the sofa. After getting her agreement that its view out the window was too narrow, we re-arranged things a little bit more.

"Oh, that's perfect," she said. "I just love the way this room looks now."

"Anything else we can help you with?"

"Well, I hope you boys can spare another few minutes. I know you're busy, but I've got a treat for you." She called us back in the kitchen, where she'd laid out beautiful china and cloth napkins and had coffee brewing. So we sat down for ten minutes and enjoyed her coffee and cranberry pastries she'd made.

"This is so nice of you," I said.

"I just appreciate your helping me," she replied.

Back in the squad car, the rookie turned to me and said, "What in the name of hell was that?"

"That lady doesn't have anybody else in this world; she needed our help. Of all the calls we'll answer, that was one of the most important. We made her day, and it took less than twenty minutes. She sees the entire department in a very positive light now."

The rookie nodded reflectively, taking it all in.

Another time, in the evening, I was riding alone when dispatch sent me a signal 58. A woman had called for help getting her husband, a stroke victim, out of the bathtub. She was trying to keep him at home instead of in a nursing home, where he probably should have been. Like many older couples, their children were grown and had moved away. In the past, with her help, he'd been able to make it out of the tub. But now he'd become too weak and uncoordinated, so in desperation she called the police. She was at the door when I arrived; I followed her inside. Seeing her husband naked and helpless was slightly embarrassing for me and intensely humiliating for him. Together we pulled him out quickly. She dried him off and we carefully guided him into bed.

"I'm so sorry to have bothered you," she said.

"Ma'am," I told her, "that's what we're here for—to help you any way possible. Don't ever hesitate to call." I tipped my hat and left, knowing I'd carry that scene to my grave. Dallas police officers provided a lot of unusual but important services like that. We considered it an honor and a crucial part of our job.

Mutual Detestation Society

Some of the people I met on patrol were worthy of attention, but not because I liked them. The most troublesome spot on my beat was the 3600 block of Samuell Boulevard, one bar after another—Jeter's, the 19th Hole, The Lamplighter, Ma Brand's, and others. My favorite gang of misfits, the Bandidos Motorcycle Club, hung out there in force, making as much trouble as possible. They'd intimidate and frighten away all the bars' other customers just to show how bad they were. But if you scratched the surface, you'd find they weren't particularly tough, just vicious. Their favorite sport was outnumbering their prey or picking on people smaller and physically weaker than them. From time to time a bar owner would call the police to report another Bandido-instigated disturbance. Large numbers of people were sometimes involved, so DPD would dispatch every available officer to the scene.

I was riding down Samuell Boulevard with Jim Halverson about 2:30 one morning. As we neared the biker bars, a woman's screams filled the air and didn't stop. The bars had just closed for the night, and a few people were still outside them. One was the person in distress, who looked to be in her seventies or eighties. Four men in Bandidos gear stood near her. One was emptying a can of beer on her head while another peed on the hood of the only car there, an old sedan surrounded by Harley Davidson choppers. The men backed off when my partner Jim and I pulled up. The woman calmed down a little but remained understandably distraught. I told the Bandidos to stay put. I planned to go to town on these guys, and wasn't worried about more of them showing up. We figured help was just a radio call away if we needed it.

I told the woman she was safe now and asked why she was there, especially at that time. She said her daughter had called from one of the bars and asked if she'd come pick her up. When the mother arrived in the old sedan, though, all the bars were closed and the daughter was nowhere in sight. I advised her to drive home, try not to worry about her daughter, and call us the next day if she still didn't show up. Now it was time to deal with the Bandidos. I walked up to the one that had poured beer on the woman's head. He'd just opened another.

"Where I come from, it don't take much guts to pour beer on an old woman's head," I said. "But you gotta be tough to do it to a man. Let's see how tough you are. Start pouring."

Jim stood nearby, keeping an eye on the other three. You never knew what they might try, but they wouldn't run off and leave their bikes behind.

My joker said, "No, no. I don't want to go to jail."

"Well you are." I took his beer, turned him around and pushed him against the squad car, where Jim cuffed him. Next up: the guy who peed on the sedan.

"Your turn, bad ass." I held the beer out. "Pour it on my head."

"No, man. I don't want no trouble."

"But you brought the trouble here, chum. I'm just giving it back to you." I grabbed his biker vest, pushed him against the squad car, and cuffed him too. Over his shoulder, I saw Jim look me in the eye, shaking his head left to right. I didn't know what he wanted, and was on a roll. After the third Bandido declined my offer and joined his pals against the car, I noticed Jim still nodding "No" at me. But I'd built up a head of steam, and wasn't about to stop. I walked over to the fourth Bandido, who all along had been standing in the background and hadn't bothered the woman.

"You got something to say?"

He looked at me, serious.

"Yeah. What's the quickest way out of Dallas?"

"Figure it out yourself. You got ten seconds, and I'm up to eight already." He jumped on that Harley in a flash and gunned it onto the street. As the rumble of his engine grew fainter, I was in an expansive mood, and went over to see what was on Jim's mind.

"What's the problem?"

He was peeved. "I'll tell you what the problem is. Our radio's not working. We couldn't have called for help if we needed it." Jim had discovered this when he tried to call in and request a van to pick up our prisoners. This was serious. We were in a nonresidential area across from a deserted municipal park in the middle of the night.

"Oh," I said, sheepishly. We'd had a close call because of me, but I couldn't restrain my sense of humor. "Let's not tell the prisoners."

Jim got in the back with two and I buckled in the third up front with me. The Fury's suspension sagging, we chugged off to jail. These three were just the latest of many Bandidos I brought there.

No wonder that gang didn't like me. The feeling was mutual.

Public Enemy No. 1

Not all of our assignments grew out of calls from outside the police department. At one point, my sergeant wanted me to go after the ice cream man for violating a Dallas ordinance that prohibited advertising with amplified music. He said that included the tinkling audio loop the ice cream truck played. "That guy's breaking the law and you're letting him!"

"Aw, Sarge," I said. "Don't make me write the ice cream man a ticket."

He wasn't fazed, though, and demanded I enforce the ordinance that day.

I went on patrol thinking, "I am not writing the ice cream man a ticket. That's not police work."

When I returned that evening, the sergeant asked if I'd achieved the objective.

"Hell, yeah!" I said. "While I was writing out his summons, he mouthed off. I whipped his ass and put the son of a bitch in jail."

The sergeant took a step backward. "Oh, my god, you beat up the ice cream man?"

"Damn right! No one gets to talk to me like that."

"What'd you do with his truck?"

"I put it in the auto pound."

"What about his ice cream?"

"Must be all melted by now," I said, and walked back to my locker.

A few minutes later, the sergeant came over.

"Ratley, did you really beat up the ice cream man?"

"No, Sarge," I said. "He outsmarted me. I couldn't catch him."

With that, the sergeant flushed and silently walked away.

"Here we are trying to protect and serve the public," I thought. "And he wants me to write up the ice cream man." Made no sense to me. The sergeant never mentioned it again.

Truth or Consequences

I had a rookie with me when we drove up on two guys fist-fighting in front of an East Dallas honky-tonk. I broke it up, and I asked them both for ID. One guy gave me his driver's license; the other said he didn't have any.

"All right. What's your name?"

"Bill Robertson."

"OK, Bill, how do you spell Robertson?"

He got this look of panic in his eyes and said, "Uh...R-o-b...i-t...s-o-n."

"Your age, Mr. Robertson?"

"31."

"Date of birth?" Again, he gave me an "Oh, no!" look and stammered out a birth date for someone 39 years old. "Wait here," I said, and took the rookie back to the squad car. Per standard procedure, we asked dispatch to query the FBI's National Crime

Information Center database, which has hundreds of thousands of records on individuals wanted on felony charges. No warrants were outstanding on the guy with the driver's license.

"I won't bother checking Robertson," I told the rookie. "He's lying about everything."

"What're you going to do?"

"Scare the hell out of him," I said, and walked back over. In Texas, giving a false name to a police officer was a class C misdemeanor with a $27.50 fine.

"Here's the deal," I said to the first guy. "Either you go home now or I'll take you to jail for disorderly conduct."

"I'll go home; I'll go home."

"Don't let me see you here again." I gave him back his license and he scrammed. I turned over to the other guy.

"Mr. Robertson, you're under arrest."

"Say what?"

"We checked your record. Houston PD has four warrants out on you—three for burglary, one for murder."

"That's not me," he said, and waved his hand dismissively.

"But you're Bill Robertson, age 31. You just told me."

The consequences of his lies seemed to suddenly dawn on the guy, who now dropped all pretense. "Officer, I lied to you about my name."

I rolled my eyes. "Mr. Robertson, I've been doing this job a long time. Don't treat me like an idiot." I moved him toward the squad car, and pulled out my handcuffs. "Turn around and put your hands behind your back."

His eyes bulged at the sight of them. "No, no, this is all a big mistake."

"Mr. Robertson, please. This officer and I are professionals, sir. We can tell when people lie. You can't change your name after we find out about your warrants."

"My name's not Robertson."

"Far as I'm concerned, it is, Mr. Robertson." I applied the cuffs and sat with him in the back seat while the rookie drove. All the way downtown, he wept and pleaded his innocence. I stepped it up, telling him that a Houston PD officer would come to Dallas and compare fingerprints. "If you're not the same Bill Robertson, they'll turn you loose."

"Will that be tonight?"

I looked at him with pity. "Oh, no. Usually two weeks. But sometimes real quick, say, ten, maybe nine days." If Robertson had been wearing a wig, it would've flipped twice and flown away.

"I can't stay in jail that long!" he said. "I'll lose my job!"

"Calm down," I said. "You can post $500,000 bond and they'll let you right out. You'll get the money back later."

"Officer, I'm not a drug lord! I don't have half a million dollars."

"You don't understand, Mr. Robertson. You've entered the criminal justice system in a democracy. The wheels turn at the same speed for everyone. You'll just have to wait until Houston gets here. You'll be fed and everything, shower once a week."

"But you have to believe me! I swear to God, I lied. I've got a job. I gotta be at work."

I assumed a sterner tone. "Well, Mr. Robertson, next time maybe you'll think twice before breaking into someone's home and killing him."

"That wasn't me," he moaned. "Why won't you believe me?"

"Mr. Robertson, some people don't think very highly of our intelligence," I said. "I can't believe you were lying. You knew how to spell Robertson. You knew your date of birth." He lapsed into a morose silence and awaited his fate while we drove to the station. There, the rookie wrote up the arrest report, and I went to see the booking sergeant—one of my favorite cops—Bill Gee, a gruff guy with a dry sense of humor. He reviewed arrest reports and told prisoners what they were charged with. I filled Gee in on the collar and what I'd told Robertson after he'd lied. Laughing softly, Gee said bring him over.

I put on a bleak face and told Robertson the sergeant would see him. We walked over to Gee.

"Sergeant, this is Bill Robertson."

"That's not my name!"

We ignored that. Gee looked at him with a mixture of pity and disgust. "Whatcha got to say for yourself?"

Robertson took a deep breath. "Sergeant, I made a horrible mistake. I lied to this officer. The phony name I gave, that son of a bitch is wanted for murder, burglary, every damn thing but holding up the air raid warden." I couldn't take it, and had to turn away to hide my laughter. But Gee kept listening with a straight face while Robertson jabbered on.

Finally, Gee sighed and cut him short. "I talk to a lot of pathetic bastards every night, fella. But you're absolutely the most pathetic one I've ever seen. This officer has known all along you were lying. You're not charged with murder or burglary. The actual charge is failure to identify yourself. As soon as you get someone to bring over your ID and pay $27.50 bond, we'll let you out."

Robertson looked over to me and smiled, tears in his eyes. "You knew all along?"

"Uh-huh."

His shoulders sagged in relief clearly greater than his embarrassment. "You scared the hell outta me," he said, and laughed weakly as we walked to a holding cell. Aside from Columbus Hardin, I never saw anyone so happy to spend a night in jail.

Double Trouble

Riding patrol with me one summer night, Daddy nearly died laughing. He would've been happy to go that way like Pecos Bill but he survived. No one was out as we rolled slowly down Graham Avenue. The streets were quiet, and aside from background chatter, so was the squad car radio. Then something made a popping sound off to our right.

"Did you hear that?" Daddy said.

"Yep." I pulled over and we listened. Again it came, weakly: pop, pause, pop. I looked in the rear view and saw a woman running across the intersection at Terry Street. I slammed the Fury into reverse. Backing up, I could just see another woman running in the same direction. The popping sound was coming from her; probably a small automatic.

"Whoo-eee!" Daddy said.

I slowed down at the intersection, shifted into drive, and turned. With my brights on and roof light flashing, I closed in on the pair, still running down the middle of the street. The second one fired another round. The first one jumped, yelled "Yow!" and kept going.

"Police! Hold it right there," I yelled, and they stopped. They looked like twins. Both about five-two, 250, and gasping for breath. I got out, drew my pistol, and yelled at the shooter to drop it. She did.

The other ran toward me, yelling, "I been shot! My sister shot me!"

Seeing I had things under control, Daddy got out and came over. I picked up the automatic and pocketed it.

"Don't move," I told the shooter, and asked the other where she'd been hit. She seemed in pain, but otherwise okay.

"In back," she said.

To find out whether she needed an ambulance, I told her to come up by the headlights. "Show me." She leaned over near the hood and pulled up her dress. Daddy moved in for a closer look. She'd been hit once, all right; her white pantyhose had a small bullet hole in them. But amazingly, there was practically no blood. Apparently, an abundance of natural padding had stopped the small-caliber round from doing much damage. When Daddy realized this, he let out a laugh so deep and long I thought he'd wake up the whole neighborhood.

"Will you *please* get a grip!" I said, dying to bust out myself when I saw she wasn't seriously hurt. Daddy staggered over to the car's hood and collapsed on it, face down, laughing hysterically.

"It's not funny, goddam it!" the victim yelled.

"Who is that guy?" the shooter said.

"Undercover," I replied. "Don't move."

It would've been too painful for the victim to sit in the squad car, so I called for an ambulance. The way Daddy was carrying on, I thought he too might need one. Leaning up from the hood, he seemed okay for a second, but collapsed in another fit of violent laughter. I put my head next to his. "You better jam a sock in it right now."

"What's wrong with that man?" the victim said.

"He's got a condition," I told her, and walked over to the shooter.

"I didn't mean it," she said. "It was an accident."

"But you were running after her, shooting."

"Well," she said indignantly, "she got me mad."

After the ambulance took the victim to the hospital, I cuffed the shooter and belted her into the front with me. I wasn't about to sit her next to Daddy.

Night and Day

Simple pleasures helped relieve some of the stress we officers experienced from being on patrol. Laughter was one; another was our Friday night routine of buying a watermelon at the farmer's market and bringing it over to 7-Eleven, where the clerks would put it in their cooler. Just before dawn, we'd pick it up. By then, all the bad guys had gone home and the drunks passed out. We'd go over to Tenison Park, a big greenspace north of Samuell Boulevard, eat the melon, and relax for a few minutes before going back on patrol. It was a nice break, and we needed it.

Both my daughters were born during my street patrol years, and I wasn't earning much. I was always looking for some kind of part-time work to make ends meet. Most often I directed traffic at a shopping center or provided security for other businesses. I wasn't alone. Every Dallas cop was horribly paid and struggled to pay routine bills, get family health care, save for retirement, and put a little aside for an emergency. My two jobs definitely weren't bringing in enough to support my family. So when DPD's Vice Squad put out a call for applicants, I jumped at the opportunity to make a slightly better wage.

And, truth be told, I'd accomplished everything I'd set out to do on street patrol. I was a field training officer, I had my own beat, and I routinely led the sector in activity each month. I wanted a new set of challenges within the police department. Ultimately, my record served me well; I got the job. All I had to do was make it through another week on street patrol before my transfer.

Right up to the End

At that time in East Dallas, a guy had been breaking into women's homes and raping them. Some said he put a knife to their throat; others said it was a screwdriver. Two nights before my transfer, the rapist struck again.

I was driving and had a rookie with me. The victim dialed 911, and dispatch sent several cars at once, including mine. Another squad car was near the victim's house when the call came in. That officer saw the suspect run away, weaving between houses, so he got out for a foot chase. As it is, most cops are out of shape from sitting in a squad car so much. Plus, they have thirty pounds of equipment on them. So, doing his best to keep up, the pursuing officer used his walkie-talkie to report.

All cars heard him holler, "We're running north on Garret Street through the park, toward Ross Avenue."

I knew the area well and realized the suspect was heading toward a nearby strip mall. "There's a tight little alley between two of the mall's buildings," I told the rookie. "That's where he'll come out."

I sped over there and parked just out of sight near the end of the alley. After killing the lights, we waited. Not a minute later, the suspect came flying out of the alley and practically ran into the squad car. He stopped six feet from me, holding a screwdriver. I drew my pistol and screamed, "Freeze or I'll blow your goddamn head off!" He raised the screwdriver and pointed it at me. My mind was racing a hundred miles an hour. I knew that if I shot him, I'd have to stay on street patrol throughout the resulting shooting investigation. I cocked the hammer and said, "Don't let that Craftsman get you sent to hell."

He dropped it, but we weren't done yet. Because I had an untested rookie with me, I had to make sure the suspect was unable to fight or run. "On the ground!" I yelled and he lay down, face up. I kept my .44 pointed at him until other officers arrived to help me. After we cuffed him, the rookie and I brought him to jail. He faced 42 counts of rape, and I was on my way to the Vice Squad.

CHAPTER 15

VICE SQUAD

The day after I left street patrol, I reported for duty on the Vice Squad. In twelve hours, I went from a blue uniform to blue jeans, along with a T-shirt and cowboy boots. Undercover, you dress to blend in—not to stand out.

After seven years on street patrol, I thought I'd seen every aspect of life in East Dallas. I knew the streets, the people, and an awful lot that went on in public and behind closed doors—or so I thought. Drug dealers, pimps, and sex workers had always been there, but the Vice Squad had dealt with them. Now, in my new role, I got a different look at the same streets I'd patrolled in a squad car. It wasn't pretty.

DPD's Vice Squad consisted of two units. One fought the illegal drug trade and the other, prostitution—that's where I worked. Each unit's head count was nominally fixed, but in practice fluctuated according to need. If the anti-drug team was short-handed, I'd run their warrants or do whatever else might be necessary.

There was no transitional training for officers entering either unit. Extensive experience on patrol was deemed adequate preparation. As soon as you reported for duty, you hit the street and were expected to make arrests. I made plenty. While observing the law and respecting suspects' rights, I took many people into custody after seeing them violate one or more drug or morals laws.

I quickly learned that undercover work exposes you to more violence than any other job on the police force. As on street patrol, I worked alone most of the time. But now I often was on foot, my partner a block or two away in a van or car that didn't have a police radio. We'd take turns driving and walking. Sometimes the one driving would stop to speak with a potential suspect, who would've immediately noticed a radio with a microphone. That's why undercover vehicles didn't have one.

There was no other way to do this job. If anyone saw two guys like us together—on foot or in a van—they'd instantly know we were cops. So one of us would stay in the van while the other, at a distance, cruised on foot. As far as helping each other was concerned, the two blocks separating us might as well have been ten miles. Back then, long before cell phones, there was no quick way for undercover cops to request backup.

Vice differed from street patrol in another important way: Instead of simply responding to crime, I now had to seek it out. To top it off, the career criminals I approached were usually armed in one way or another. Many had lengthy records and a lot to lose if arrested again. I faced these challenges head-on.

Close Call

My first day in Vice was cold, rainy, and anti-climactic; bad weather depresses the street trade in sex and drugs. Sunshine filled a pale blue sky on my second day. It was nice not having to wear a hat on the job. Because most vice crimes happen later in the day, I didn't get out and about until after lunchtime.

It had just gone two o'clock as I walked by a cluster of low-income apartments on San Jacinto Street in Old East Dallas, a high-crime area. As I passed them, a stocky young woman stepped out of one and winked at me. I paused and we spoke briefly. Under the law, it wasn't entrapment to ask for sex. When I told her I needed some loving, she encouraged me to follow her back inside. I agreed but knew that her pimp might be waiting to ambush me. I resisted a nervous urge to lean down and touch the shiny .38 tucked into an ankle holster I'd just bought for my new line of work.

We entered the building's small lobby. No one else was there as she turned to me. "You got twenty dollars to spend?"

Bad move. By bringing up money, she broke the law. I badged her. "Dallas police. You're under arrest for prostitution."

Instantly she yanked a long knife out of her purse and lunged at me. I sidestepped, barely evading the blade, and for a few long seconds we struggled for control of it. Finally, when I got the knife away from her, she flung the door open and ran outside. Before I could follow, I stooped down to yank my pistol out of the leg holster. If I hadn't, it might have come out while I ran. Arms pumping, I sprinted to catch up with her.

After flying around a blind corner onto Holly Avenue, I saw too late that she'd stopped short and bent over. Caught by surprise, I slammed into her, flipped into the air, and landed hard on my back. As I lay there stunned, the wind knocked out of me, she snatched my gun and aimed right at me. I swatted it away just as she pulled the trigger; the bullet grazed my forehead. My ears were ringing and my heart pounding as I yanked the pistol back and wrestled her to the ground while she bit my forearms. I pulled my arms away and suddenly felt something hard and cold pressing on my neck.

Then a loud voice behind me boomed, "Drop it or you're a dead man!" I looked down and to the left. Blue trousers with a gold stripe—a cop; someone had called 911.

I stretched my arms out straight, holding the gun butt with two fingertips. "I'm Dallas police!" I yelled. "I'm police!" In the movies, anyone told to lay down his weapon just tosses it aside. But mine was nice, and I didn't want to scratch it.

The cop wasn't buying it. "Drop it now!" he shouted.

I also was worried my quick-handed prisoner might snatch it from the ground. So I looked around at the officer, and saw it was someone I knew—Jerry Womatt.

He hadn't yet heard of my transfer. "Aw, hell, Ratley, it's you! What's with that getup?"

I got to my feet and told him. Meanwhile the hooker scrambled up and bolted.

"She's getting away!" Jerry said. I turned, still out of breath, and started after her. But Jerry was a marathon runner and left me in the dust. "How far you want to go today, darling?" he asked, loping along effortlessly beside her. Seeing it was futile, she surrendered. I caught up, read the woman her *Miranda* rights, and hitched a ride downtown with her handcuffed beside me in the back of Jerry's squad car. If she'd come along peaceably at the outset, her only charge would've been a misdemeanor. But the shot she'd taken at me had also earned her a far more serious one: attempted murder of a police officer.

There was no time to be scared while all this was happening. But afterward, putting alcohol on my bite wounds, I was shaking like a leaf. This was far more excitement than I'd bargained for.

Battle of Attrition

About five days later, my partner Larry Paul Reed and I left Central Station in an unmarked van. It was about 10 p.m.; we'd just switched over to the night shift. Our destination, Ervay Street, was just a few blocks away. Despite its proximity to the station, Ervay was a prime hook-up spot for streetwalkers and johns. It was Larry Paul's turn to be on foot that night; I dropped him off a few blocks before Ervay and drove on. Two minutes later, I saw a tall woman walking back and forth on the corner of Ervay and Jackson. When I pulled up beside her, she walked up to the van. I reached over and rolled down the passenger window.

"What you looking for, baby?" she asked.

I told her, and she got in.

"Twenty-five dollars," she said.

I showed her my badge, told her she was under arrest for prostitution, and stepped on the gas. Before I could get up to speed, though, she jumped out and high-tailed it down Ervay against the flow of traffic. Furious, I slammed on the brakes, threw the transmission into park, and ran after her, hoping my pistol wouldn't come out of its ankle holster. It took me a half block to catch up and grasp both her arms.

"I'm sorry I ran," she said. "I'm scared."

"It's just a Class B misdemeanor," I told her. "Put your hands behind your back, and everything'll be all right." She seemed to relax, so I released one arm to pull out my handcuffs. Right away, she whirled around, knocked me down, and ran off again. Once more, I caught up, but this time was different—she fought me like a demon. Outclassed, I tried to push her away. I was willing to let her escape, but she seemed possessed and came right back at me, landing solid punches everywhere.

Several times, I reached down to get my pistol. And every time, she banged sparks off my head. One of her blows knocked me on my back again, and she jumped on top of me, flailing away. I managed to wrap my legs around her waist and reach the leg holster. But as soon as I pulled out the pistol, she jerked it almost out of my hand and was about to kill me with my own gun.

Still, I wouldn't let go of the revolver. By wrapping my hands tightly around the cylinder, I kept it from turning. And that stopped the hammer from striking the round. Marshaling the last of my fading strength, I wrenched the gun from her hands, and hung onto it for dear life. I knew that if she got that pistol again, she'd shoot me.

By now we both were exhausted and lay gasping on the sidewalk. When I told her to put her arms behind her back, she told me she couldn't move them. I felt the same. A round of boxing lasts three minutes; we'd been at it much longer. I stretched her arms out on the ground and hastily cuffed both hands as best I could. But they wound up in front of her—an error I'd never made before. I knew it was dangerous, but I was desperate and proceeded anyway in case she went wild again. "Get up," I said. "We're going back to that van." But now she said she couldn't walk, so we sat down on the curb.

The street was silent as a tomb; I saw no sign of Larry Paul and didn't expect to. I had the wheels, so he was waiting for me to come back to him. Distracted for a second, I let my attention waver and paid for it when she jumped to her feet and kicked me in the head. But it was only a glancing blow and left her off balance, enabling me to pull her back down. Again I restrained her until she stopped struggling. But I still didn't dare reposition the cuffs until I had backup.

We both were ready to drop, so I waited a minute before hoisting her up and walking her back to the van. I opened its sliding door and told her to get in. When she flopped down on the floorboard, I helped her into a seat and belted her in. With the physical battle over, I resumed the legal process I'd barely begun before all hell broke loose. I repeated the charge, spelled out her *Miranda* rights, and said where we were headed. After wearily closing the door, I lay back against it, wondering how I'd survived the most violent incident of my life. I couldn't understand why she'd repeatedly attacked me instead of fleeing. It seemed clear that I'd given up and wouldn't have chased her. But instead, for some insane reason, she went into attack mode.

I got behind the wheel and drove back to where I'd dropped off Larry Paul. About thirty minutes had passed—longer than we'd normally stay apart. When I pulled up, he saw the hooker in the back seat and nodded at me. Of course, there was no way he could've known of my brush with death.

"Another woman just whipped my ass," I said when he got in. He smiled, but I didn't. Blood and dirt made it plain I'd been in a battle royal.

When we arrived back at Central, the lieutenant came out, looked me over, and asked me what had happened. I gave him a brief recap and sat down to catch my breath while Larry Paul took the prisoner to a holding cell. The lieutenant and I went into his office to continue the debriefing.

Five minutes later, Larry Paul popped his head in. "I think the prisoner's dead."

"No!" I said.

We all ran back to the holding cell, and the lieutenant checked for a pulse. "Nothing," he said.

I called the emergency medical unit while the lieutenant opened her blouse to apply CPR. What we saw stunned us: a hairy chest and masculine torso.

The lieutenant looked at me. "You arrested a man, not a woman."

While that made sense, it also made my mind spin, and I sat back down. A minute later, the medical team arrived. Despite our efforts, it was too late to resuscitate the prisoner.

By then it was near dawn, the shift over. Gratefully I got into my Ford LTD for the drive home to Mesquite. On the way, I un-strapped the leg holster and threw it out the window. For someone with my job, it was worse than useless; it was dangerous.

That afternoon, news of the incident hit the papers. DPD's investigation revealed that the prisoner was 21 years old and had a long rap sheet. Later the autopsy report said he'd been heavily intoxicated by a mix of drugs and had died from a heart attack.

My first two arrests were difficult, to say the least, and this was only my first week in Vice.

The Aftermath

These days, after a fatal incident, a police officer will get time off and psychological counseling. In my day, though, you had to suck it up and get back to work. The next night, I was shaky and hadn't slept at all. In the locker room, Larry Paul told me to take it slow and concentrate on backing him up when he made a bust. That worked all right for a few days, but I hated it—not least because it wasn't fair to my partner.

So at the end of my second week, I asked my sergeant for a transfer out of Vice. "I get physically sick when I come to work. I can't handle this job."

He shook his head in empathy. "I completely understand," he said. "But I won't transfer you while you're scared. If I did, you'd regret it for the rest of your life. So don't worry about making arrests for the next couple, three weeks. Just go back out there and give it some time. Next month, if you still want a transfer, I'll sign the paperwork."

I appreciated that and said I'd try. But secretly I intended to see him again in a week and say it was all over. Meanwhile, though, I took his advice. And to my surprise, my confidence gradually returned, and I resumed making my share of arrests. It took longer for me to master the anxiety that lingered from these first two violent incidents. But from then on when suspects pulled guns, knives, or both, I was prepared—mentally as well as physically—and knew how to handle them.

A New Era

After I'd been in Vice for a couple of years, my sergeant asked me to train new arrivals as an FTO. With plenty of experience as a Vice officer, and even more as a trainer, I agreed.

For some time, DPD had been integrating women into non-clerical positions; I'd trained some at the academy. One recruit, Jill Muncy, had performed particularly well on a field exercise I supervised in which she responded to a simulated shooting incident. Since then, Jill had racked up a couple of solid years on street patrol and was happy there.

At that time, though, the Vice Squad had no permanent female staff members. A few women, including Jill, had completed temporary assignments in Vice, but none had been brought back to stay. Now top brass decided the time was right to bring a female officer to Vice permanently. They picked Jill on the strength of her long-term record on street patrol and her brief performance in Vice.

Back in 1971, when I joined DPD, only men wore guns. Now, nearly a decade later, that had changed, but without personally affecting me; I'd never depended on a woman for backup. It became very personal, though, the night I learned Jill would routinely join me undercover, armed, and posing as a prostitute. I worried that some women's lack of physical strength might endanger them and their partners in violent physical encounters. Still, I greeted Jill professionally and was fully committed to working closely with her. It helped that I remembered how talented she was.

While few male police officers welcomed the advent of women to their ranks, we all knew that women listened more closely and spoke more clearly and tactfully than men did. That often gave them an important edge in resolving disputes and completing arrests without resorting to force. So male officers gave women a fair chance to bear their share of the workload. Overall, the women

215

performed as well as the men did, and we all moved forward together. And during the two years we worked together, Jill became the best partner I ever had.

Tough and brilliantly smart, she impressed me as someone who'd rise to the top of our profession—and she did. As my trainee, she learned from me; but I learned much more from her, especially about how to approach and communicate with people. Not long after we'd each left Vice, Jill made sergeant. Later, she became a lieutenant and ultimately retired as deputy chief of police.

Not one to sit on the sidelines, Jill then moved on to a bigger arena. In 2003, the U.S. Department of State selected her as deputy commissioner of operations for the United Nations Police (UNP) in the Republic of Kosovo. Commanding 9,000 officers, Jill was the first American woman to hold an executive position in the UNP. Following that assignment, she set up and ran a training program for the Internal Security Forces of Lebanon.

We still stay in touch and will be friends until we die. We faced some pretty tight situations together in Vice.

Jim Dandy to the Rescue

Vice's prostitution unit consisted of four teams of two cops; Jill and I formed one. Before hitting the streets, we'd plan the night's work with our sergeant. Generally, we focused on locations where the public had complained about prostitution activity, as well as the drugs and violence that came with it. On the street, in addition to my cruising to engage hookers, Jill would stand on a corner, posing as one until a john approached her. In contrast to my practice with male partners, Jill and I could stay within eyesight of each other. When someone violated the law, we'd regroup, arrest the perpetrator, and transport him or her downtown. We also posed as a drunken couple in clubs suspected of hosting gambling or selling liquor without a license.

One memorable incident took place in a bad part of West Dallas near the Trinity River. According to a tipster, a cockfighting crew from Laredo had just set up shop in The Double Eagle, a rough cowboy bar on North Industrial Boulevard, the desolate west side of Interstate 35E, which runs through the center of Dallas. Just a few blocks away, on the much more developed east side of the Interstate, lay the Texas School Book Depository at 411 Elm Street, facing Dealey Plaza, where assassin Lee Harvey Oswald committed the biggest crime in Texas history.

Acting on the tip, our sergeant asked Jill and me to investigate. Our strategy this time was to travel there together and separate before we entered the bar. We pulled up in its parking lot; Jill walked in first and I followed five minutes later. While she put sly questions to the bartender and then mingled with four cowboys, I watched surreptitiously from the other end of the bar, nursing a beer. As usual, we blended in smoothly.

Depending on whether we discovered anything illegal, we'd either jointly make arrests or leave separately a few minutes apart. So it surprised me, after we'd been there about twenty minutes, when Jill pretended to see me, an old friend, for the first time that night. I searched her face for a clue when she walked over; this wasn't what we'd planned.

Jill quickly came to the point. "We need to get out of here now," she said. "Those guys want me to be their entertainment tonight. I told them no thanks, and they ain't happy."

I spotted the four out of the corner of my eye. They were downing tequila shots and staring right at us. "C'mon, sweetheart," I said loudly as I put my arm around Jill and headed for the door. Outside, I hugged her and turned so I could see whether anyone was following us; all four guys were. I quickly turned again, and we headed for the car. But, realizing they'd catch up to us before we got there, I stopped and hugged Jill again. At the same time, I pulled the .38 out of my pants and slid it under the back of her loose blouse.

Jill jerked her head away from mine. "What the hell are you doing?" she said as the four closed in on us.

"We're still too far from the car," I replied. "That's my gun you feel. Anyone messes with us, I'll blow his ass off."

"All right," she said. "But don't you shoot through my new blouse, Ratley!"

I sweated it out as the cowboys drew closer. At the last minute, they split up and sauntered past us, two in front, two behind. I couldn't believe it; they just walked away. I was glad we'd gotten off without a fight and even more relieved that I didn't have to deal with Jill about putting a bullet hole in her blouse. Not having found anything illegal in our brief visit, we decided to leave The Double Eagle alone for that evening at least and to turn our attention to other vice hotspots people had complained about.

A Rock and a Hard Place

I wasn't making much money on street patrol when my two daughters were born, and now in Vice, I wasn't making much more. This caused a lot of tension between me and my wife, Mary Ellen. Working undercover and sometimes a second job brought in much needed money, but it also put a great strain on our marriage. Our girls still hadn't started school, and had little idea of what was going on. But they seldom saw me, and I'd gradually become a stranger at home. When I was there, Mary Ellen and I argued incessantly.

To spare our kids the unpleasantness of it all, I moved out, even though I had nowhere to go. Sometimes a cop would spend the night in an empty holding cell. I couldn't bring myself to do that, though, and chose a less unpleasant alternative—living in my car. While that was undeniably a comedown, things could've been worse. For starters, I loved that 1976 Ford LTD. It was one of the best rides I'd ever had, with a gold vinyl top and nice soft seats that were comfortable for sleeping. As it turned out, I lived that way for six months. And if I ever have to move into a car again, I hope it'll be a '76 LTD. Mr. Ford makes an excellent automobile.

Not long after I moved out, Mary Ellen and I divorced, and she got custody of the kids, with weekend visitation rights for me. After a bit, I went back to the house while she was out with the kids. Desperate for a change of clothes, I headed for my dresser and closet. Both were empty. I cursed myself for not coming before she apparently threw all my stuff in the garbage. I remembered, though, that my favorite tool kit might have escaped her attention and still be in the garage. I went to look, and it was there—along with my clothes, which were laid out across the garage floor and covered with tire marks. She'd been driving all over them ever since I left.

I wasn't happy about this, but realized she was acting and thinking the same way I was. When you're going through a divorce, you lose about half your brain. So gritting my teeth, I gathered up my clothes in grocery bags, washed them in the men's room sink at the station, and then laid them out in the back seat of my car. The trunk was too dirty, and no one was going to steal a bunch of T-shirts, jeans, and drawers, which is all I had.

Wheels of Justice

Just as patrolmen have to write a certain number of traffic tickets each month, we on the Vice Squad had to average a couple of arrests each night to satisfy our monthly quota. Sometimes walking through a high-crime area would put us among drug dealers and streetwalkers who were breaking the law and subject to arrest. But because a car enabled us to cover more ground and encounter more criminals, I most often chose to drive.

I liked making deals in a car because, being left-handed, I could hide my pistol under my left thigh. When hookers or drug dealers got in the car, they'd ask if I were a cop and I'd say I wasn't. "Then pick up your shirt so I can see if you've got a gun," they'd say. So, I'd pull my shirt up and show them I didn't—at least not there. No one ever asked me to stand up to see whether I was *sitting* on a gun.

Working out of a car, however, had its own challenges. Once we'd been seen using a certain car during an arrest, it was useless because it had been "burned"—recognized by street criminals as an undercover police vehicle. We couldn't use unmarked DPD cars because they were all equipped with police radios, a dead giveaway of who we were. So we used older cars from the local Rent-A-Wreck office. But eventually the hookers and drug dealers recognized them all on sight.

We could fill out a request to use our own cars. If it were approved, the city would pay for any damage. But I was impatient with bureaucratic procedures and never bothered to request permission. I just used my car, and accepted responsibility for repairing anything damaged on the job.

Because Rent-A-Wreck cars were several years old, they looked like something owned by an individual, not a government agency. Hookers and drug dealers were less wary when we pulled up in a beat-up crate instead of a relatively new model. My car had the drawback of being only a year old. But my shabby wardrobe in the back seat more than made up for that. I'd drive up to someone and say, "I need some comforting. My old lady just kicked me out, and I'm living in my car." After one look at my pile of clothes, prostitutes would fall all over me and drug dealers would show me their wares, no questions asked. They'd sell me whatever I asked for, and I'd whip my pistol out from under my leg and bust them.

One time, near the end of the month, my sometime partner, Jim Halverson, was well short of meeting his quota. I'd already satisfied mine by using my clothes-equipped LTD. So I told Jim to borrow it and spelled out the pitch I used with it. I got out and waited on the street while he gave it a try for twenty or thirty minutes. An hour and a half later, he still hadn't returned, and I began to worry.

Then a squad car pulled up. "You Ratley?" the cop asked. When I said I was, he told me to get in. "Your partner's been involved in a shooting on the 5000 block of Ross Avenue." We got there in no time, and I was glad to see that Jim was all right. At first, my car seemed unharmed. But I saw a guy in the passenger seat, and he wasn't moving.

Halverson had attracted a drug dealer, who tried to stab and rob him. During a violent struggle in the front seat, Jim had shot the guy who kicked furiously in every direction before dying. The radio knobs were broken off, as was the glove box cover. After an ambulance crew removed the body, I noticed a bullet hole in the front seat. After passing through it, the round had also gone through most of my clothes.

I made sure Jim was in decent shape; I knew just how he felt, and gave him a ride back to Central. Then I drove to a quiet street nearby where I hoped to get some sleep in the car. When the sun came up, my spirits remained low. Not only was I living in my car, but it and my clothes had been—there's no other word for it—violated.

Soon stores opened for business, and in one I found a new product called Superglue, which I bought with two of my last dollars. I went back to the car, glued the knobs back on the radio and ran a bead of Superglue along the edge of the glove box cover. Then I pressed my hand against it while the glue set. After waiting about five minutes, I glanced at the tube and noticed big block letters on its side: DO NOT ALLOW TO COME IN CONTACT WITH SKIN.

Not worried, I tried to pull my hand away, but it wouldn't come loose. I tugged harder, winced in pain, and began to panic. For about an hour I sat there, unable to free myself. Finally, I literally ripped my fingers away, tearing off flesh in the process. I wrapped a sock around my hand, climbed into the back seat, and fell into a fitful sleep.

A few hours later, I woke up and drove back to Central to get a few packets of ketchup from the cafeteria. Mixed with water, they made a thin soup that quelled my hunger for an hour or two. I knew I couldn't go on like this; I'd lost sixty pounds since moving out from home. It would've been nice to just disappear—move to Hawaii and walk around in shorts and a T-shirt. But I never forgot that people were counting on me. My kids needed my support, and so did my colleagues at work.

Jill offered to let me stay in a spare room at her house. "Thanks, but no," I told her. "I got myself into this mess, and I'll get myself out of it." I realized I had to go about life in a different way, although I wasn't sure how.

A New Direction

The change I needed finally came, but not because of anything I'd done. Instead, after a DPD probe into corruption in the Vice Squad, all its personnel were transferred to other units, even if—like me and virtually all my colleagues—they had no part in the bribe-taking and other violations that prompted the shakeup.

At the time, any new assignment would have appealed to me. But as I described in Part One, I wound up processing cases in the Youth Division, a thankless and frustrating task. A few months later, however, I jumped at the opportunity to co-found the Child Abuse Unit. And from there, I eventually moved to Internal Affairs, where I initially investigated corruption allegedly committed by DPD officers. But later, while temporarily assigned to a special task force, I came face-to-face with a type of criminal I'd never seen before: the non-violent, white-collar perpetrator of occupational fraud.

CHAPTER 16

A MORE NORMAL LIFE

After leaving the Vice Squad, I saved up enough money to move out of my car and into a house back in Mesquite, where I lived alone, preoccupied with co-founding and running the Child Abuse Unit. Later, after I was transferred to Internal Affairs, my hours mostly became those of a normal 9-to-5er, with weekends off. The best part was that it helped pave the way for me to gain custody of my little daughters, Sarah and Leslie, who were still early on in grammar school. The combination of my new work schedule, comfortable home, and various changes in my ex-wife's circumstances led us to switch roles. We agreed that it'd be better for the girls if they moved in with me and visited her on alternating weekends.

My happiness was tinged with more than a little anxiety, though. I wasn't much of a cook, and still had plenty to learn about raising small children, especially girls. But thinking things through calmed me down. I knew I could feed my kids by following recipes; all I needed was a good cookbook or two. Dressing them was another matter. So I turned to my mother and sisters, who pitched right in with detailed advice and suggestions that made all the difference. For the moment I rested easy, knowing that in addition to being loved, my girls would be fed well and dressed properly.

I soon developed routines for my various duties as an honest-to-goodness Mr. Mom. On Saturdays, I'd take the kids grocery shopping. Sundays, I'd prepare a few casseroles and freeze them. Then, weekday mornings, before leaving for work I'd put one in the microwave and set the timer on low. By the time we got home, our dinner was ready.

Happy Together

Because Sarah and Leslie were only in the third and fourth grade, respectively, I had a babysitter bring them from school to her house until I high-tailed it over there after work and picked them up. On the way home, we'd drive back past the school. Most days the drill team would still be out practicing their moves. That sight and the sound of the band lit Leslie and Sarah's eyes right up. "Daddy, we want to do that!" they cried in unison. Every time we drove by, they piped up again.

Their enthusiasm was so contagious that finally one day I said, "Girls, let's do it!" So we walked out on the drill field, met the team director, and signed up.

"They're just the right age," she said, welcoming us. My daughters were ecstatic.

Next the director introduced us to the drill coach, an attractive professional named Gloria Ausley. Leslie and Sarah quickly took to her warm and supportive manner. I too was impressed. So much so, that within a few months I proposed marriage. Things worked out magnificently; the girls got a great coach, and I got a wonderful wife and two new stepchildren, Matt and Nikki. More than 30 years later, Gloria and I are still happy together.

But back on that first day on the drill field, a big challenge lay before me, and I didn't handle it well. After introducing us to Gloria, the director got down to business. "Image is a key factor in drill team success," she said, looking me in the eye. "We pride ourselves on our uniforms, which are custom-fitted by an expert tailor." Leslie and Sarah listened wide-eyed.

"Sounds great!" I said, envisioning it all. My girls would march proudly across the fifty-yard line while I told everyone in the stands around me that those were *my* kids.

Back on Earth, the director said, "I'm so glad for your support. Now, each uniform, plus custom fitting, final adjustments to en-sure perfection, shoes and socks comes to…three hundred. Times two is six hundred."

I heard what she said, but it didn't make sense. I stared at her, waiting for clarification.

"Your check will put everything in motion," the director said.

Coach Hartzel's philosophy came to mind. *Never let 'em see you're hurting.* I wasn't about to start now. "Mighty fine," I said. "I'll…get my…checkbook." Slowly I walked back to the car and opened the glove compartment, wondering how kids' play clothes could cost more than a week's take-home pay. The check I wrote her was so hot steam was coming off it. But the director, Leslie, and Sarah were all smiles, so I showed my teeth and hoped I didn't look as pale as I felt.

Next morning, sleep-deprived, I headed straight to the bank on my way to work. I strode resolutely to the manager's office and showed his assistant my badge.

She buzzed, and he came right out to me. "Is there a problem?"

"Afraid so," I said, and hastened to clarify that I'd caused it. When I explained and promised to deposit the shortfall first thing payday, the manager graciously said he'd hold back my check to keep it from bouncing. I kept my word and promised myself I'd never do such a dishonest and foolish thing again. At that point, though, I didn't know how I'd keep up with the soaring cost of raising a family.

My kids were depending on me, in some ways more than I realized. One extra busy Saturday, I postponed my usual grocery run until Monday. As a result, I was an hour late after work to meet the girls at drill practice. When I drove into the school parking lot, they both ran up to me in tears, having feared I'd been in an accident. That's how punctual I'd always been. I hugged them, said I was sorry, and we headed home together, happy again. Sarah and Leslie were the best behaved, politest, sweetest young girls. We did everything together, from cooking to watching the *Wizard of Oz* on TV. Those days were among the best of my life.

Catching Up on the News

Saturday mornings, before the kids and I went food shopping, I'd take my sweet time reading *The Dallas Morning News*. It felt good to take a break and find out what was happening in the world. Sometimes, however, current events were particularly frustrating. A prime example was when the *Morning News* reported that the chief executive of Dallas/Fort Worth International Airport (DFW) had put a $4,000 alligator skin briefcase on his monthly expense report.

When DFW opened back in the 1970s, I saw the good sense in building a modern airport to serve both cities, which are only 35 miles apart. But because a smart idea and its implementation sometimes differ radically, I'd wondered whether taxpayers would get their money's worth from the enormous investment in DFW. Reading that its CEO was so irresponsible renewed my fears that hard-earned tax dollars were going down the drain. At the same time, though, I was thankful that investigative journalists had somehow obtained the CEO's expense report and exposed it to much-needed public scrutiny. I wondered what other unsavory things were going on at DFW. The answer would come sooner than I expected.

Battle Stations

The minute I arrived at my desk in Internal Affairs the following Monday morning, I sensed something extraordinary was underway. As I hung my jacket on the back of my chair, I noticed the chief of police leaving my lieutenant's office. The chief didn't visit often, and his steely gaze told me big news was coming. The lieu wore an equally determined look as he watched the chief leave his office. Minutes later one of our two sergeants called me and the other ten investigators into the detail room. The long and the short of it, the lieutenant told us, was that the *Morning News* story had touched off cover-your-ass firestorms in Dallas and Fort Worth, whose mayors had ordered an immediate, well-publicized fact-finding mission at DFW.

Accordingly, the two cities' police chiefs were hastily assembling a joint task force. I and two other investigators from DPD Internal Affairs would join three officers from the Fort Worth PD on temporary assignment at the airport. We were empowered to interview DFW management and staff, examine operations, and report any suspicious or unauthorized practices and expenditures. The lieutenant explained that DFW's CEO hadn't committed fraud or otherwise broken the law by "expensing" his luxurious briefcase. But his misallocation of DFW discretionary funds was unacceptable in any executive post, especially at the helm of a public entity like a municipal airport. Given the CEO's poor judgment, it made sense to assess the entire operation at DFW.

I listened, pondering my role in this highly politicized situation. What first came to mind was my recent futile exposure of timecard fraud by numerous DPD motor jocks. The outcome of my investigation—hushed-up administrative slaps on the wrist for the guilty parties—made it clear that at that time DPD valued its public image more highly than its actual integrity and would do anything to avoid open scandal. I didn't expect either city's government to approach negative publicity any differently than DPD had. That meant the task force's primary purpose was not to root out fraud at DFW, but to convince the press that the situation was under control and no longer worth covering.

It shouldn't have been surprising, then, that no one on the task force had ever investigated the kind of offense we'd be looking for—white-collar crime. I'd been picked for the team because I had earned an accounting degree at the University of Texas at Dallas while working at DPD. But that wasn't much help in identifying the fraud we encountered at DFW. Much more useful was investigative skill, including the ability to conduct admission-seeking interviews. I'd been investigating corruption and other malfeasance in DPD for the last three years and had been with the department for 15 years. My task force colleagues had similar backgrounds.

Despite our lack of experience investigating civilian corruption, it wasn't hard to pick the low-hanging fruit. We found barely concealed fraud everywhere—inventory theft, kickbacks, falsified reports, and bogus changes in key provisions of lucrative contracts. From what we could tell, these things had been going on for quite some time and could have been detected easily—if someone had bothered to look for them. But no one had looked, and that's why press coverage was so important—it forced the two cities to take action.

When it came to uncovering the less obvious but often costlier frauds, though, we on the task force realized that fraudsters were vastly different from criminals we'd encountered elsewhere. To better understand how they came to thrive at DFW, I did some quick background research on the airport. I knew that you can't eradicate a parasite if you don't understand its host.

The Lay of the Land

First, I located a *Dallas Morning News* front-page clipping about the airport's dedication ceremony in 1973. It had been quite an affair, with 50,000 people in attendance to see the ribbon cutting and the first U.S. appearance of France and Britain's Concorde, the world's only supersonic commercial aircraft. All the fuss was justified. DFW was the world's biggest airport; planning and building it had taken ten years and cost $700 million—an astonishing sum at the time.

Right from the get-go, nine airlines offered service from four passenger terminals, complemented by a 600-room hotel, a post office, and numerous shops and restaurants. Including the extensive system of runways needed to handle the thousands of flights anticipated, the airport covered more than 15,000 acres. Building those runways had required as much concrete and asphalt as would have been needed to construct hundreds of miles of ordinary roads—and that was just the beginning.

By the time our task force arrived in 1985, DFW had contracted with construction companies for another several hundred million dollars' worth of additional structures and other enhancements. At any one time, three to five major contractors were working on multimillion-dollar projects at the airport. Yet with all that money changing hands, DFW had few if any safeguards against embezzlement, theft, and other financial crimes.

To find out why, all you had to do was look at the audit committee. In organizations that take ethics seriously, audit committee members are independent of management and experienced in one or more essential areas, including internal and external audit, corporate governance, financial reporting, regulatory compliance, and risk management. Not at DFW. There, a political connection to senior management was the primary qualification for appointment to the board of directors and its various committees.

To make matters worse, these hacks weren't just incompetent; they were lazy as well. Many didn't want to attend quarterly meetings at which the audit committee would discuss operations and policy with management. The airport CEO was happy to oblige them, and volunteered to meet separately with the audit committee and inform the board of any important developments. But he soon tired of this role, and assigned it to a vice president who had neither the authority nor the interest to act on any problems or concerns the audit committee raised. So on the few occasions when there were audit findings, they fell on deaf ears and no one did anything about them. It was a perfect storm of unmitigated risk. As I uncovered one scheme after another at DFW, I saw how deeply corruption had seeped into and overwhelmed its organizational culture.

That brought to mind a news story I'd seen next to the 1973 DFW article on the front page of the *Morning News*. It reported that then–Vice President Spiro T. Agnew was negotiating a plea deal with the U.S. Department of Justice. According to the criminal charges against him, Agnew received highway construction kickbacks while governor of Maryland and had continued to accept such payoffs even after assuming the vice presidency.

I of course remembered that Agnew had resigned, and I learned that later a federal judge in a separate civil trial had ordered him to pay more than a quarter-million dollars to the State of Maryland as restitution for the kickbacks he'd taken. In the civil trial, Agnew's former lawyer testified on Maryland's behalf that in 1973 when he'd confronted Agnew with evidence of taking the kickbacks, Agnew had replied that such payoffs "had been going on for a thousand years" and that the amounts alleged were exaggerated. "It was only $2,500," he said Agnew told him. Talk about missing the point.

The parallels with DFW were clear. Even high-ranking, apparently respectable officials might be corrupt. That meant we had to be alert for *any* signs of fraud at DFW, no matter how improbable our prior investigative experience and our own moral code might make them seem.

Something for Everyone

The vast majority of workers at DFW were honest; but for many, fraud had become a routine part of business. At Christmas time, the construction contractors gave DFW employees cowboy hats and filled their stockings with whiskey and other gifts. While that might have flown in private industry, it certainly wasn't appropriate in the public sector. But many employees, following the tone at the top, rationalized their acceptance of these illegal gratuities. Unfortunately, those who took small bribes were more susceptible to big ones—and not necessarily cash or goods.

As I got to know more people at the airport, I picked up a lot of scuttlebutt. Unless there was reasonable support for rumors and gossip, I'd file them away for future reference. But whenever I got a credible tip about an important matter, I'd make an extra effort to evaluate it. Sometimes additional information simply landed in my lap.

Right after DFW's chief engineer left for a post elsewhere, the senior vice president of the division astounded everyone when he appointed a clerk as the new chief of engineering. That led several outraged civil engineers, who now reported to her, to pay me a visit. Not only was their new boss not an engineer, they said, but she was having an affair with the SVP, who was married. I wasn't there to root out adultery, though, and kept my eye on financial fraud.

When it was the engineering department's turn to be examined for potential fraud exposure, I spoke with its new chief, the former clerk. Together we reviewed her area, and I found nothing amiss. But she apparently feared I'd heard the rumors about her and the

SVP. She blurted out that everyone thought she'd been promoted because of a personal connection, rather than merit. I just sat there and let her talk.

Despite not knowing what, if anything, I knew about the situation, she felt compelled to discredit her rivals' claims. "Just lies," she said. "I might not be an engineer but I'm serious about this job. I'm even taking college courses at night so I can understand what my engineers are talking about."

That told me a lot, but not what she wanted. Clearly she felt the need to convince me she deserved her promotion. Like the unsophisticated criminals I'd previously dealt with, this white-collar worker revealed what she wanted to hide: that she didn't get the job by merit. And I hadn't asked a single question about it. If this matter had fallen within the task force's mission, her statements would've spurred me to look into it. Yes, I was new to DFW and white-collar crime, but some of the interview skills I'd learned earlier would work here too.

One of the more obvious cases I came across at the airport involved a secretary who'd written herself dozens of DFW checks and charged them to her department's various high-activity expense accounts. What tripped her up wasn't the crime; DFW's internal controls and audits were so feeble that no one noticed the embezzlement. But when she cruised into the DFW parking lot in a new Mercedes convertible, other employees wondered how a person making $20,000 could afford such a car. One of them reported it to the task force. I jumped on that lead and visited the local Mercedes dealer, who fondly remembered the $80,000 cash sale and told me, with some regret, what I needed to know. The next day, I quietly confronted the secretary in a surprise interview and took down her tearful confession.

"I'm not the only one stealing," she told me. "I work hard and needed a treat. Besides, no one missed that money." It was true; if she'd been more discreet, her fraud might have remained undetected. But when her first embezzlements weren't noticed, she couldn't resist stealing more, and even had to show off.

Competition Among Thieves

As the task force's efforts led to more arrests, an increasing number of honest employees were encouraged and contacted us with tips. Soon we had so many it was hard to keep up with them. And, although I still had plenty to learn about investigating fraud, my initial successes had swelled my head.

One morning, a woman in DFW's vehicle maintenance division called me with a tip. According to her, the shop manager had been stealing company property—hydraulic jacks and other equipment used to service the airport's trucks and buses. "I've seen him load the stuff in his pickup and drive off," she said. I took down the information, said I'd get right on it, and put a sticky note on the wall to remind me. After hanging up, I recognized the name and remembered I'd met the guy once.

The following week, she called again. "I've been real busy," I told her. "Don't worry; I'll look into it." I put up another sticky note to ensure I didn't forget. A week later, I'd been working on yet another investigation and still hadn't gotten to the maintenance shop. When the tipster called, I broke a pencil in half and said, "Ma'am, I really have been very busy."

"I doubt it, Mr. Ratley," she replied. "You're not important enough to be that busy."

I almost dropped the phone. It was like she'd slapped my face with a cold fish. "You're right," I admitted. "I'll come over today." I was furious with myself and embarrassed as hell. But I wasn't going to take it out on the suspect, and went to see him with an open mind. I brought another investigator with me, and we walked out on the shop floor. The manager was yelling at one of his staff, but stopped and put on a big smile when he saw us.

"You know what somebody told me?" I said.

"What's that?"

"That you drove off with a hydraulic jack and a bunch of other equipment that belongs to the airport."

"Naw," he said. "I'd never do something stupid like that. I didn't even finish high school, but they got me managing this place. I'll be here 'til I retire."

I believed him. "Glad to hear it. But you understand I'm obligated to confirm that. So if you'll authorize me to search your home, we'll go settle this and I'll buy you lunch on the way back."

I put the form in front of him. "Sure thing," he said, and signed right away.

The three of us rode out there in my car. On the way, I noticed he was pale and sweaty. "You okay?"

Oh, yeah," he said weakly. I started thinking sandwich at my desk.

"If you're having a heart attack, tell me now and I'll call an ambulance," I said. "Don't expect me to give you mouth-to-mouth."

"I'm fine," he insisted, looking awful.

When we pulled up in front of his house, I saw a hydraulic jack in the driveway, rusted from being out in the rain. That wouldn't have happened at the airport. I got him to open his garage, and saw why the jack was outside—there was no room inside. My partner and I estimated that the manager had roughly a quarter-million dollars' worth of stolen DFW property in there. I arrested him on the spot, and brought him downtown for processing.

Afterward, I called the informant and thanked her for the tip. She suggested I speak to other people in the vehicle maintenance division. This time I followed up immediately, and over the next few days was told by more than one employee that both the manager and the assistant manager were taking everything not nailed down. According to people who worked with them, the two fought constantly over who got to steal what. On one occasion they'd allegedly exchanged blows in the parking lot after the assistant manager stole something the boss wanted, and wouldn't bring it back. I was able to confirm these reports, and arrested the assistant manager as well.

I also found that most of the mechanics there owned cars that were the same make and model as those in DFW's fleet. That enabled them to pilfer company parts and supplies for their own cars, which they serviced at the airport during work hours. The manager outdid them all; he had the mechanics refurbish two of his trucks. You couldn't make this stuff up. Things really had gotten that bad at DFW. I just didn't realize that so far I'd only been scratching the surface.

Rocky Roads

After breaking up the larceny ring in the vehicle maintenance division, I focused on finding out how they'd been able to get away with it for so long. I figured that might help explain why fraud flourished at DFW. Since the division had been audited just before I intervened, I got a copy of the report so I could check its findings. As I feared, the internal auditor had found nothing wrong.

Well, I told myself, auditors aren't trained to detect theft. I kept on reading, though, and saw that the auditors had checked whether reported expenses corresponded with items purchased. Everything, they said, matched up. The report went into a lot of detail, too—right down to how much had been spent on replacement parts for specific vehicles.

At first, it seemed thorough, but the more I read, the worse it looked. For example, the division had purchased one hundred sets of tires for a single van used to transport passengers from the airline terminals to the car rental offices. The auditors confirmed that DFW had actually received the tires it paid for. And a DFW car needed 258 carburetors in the same time period. Again, the auditors confirmed the carburetors paid for were actually received.

Sure, the numbers added up, but there wasn't a shred of sense in them. At that point, there was no telling whether the auditors were knaves or fools. But I was going to personally put the divisional vice president on notice of the sorry state of affairs. I expected that would light a fire under him. Even a few proactive steps would've helped stem the tide of taxpayer dollars flying out the window.

I called his office, and left a brief message saying why I'd be coming over the following morning. The next day, when I walked in, he looked worried.

"You know," he said, "I think you're overstating the problem."

I couldn't believe my ears. The thefts and overbillings in his division added up to half a million dollars.

Believing the audit report would state the case for me, I opened my briefcase and gave him the page that found no problem with putting four hundred new tires on one van in six months. "Give me a reasonable explanation, and that'll be the end of it," I said. "I'll walk right out of here, and you won't see me again."

He looked at me, dead serious. "Jim, these roadways are *hell* on a set of tires."

I looked at him, then at the framed diploma on his wall and wondered how an educated person could make such an asinine statement. "You're a college man," I said. "Can't you do better than that?"

He looked away. "I'm sorry you feel that way."

"Likewise," I said, and took back the audit report before leaving.

This meeting showed me it was folly to expect impartiality from someone with skin in the game. The vice president didn't want to be part of the solution because that would involve admitting he was part of the problem. And he was just the tip of the iceberg. I'd now seen unethical behavior at every level of the airport's workforce—the C-suite, senior and middle management, and the rank and file. What worried me most about DFW's fraud epidemic was not just its extent, but how different most of it was from everything I'd worked on before being assigned to the task force. Unless I adjusted quickly, I wouldn't be a strong enough part of the solution either.

Uphill Battle

Although I hadn't been able to light a fire under that weasel of a vice president, his irresponsible passivity set me off like a rocket. I was determined to maintain the momentum of my latest fraud busts. As soon as I got back to my desk that morning, I pulled the file on every pending case and lead I had. No longer taking anything for granted—not even management's support—I resolved to let nothing even remotely suspicious escape my scrutiny. With an eye even more skeptical than before, I reexamined each report and red flag, and found several situations worth double-checking. Soon, without realizing it, I'd worked through the rest of the day without breaking for lunch. Tired and hungry, I felt a wave of doubt flooding into my mind…but not about the cases and leads; they definitely were worth looking into. No, my concern was the resistance or apathy I might encounter when I started asking other senior managers and executives about potential red flags in their units and divisions—perhaps in their very own activities.

It wasn't that I hadn't faced difficult opponents before. Hell, more people than I could count had done their best to maim or kill me, and I'd put them behind bars. But tracking down and busting white-collar criminals was altogether different. For one thing, many of the frauds at DFW involved millions of dollars. Investigating cases of that magnitude was a big responsibility, and at first the pressure nearly overwhelmed me. Before I was assigned to the task force, most of my cases were relatively straightforward. In contrast, many white-collar crimes are hard to detect. If the DFW secretary who'd embezzled her way into a Mercedes had instead bought a car like my Ford, her scheme just might have escaped notice. And while some frauds like hers leave a clear paper trail that will easily convince a judge and jury, others are so mind-numbingly complex they seem like an investigator's pipe dream.

In several of my DFW cases, all I had to go on was an allegation of fraud and boxes full of documents about complex financial transactions.

Many of the suspects were high-powered executives with an MBA or degree in finance. Some were generous supporters of Dallas and Fort Worth political leaders, and all looked like model citizens. I and the other members of the task force each made $30,000 a year. Going nose-to-nose with well-connected suspects earning several times that and perhaps stealing even more wasn't easy. So we dug our heels in and didn't relent until we got conclusive answers to our questions. Fortunately, press coverage of the investigation helped prevent a cover-up that would have sacrificed a few low-level DFW employees, declared victory over fraud, and quietly disbanded the task force. But even with that support, my colleagues and I still had a lot to learn.

One of the greatest adjustments I had to make related to the very documents I now found myself buried in. It wasn't just that there were a lot of them and that they were complicated. The new wrinkle was that the documents in question were created by other people. In my past investigations, I put together most, if not all, of the documentary evidence myself, which typically consisted of transcripts of suspect and witness interviews I'd personally conducted. I knew my documentation was reliable. It might not contain all the answers I needed, but it never asserted anything I hadn't personally verified. And when I couldn't confirm something, my report identified it as an open question.

At DFW, though, someone else had prepared the financial statements, purchase orders, accounting records, and other documents

I reviewed in my search for evidence. And because some of those records were riddled with falsehoods, inaccuracies, and omissions of key information, I had to broaden the scope of my professional skepticism. Everyone and everything was potentially deceptive. A prime example: the auditors' nonsensical, see-no-evil report on the corrupt vehicle maintenance division. Like it or not, though, the answers to my questions were often in those potentially unreliable documents. So I did the only thing I could do—wade deep into their details, much of which I didn't understand. In some cases, I scoured a hundred or more complex documents, going over them backward and forward until I'd virtually memorized them. I couldn't take the chance of missing key items that would tell me what I needed to know.

Day by day, I learned the value of patient analysis and the power of pure reasoning. Sometimes a single bogus entry in an expense account or financial statement helped me expose a fraud scheme. And when I couldn't understand a suspicious transaction or document, I'd interview whoever prepared it. "Tell me what this paperwork's all about and how it fits into the workflow," I'd say. When they gave me some insights, I'd press them for more. "If someone wanted to commit fraud," I'd ask, "how would they change this document to support their scheme?"

Of course, I had to be alert for answers designed to hide the truth, not reveal it. But even when I was close to positive that someone was guilty, I didn't let it show until I had a strong case. During investigations before DFW, I'd learned that a suspect's answers are seldom completely false. The challenge for the interviewer is to distinguish the lies from the truth. If you succeed, you learn what the suspect doesn't want you to know—and might not realize he's revealed to you. And that helps you expose his falsehoods, making further denial futile and confession nearly inevitable. This approach worked well for me in Child Abuse and Internal Affairs, and case by case, I was adapting it to my fraud cases at DFW.

Along the way, it became clear to me that an accounting degree isn't the most useful thing to have when investigating white-collar crime. Yes, I had to interpret and evaluate my share of financial statements. But if I had arrived at DFW with just my accounting sheepskin, I'd have been at a serious disadvantage. Instead, my prior interviewing experience enabled me to solve some cases quickly while adjusting my technique to the white-collar environment. The bottom line was—and still is—that you don't need accounting expertise to be an effective fraud examiner. Unless you're a good interviewer, though, you'll have a hard time investigating fraud. Unfortunately, few people have innate interviewing skills; like me, most have to develop them. As always I was dead serious about my work and wanted to learn more.

A New Landscape

Communication skills had been essential to me back when I was on street patrol, and I became adept at reading people's facial expressions and body language. This helped me tell when a witness or suspect was withholding information or outright lying to me. Even so, as a street cop, it wasn't my responsibility to formally interview anyone. Whenever I found prima facie evidence that a certain person had committed a crime—that is, there was enough evidence to warrant an investigation—I put him or her in jail. It was the investigator's job to further weigh the evidence and, if appropriate, perform an admission-seeking interview. And when I transferred to the Vice Squad, my role was trying to buy sex or drugs; I still didn't have to interview the people I busted.

That changed when I began working child abuse cases. As I said earlier, I wasn't very good at interviewing. But because it's the backbone of investigation, I had to improve. So I made it my business to get the help I needed, and that's how I found Gus Rose, who showed me the way forward. Before meeting him, I hadn't known how to succeed in my new assignment in the Child Abuse Unit. Now, investigating fraud at DFW, I was at a similar crossroad: I didn't know anything about white-collar crime, but I had to interview people suspected of committing it. The difference from my earlier predicament, though, was that this time I *knew* I could find someone to help me improve my interviewing skills. Gus had retired, but I quickly came up with a list of other people to consult. Then I got on the phone and started making appointments with them.

A Better Roadmap

My first call was to Bill Parker, a veteran DPD homicide detective, widely regarded as the department's next best interviewer after Gus Rose. Bill welcomed a visit from me, and gladly shared everything that might apply to white-collar crime. As I knew from personal experience, murder and fraud investigations shared some common ground. Bill had been doing the former for decades, so I took his advice to heart.

Perhaps the most important tip he gave me was this: It's self-defeating to slavishly imitate someone else's interviewing style. "What works for them might not work for you," he said. Naturally, I took detailed notes while Bill spoke. But going over them later, just as he predicted, I decided that some weren't right for me.

My next call was to the police department's psychiatrist. I'd spoken with him in the past about the psychology underlying officers' misconduct, and he'd given me some useful insights. This time, though, my focus was on civilian fraudsters. "I've done a few successful white-collar admission-seeking interviews," I told him. "But the more I see of these people, the more questions I have about what makes them tick. They all look like upstanding citizens, including the ones who turn out to be guilty of fraud. Married with a family; never been arrested. Same profile as me."

241

The psychiatrist nodded in acknowledgment. "Picture a guy who's been on a job for two or three years," he said. "Every day he has the opportunity to steal from his employer, but he doesn't do it. Then one day, for whatever reason, his resolve weakens, and he submits a phony expense item. He's still the same guy who works hard, pays his bills, and loves his family, but now he's a thief too. Who can see all that just by looking at him?"

Having recently written a rubber check to pay for Leslie and Sarah's drill team uniforms, I couldn't disagree. The only difference between me and the Mercedes-driving secretary was one you couldn't see: I fully intended to make it right, while she didn't. But why did she think that way while I didn't? This wasn't just a theoretical brain teaser. To match wits with a fraudster during an admission-seeking interview, I needed clear insight into why he or she stole and often kept stealing until caught. That would help me interpret what the suspect said or didn't say, as well as understand how to persuade him to level with me.

On occasion, I read articles on why crooks committed a variety of crimes, and now my interest was surging. So I called the University of Texas in Dallas and asked for an appointment with Dr. Larry Redlinger, a highly regarded criminologist. When we met, he explained that although he didn't specialize in white-collar crime, he knew of two books that might help me.

"Bring this over to the UT library," he said while scribbling the titles and his signature. "Tell them I'd appreciate it if they let you borrow them. The more important one is Dr. Donald R. Cressey's *Other People's Money*. It explains who embezzles and why." He added that Cressey had co-authored the second book—*Principles of Criminology*—with Edwin H. Sutherland. "It's the standard text. Sutherland coined the term *white-collar crime* to describe this particular type of offense."

I thanked him and hurried to get those books before someone else did. That evening I began devouring both. They would eventually change my professional life.

242

Applied Science

Over the next several nights, I immersed myself in Dr. Cressey's discussions of why and how people steal from their employers and others who trust them. The key factors that he said cause and permit fraud—*need, opportunity,* and *rationalization*—figured prominently in the cases I'd investigated at DFW. Together these three elements formed what Cressey called the *Fraud Triangle*. Now, thanks to him, I understood what really linked white-collar criminals, their schemes, and the businesses they defrauded. First, *need*. In the vehicle maintenance division, the manager and assistant manager envied each other's thefts, and began to perceive that they "needed" the things they pilfered, when in reality each simply wanted to steal more than the other. Second, *opportunity*. Of course, they wouldn't have been able to steal so much if DFW's toothless controls hadn't let them take whatever they wanted. Last, *rationalization*. Because the embezzling secretary worked hard and earned less than others who also stole, she had no remorse.

At first it was hard for me to believe that people who didn't appear to be criminals really were. They stole again and again; if they had second thoughts, they were only about getting caught, not about taking things that didn't belong to them. But reading Cressey revealed to me how rationalization stimulates and perpetuates fraud. I remember thinking to myself, "You can't judge these people by your standards. They don't have your standards." And that's how it is. White-collar criminals often don't feel like they've done anything wrong. Once I understood that, I changed my entire approach, tailoring my interviews to their rationalizations.

Before reading Cressey, I would have said to a suspect I had strong evidence against, "I know you took that money, so just tell me how you did it." But it's hard getting someone to admit he committed a crime; sometimes I'd be at it all day and wind up with nothing to show for my efforts. My new method was to ask the suspect how he felt about his job and the company. If he expressed resentment, I'd probe for specifics. That tended to induce the suspect to vent, for example, about working long hours and not getting a raise. Then I'd shift gears, no longer trying to get him to admit doing something wrong. "All that extra work, and they didn't give you anything for it?" I'd say. "How did you manage to get the money they owed you?" When I got a suspect to answer that question honestly, I knew I'd made real progress, far more than by being confrontational or accusatory.

The next step was to get a written, signed statement from the suspect, as I'd done many times for nonfinancial crimes. In fraud cases, though, there's no point in charging someone unless you can prove intent.

Some suspects admitted committing a fraudulent act, but said it was the result of an honest error or ignorance. To counter that, I'd appeal to the suspect's vanity, encouraging him to explain how he'd cleverly managed to conceal his fraud. I'd also ask nonconsecutive questions about specific aspects of the fraud, seeking contradictions in the suspect's account that might lead him to tell lies I could disprove by comparing them to known facts or witness testimony. In this way, even when the suspect didn't realize it, I'd obtain ample proof of his intent to commit fraud. And that gave me a solid case for the Dallas County D.A.

Hidden in Plain View

Perhaps the most pernicious fraud exposure in massive undertakings like the construction of DFW is the *change order*, a formal modification to an existing project contract. Change orders are not only inevitable; they're desirable, providing essential flexibility as project requirements change or emerge for the first time. Without change orders, initial plans would take years longer to prepare and almost certainly still require modifications for critical,

244

impossible-to-foresee contingencies. While either the contractor or the client can request a change order, both must approve it. In a complex project, it might be necessary to issue hundreds of change orders. And unless the managers of a project apply rigorous controls, the flow of change orders can easily devolve into a flood of unchecked expenditures.

At first glance, almost all transactions seem routine and necessary. But closer analysis might reveal some that reflect inefficiency or even abuse. As we on the task force discovered, DFW's poor controls invited some of its managers and certain construction contractors to collude in kickback schemes that cost the airport millions in unnecessary expenses. And they did it with change orders—the most common fraud technique I encountered at DFW.

To detect such schemes, we audited many of the airport's contracts with construction companies working to expand and enhance airport facilities. In one such deal, DFW laid out $8 million for the construction of additional runways needed to accommodate the rapid increase in airline traffic. Before our audit, my colleagues and I closely reviewed the contract's provisions. We all were struck by how strongly it favored the contractor. Satisfactory performance was generously rewarded, and deficiencies drew light penalties. This didn't seem like the product of an arm's-length negotiation. And since we'd already discovered a lot of fraud at DFW, we suspected this contract might be yet another instance of collusion. At that point, though, there were no details or proof.

That changed abruptly when I got an anonymous, type-written tip that the construction companies were paying several airport managers to issue numerous change orders for large quantities of concrete—perhaps more than was needed for the planned runways. On the surface, this was plausible. So we ran background checks on the managers, and we found that their lifestyles matched their known income. If the managers were receiving kickbacks, what form did they take? It didn't seem to be financial.

When we dug deeper into the background reports, we noticed that each manager owned residential property near the airport. A light of inspiration went on in our minds. But reading further, we saw that the land was undeveloped. Still, we told ourselves, the construction companies might compensate the corrupt managers by building houses for them. Yet a closer look at the construction companies clearly showed they had no home-building experience or personnel. They built runways, not houses. The light of inspiration went out as suddenly as it had lit up.

And then another tip came in, perhaps because the anonymous informant, impatient for us to break the case, realized we couldn't see what was obvious to him. The unsigned typed note on my desk said, "Hello, stupid. Try looking at how nice the roads are where the managers own barren land. You ever seen such perfect streets in an empty subdivision?" This time the light stayed on.

We sped out to the site and saw that while the streets weren't paved with gold, they nonetheless were high-quality work. When the airport managers eventually had homes built there, they'd save tens of thousands on roadway construction costs. We probably had enough evidence to get an indictment from a Dallas County grand jury. But I wanted more—something directly tying the airport managers to the delivery of the concrete to their subdivision.

It occurred to me that the driver of the cement mixer would be a good person to interview. I was confident I could get him to tell me which managers had shown him and the construction crew where to deliver the concrete and build the roads. Because I figured the driver had innocently followed orders from the real culprits, I considered him a witness not a suspect. I didn't want anyone at the airport to know of my conversation with the driver, so I obtained his home address and brought another investigator there with me late one afternoon.

When I knocked on the door, the driver answered right away. Our dress code was discreet—suit and tie, shoulder-holstered pistol. We told him who we were and showed our badges. To our surprise, the color drained from his face and he started crying. "I knew it!" he said, bending over in anguish. "I'm going to prison. I don't know why I did something so stupid."

My partner and I exchanged glances; we'd both seen this kind of reaction before. A nervous perpetrator can mistakenly think the police know everything about his crime. But not only had we not suspected him; we didn't even know what he was confessing to. So we played along, trying to act like we really did know everything. That was easier said than done.

I offered some reassurance. "Don't worry," I said. "You'll be fine if you answer our questions." For a second, I considered just shutting up and letting the silence pressure the driver into saying more. Instead I found myself saying, "Tell me about the concrete." This seemed to stun both the driver and my partner, who elbowed me in the ribs. But by then it was too late. The driver wiped away his tears and looked at me with hope.

I knew why, and my blood went cold; I'd just committed a major interviewing blunder. Anyone who's found words coming out of his mouth while his brain is yelling "Shut up!" knows exactly how I felt. By mentioning concrete, I'd revealed how hopelessly ignorant we were of what the driver had been about to confess doing, which apparently was much worse than the kickback scheme we were investigating.

"Concrete!?" he said. "That's all you want to know about?"

"No, no," I told him. "You go ahead with what you were saying."

"Forget it, man," he replied, standing straighter and smiling. "I ain't saying jack."

I cursed myself; he'd been about to tell us something important about fraud at DFW, but I'd shut him down. And there was no way he was going to open up again. After a dispirited huddle, my partner and I told the driver that was all for now, and that we'd be in touch. But we and the driver knew that was BS. We had no idea what he was hiding and no reason to suspect him of any crime. I hadn't approached this as an admission-seeking interview, and there was no probable cause to bring him in for further questioning. The most we could do was keep an eye on him. But with all the other leads we had, that was unlikely.

"Sorry," I said when my partner and I got back in our car.

"It happens," he answered.

I noticed with chagrin that he didn't say "...to us all."

In an effective interview, the information flow is one way: from the interviewee to the investigator. By not paying attention, I'd reversed that flow, ceding control to a knowledgeable source and potential culprit. Many more interviews awaited me at DFW, and I promised myself I'd focus more intensely and handle them better. There was too much at stake not to.

CHAPTER 17

CHECKING THE CHECKERS

Despite my bungled interview of the concrete truck driver, I'd gathered enough other evidence to prove the first DFW kickback scheme I'd uncovered. Dallas County prosecutors used my findings to obtain indictments against the DFW employees who had accepted construction company kickbacks for approving unnecessary contract changes. That ended the diversion of concrete from DFW runway projects to the building of roads serving airport managers' personal real estate holdings.

While I worked practically every kind of fraud case at DFW, those involving construction kickbacks were the biggest. So I pored over every contract, particularly those for expanding DFW's network of runways. I feared they might contain even more bogus change orders—especially because there was another costly runway component I hadn't at first been aware of.

As I learned, paving thousands of acres to create runways prevents rainfall from seeping directly into the covered ground. Instead, during any good-size storm, a flood of rainwater builds up and surges horizontally. Unless guided in some way, the torrent can damage lights and other critical structures as it flows across and eventually off the runway. Most important, water on a runway makes it harder for pilots to control their aircraft during takeoff, landing, and taxiing.

In response, airport planners and civil engineers over the years developed increasingly effective ways to channel rainwater off and below runways and through the open areas surrounding them. In keeping with DFW's massive size, its surface and underground drainage systems were extensive. The difficulty of designing and installing concrete culverts and pipelines was reflected in both the contract's cost and the number of change orders required to finish the complex project. Knowing what I did about DFW's often-corrupt business environment, I carefully scrutinized the entire runway drainage contract and every single one of its change orders.

As it turned out, there were 71 change orders. The red flag wasn't the number of them, though. It was the documentation or, in one particular instance, the lack of it. The first seventy changes were thoroughly documented. But the final order—for a $1.2 million increase in the contract—was altogether different. When I opened its documentation folder, I saw that the paperwork consisted of a solitary yellow sticky note. On it was written a single word: "Miscellaneous." Red flags don't come any brighter than that. But did it signify anything crooked? Or was it merely an oversight? Only a fraud investigation would tell, so I got started.

First, I paid a "surprise" visit to the contract administrator. When I asked for the documentation for change order 71, he blanched and quickly said, "I don't think I can find it." That spoke volumes. I figured that if he weren't hiding anything, he would've at least tried to locate the folder. But his immediate resistance told me he didn't want to find it.

As in other situations like this, I let time and the suspect's anxiety move things forward.

"I don't think you're leveling with me," I said. "But there's no law against lying to the police." Silently he stared back at me.

I tightened the screws. "Lying to a grand jury, though—that's a felony punishable by two to ten years in the state penitentiary." With a dire expression, I told him he'd face a grand jury if he didn't cough up the full documentation by the following Monday. "If you give them the same hogwash you gave me," I said, "You *will* be indicted." His eyes widened in fear, and I walked out. Let the slow roast begin, I said to myself. Over the weekend, it cooked to perfection.

When I got to my desk Monday morning, I saw that the contract administrator had left me the details I'd asked for. According to the full documentation, the construction contractor had needed more than a half-mile of additional reinforced concrete drainpipe to finish the underground portion of the runway drainage system. The order had called for pipes with the biggest diameter available—six feet. Pipe sizes varied according to their position in the system.

Where water flow was just beginning, smaller diameters—less than two feet—sufficed. But at points farther along the line, where the accumulated surge was far greater, six-footers were essential. The order apparently made sense; extending an existing drain line would require the widest diameter pipes. So far, so good—in principle. My next step was to see whether the contractor's completed work matched the change order documentation. I knew that wouldn't be easy, though.

While reviewing the contract, I'd done more research and picked up a little technical knowledge. To facilitate the flow of water, drainage systems are laid out at a slope of approximately one inch downward for each hundred feet of pipe. At the project position this change order addressed—the end of a long pipeline—that slope had required burying the pipe as much as forty feet beneath the runway. I'm not claustrophobic, but the thought of crawling down there to check it wasn't appealing. Still, I didn't see any other way to determine whether the contractor had done what DFW had paid $1.2 million for.

Daddy's work on the Amistad Dam had made me very familiar with how dangerous flash floods were. The runway drainpipes were confined spaces and I didn't want to find myself surprised by a storm surge. Even after scrambling back through hundreds or thousands of feet of pipeline, I'd still have to climb a forty-foot ladder to get out. So the first thing I did was check the weather forecast with several different sources. They all agreed: no rain anticipated for at least a week.

Now it was time to find out how and where I'd gain entry to the underground system. I visited DFW's facility maintenance chief, told him my objective, and he assigned a crew worker to get me started. After studying a map of the inspection and maintenance manholes on or near the runways, he identified the one I was after. Early the following morning, I arrived at the maintenance office, wearing my oldest jeans and boots and packing my Kel-Lite and a long measuring tape, the kind DPD used to document traffic accidents.

I jumped in a van with the worker, and we headed for the target manhole, out in no-man's land amid several runways. When we pulled up next to it, I noticed two things about the cast iron cover: Embossed letters on it said "STORM DRAIN," and it was bolted to the manhole. The first reassured me; I didn't want to mistakenly climb down into a power line junction. The second, however, puzzled me.

I turned to the maintenance worker. "Why the bolts? Security?"

"Partly. But a flash flood can fly up that hole and blow the lid right off. Bolts hold it on."

He loosened them and with some effort, we slid the cover aside. I pictured a sudden storm and saw myself flying through the pipeline like a cork. Not a happy thought. But I'd double- and triple-checked the forecast, and it was game time.

The pre-cast concrete hole was about five feet wide. Down one side, a series of built-in metal rungs disappeared into the darkness. I shone my light straight down but couldn't make out the bottom. Tossing a pebble in might've helped, but I couldn't find one. So I exhaled deeply, stuffed the light and tape in my pockets, and stepped onto the first rung. As I descended, the sunlight grew dimmer and the air cooler. Soon I was on the bottom, four stories down. It was dry and littered with gravel.

"You okay?" the worker called down. His head was a speck in a small circle of blue sky.

I said yeah, and pulled out my Kel-Lite. At five-eleven, plus boots, I had to stoop just a little to fit inside the pipeline. Pitch-black darkness and silence surrounded me. Above ground the task ahead had seemed tedious, like measuring a long driveway. Now, far beneath the surface in darkness broken only by my light, it was a bit more complicated. But I pushed aside distractions, keeping track of how many times I extended the tape to its full length. Soon I'd measured the first hundred feet of pipe. Then suddenly a rustling noise ahead shot my pulse up high. I pointed my light that way and saw an enormous brown rat, frozen in the beam not twenty feet off. Sherlock Holmes' Giant Rat of Sumatra had nothing on this monster, which must've weighed ten pounds. When I stomped down hard on the concrete, he chirped at me, turned tail, and scooted off into the blackness.

With a long way to go, I got back to measuring. Just when I figured the worst was over, a massive ka-thump shook the whole pipeline, followed by a long, roaring vibration. It's collapsing, I thought, and scampered back toward the ladder. By the time I got there, the violent, deafening shaking had begun to subside, and I realized what had caused it. I pointed my Kel-Lite at the sky.

"How's it going?" the worker yelled.

"What kind of plane was that?"

"DC-10."

"All done!" I called back. No way did I want to be down there when a 747 came in. There had to be a smarter way to evaluate change order 71, I told myself.

Let There Be Light

That weekend, my dad came over to see me and my family. He and I had an understanding: I wouldn't let him near the kids when he'd been drinking. Because seeing them meant so much to him, though, he'd put the bottle aside well before he called me about visiting. When Daddy asked about my latest case at DFW, I briefly described the one I was working on. He got a laugh out of my journey to the center of the earth and was particularly interested in change order 71, which I still couldn't make heads or tails of, fraud-wise. But Daddy's entire career had been in construction, a lot of it working with concrete.

"Get that paperwork out, son," he said. "Let me have a look at it."

I stared at him and thought, "I'm a trained detective. If I can't figure it out, there's no way in the world you can." I hemmed and hawed, but to no effect. He just wouldn't give it up. So I dug into my briefcase and put the change order on the dining room table. Daddy and I sat down there, side by side. After eyeing it for maybe thirty seconds, he rested his index finger where the specific amount of concrete pipe was listed. Its total length was a long, odd number, extended out to two decimal places.

Daddy turned over to me and smiled. "Boy,"—he called me that 'til the day he died—"no one orders pipe in fractions of a foot."

My mouth fell open, but I was speechless. Daddy was right: The length didn't make sense. That meant it might not correspond to the work the change order described. Maybe it was an error, but I didn't think so. A feasible length would be a multiple of the eight-foot-long size pipes came in. What's more, the total price—an amount you *would* expect to be an odd number—was an even $1.2 million.

Looking at it from a fresh perspective, I suspected the total length was simply made up to arrive at the total price. A fraud theory began to form in my mind: *If the contractor and contract officer wanted to steal $1.2 million, perhaps they simply divided their target haul by the pipe's price per foot. That would explain how they came up with the bizarre length.* In a normal—that is, an honest—business transaction, you start with the unit price and the total length you need. Then you derive the total price from the total length—*not* the other way around. The scheme seemed obvious, now that Daddy had pointed out its inherent absurdity. But I wouldn't have caught it if he hadn't shown me.

I reflected yet again on how important it is for an investigator to understand each case's business context. There isn't an investigator who hasn't found himself in new and unfamiliar territory. Often, you get experience the hard way—by probing and brainstorming your way from one breakthrough to the next. This time I was lucky to have Daddy's help. He'd never done an investigation in his life, but he solved this one for me. For years afterward, when we were with others he'd say, "Son, tell them about that case I solved for you." He was just tickled to death, and I gave him all the credit; he deserved it.

The following week it took me 15 minutes to get that contract administrator to confess. When I questioned the absurd amount of pipe on change order 71, he assumed I knew everything there was to know about the scheme. Confirming my suspicions, he admitted the change order was totally unnecessary—a fraud. The fully documented first 70 change orders covered the additional pipe necessary for the drainage project. But change order 71 described pipe that was neither delivered nor laid, and it bilked DFW out of the exact amount the fraudsters had wanted to steal: $1.2 million. At this point, I couldn't get the contract administrator to reveal exactly who had paid him off and how, but he knew I'd be back to find out.

You Scratch My Back...

Through additional research, I learned that the quality of the concrete used in runway construction was a variable factor that greatly influenced total cost. The higher the quality of the concrete, the higher the payment to the contractor. Who made the all-important quality assessment on each batch of concrete? DFW engineers— through formal stress-testing procedures. Playing devil's advocate in search of a potential fraud theory, I asked myself a question: *Who's checking the checkers?* The answer was *no one.*

According to the terms of the contract, if the stress test results indicated the concrete could bear a certain amount of wear and tear, DFW would pay the full contract price. But if the score fell in a lower range, the contractor would receive only 75 percent of the full price. And if the score was in an even lower range, DFW wouldn't pay anything at all for it. Concrete rated at any of these levels was still safe to use, but the lower the score, the sooner the runway would wear out and have to be repaved.

After what I'd seen in recent weeks, I wasn't surprised at what my review of the stress test results revealed. In every instance, DFW's engineers had rated the concrete samples as top quality, which awarded the highest possible payout to the contractor. To see whether the engineers were falsifying their stress test results, I had every sample retested by an independent laboratory unrelated to DFW and the contractor. The result: not a single sample was good enough to qualify for any payment to the contractor. By all rights, DFW should have gotten it all for free, and had been defrauded of every payment it had made.

Once again, I'd uncovered fraud, but had to dig further to reveal the kickback method. As usual, my colleagues and I conducted financial background checks on the crooked engineers. And again, we found they all were living within their means. But as in other situations like this one, an honest DFW employee, troubled by the corruption all around him, helped us root it out. An older man, he'd at first kept quiet, reluctant to blow the whistle on his colleagues.

When I spoke with him confidentially, he told me to "look at the paperwork," and would say no more. I saw that pressuring him wouldn't work, and gave him a little time and space to think it over. A few days later, I spoke with him again, emphasizing the urgent ethical and safety issues I knew had motivated him to contact us in the first place. And gradually, I got him to give me something I could work with.

The paperwork he'd referred to was the guest register for a sportsmen's lodge that was owned and operated by the construction contractor for entertaining its employees and, in some cases, its clients. That was fine and dandy, the informant and I knew, except when it came to municipal employees—such as everyone at DFW—who were prohibited from accepting gifts or other inducements. Unfortunately, the informant said, his fellow engineers had been unable to resist the temptation of VIP privilege.

In return for falsifying the concrete stress test results, the contractor had flown them on its corporate jet to and from free hunting and fishing excursions at its lodge. As in earlier, related cases, the contractor used noncash kickbacks to achieve its illicit goals and cover its tracks. Armed with this intelligence, I popped in on the contractor's office manager.

"I want to see the guest register for the lodge," I said, and watched her panic. She tried to speak, but couldn't; she'd lost her voice. Finally, she gave it to me, and right away, I found what I was looking for: all the details on who visited the lodge and when. Among them were the names of the contract officer for change order 71 and of the engineers who'd falsified the stress test results. I had enough for the county prosecutor to obtain indictments, and I hadn't even needed a subpoena to obtain the documentary evidence, which was essential in proving the case. The police task force was working on behalf of the airport, which owned all the key documents and had wisely embedded *right-to-audit* clauses in every contract. Fortunately, DFW had implemented this particularly important anti-fraud control.

Among those who hadn't played it so smart was one of the engineers my evidence implicated. When it became apparent he'd not only get charged, but also would lose his job and benefits, he blamed it on me.

"You've signed my little daughter's death warrant!" he said. She had a nearly always fatal medical condition that, with the right care, some patients survived. "Thanks to you, I'll lose my health insurance. That was her last chance, and you've stolen it from her."

His daughter's plight deeply saddened me. So I said nothing, and let him vent. Facing illogical, unfair outbursts like this was part of the job, but it wasn't easy. That fraudster's lie would haunt me for many years to come.

Less Is More

It felt great to crack those kickback cases and help stop so many fraudsters from stealing public funds at DFW. My professional ego still smarted, though, from the memory of screwing up my interview of the concrete truck driver. But I learned along the way that my errors and defeats taught me more important and enduring lessons than my triumphs. That's how it was when I investigated a high-level DFW official who reportedly was perpetrating a long-term theft of services and materials scheme.

As chief architect, the alleged culprit held a position of power and responsibility. According to an informant on his staff, the chief repeatedly abused that authority and betrayed that trust in two ways. First, he routinely assigned staff architects to non-DFW projects serving his personal clients. The revenue from those assignments, completed on company time, flowed solely to the chief's private practice. Second, he habitually and inappropriately used DFW architectural materials and supplies to serve his private clients.

Of course, until I'd investigated the tipster's allegation, I gave his boss the benefit of the doubt. But that doubt just about evaporated during my interviews of several other staff architects, who also said the chief had forced them to design *churches* on company time. It sounded persuasive, but I wasn't about to approach the DA without physical evidence, so I went for a look-see. The informant and his colleagues told me the chief sometimes worked weekends, but never stayed late during the week. So one Thursday afternoon, well after he'd gone home, I stopped by his office at DFW and discreetly went through his papers. It didn't take me long to find hard-copy evidence of the "outside" work his staff had told me about.

Some of it was status reports and other correspondence, which didn't prove anything. They could've been prepared by anyone, anywhere, at any time. But that wasn't all I found. The chief also kept in his office the blueprints for his non-DFW projects. His scheme had been going on so long that a large number of these Mylar polyester sheets had accumulated in a row of accordion folders against one wall of his office. After examining several, I noted that each bore an official DFW seal. Rashly, the chief had inscribed on each DFW Mylar sheet the date, his own name, and that of the outside client and project.

I was holding evidentiary gold. But what, I wondered, was the best way to maximize its prosecutorial value? I pictured the admission-seeking interview I'd do with the chief. Of course, it would be a surprise, and I'd do my best to make him spill his guts completely. I knew just how to make that happen. Because there were so many unauthorized blueprints, I didn't think he'd notice it if I borrowed some of them.

The very next morning, I paid his office another visit—this time when he was in it. I gave him my usual speech about the task force's investigative mission. He didn't appear nervous, but that changed when I posed a leading question.

"What would you say if I told you I had original blueprints—on official DFW Mylar—of your work here for personal clients?"

His eyes flashed toward the accordion folders I'd searched, and quickly swung back to meet mine. "I'd never do anything like that," he said.

I stepped up the pressure. "I'd like to believe you, but the blueprints I have say otherwise. Can you think of any way this might have happened?"

Right then, he should've shut up and asked for an attorney. Instead, he talked until there wasn't anything a lawyer could've done to help him. "Come to think of it," he said, "I do personal work here in my office on the weekends. If urgent DFW business comes up, I want to be here whenever they might need me. I guess I got my materials mixed up with the airport's."

"Well, that might explain everything," I said. "Just so I understand, could this kind of mix-up have happened often?"

"Oh, no," he assured me. "Maybe once or twice."

"Is it possible you asked any of your staff architects to work on your private projects?"

His eyes blinked rapidly. "I told you I wouldn't do anything like that."

"Well, I'm sorry, but what you're telling me doesn't agree with all the physical evidence I've gathered and extensive interviews I've conducted."

He paused for a few seconds before yelling, "Good God! All right! Perhaps I took some liberties I shouldn't have."

"I already know that," I replied. "This is an opportunity to explain yourself. More lies will dig a hole far deeper than the one you're in."

Stunned, he admitted not only what I knew, but also provided numerous details on other aspects of his fraud scheme. If I'd told him exactly who I'd talked to, what they'd said, and what documentation I had, he probably would've confessed—but only to the charges I had proof of. Instead, I wangled a full confession out of him. Besides revealing all his fraudulent acts, it exposed his initial attempt to hide the fraud by lying to me. And that demonstrated the criminal intent necessary for an indictment and conviction.

What gratified me most about this case was that I kept the information flowing *to* me, not *from* me. I'd done many an interview before I revealed too much to that concrete truck driver. But no matter how experienced you are, you have to stay focused. Revealing information to a suspect gives up an advantage the interviewer must absolutely retain. So gradually I learned to ask suspects questions without giving them information.

On the Lookout

After I'd been out at DFW for several months, I dropped by Internal Affairs to say hello. To my surprise, some new guy was sitting at my desk. I introduced myself, and asked him who he was.

He told me, and added—as if he'd been there for years—all about my future in DPD. "You're not coming back here. They'll transfer you when that task force folds up. There was no sense in leaving this desk vacant for a year."

"Is that so?" I said dryly, figuring he was just blowing smoke. I had a pretty high opinion of myself and my accomplishments.

Despite my skepticism, my discomfort must've shown because the guy tried to console me.

"Don't worry!" he said cheerfully. "They'll ask you where you want to work."

"But I belong here!" I almost blurted out. Not wanting to believe any of it, I feared the worst. Having seen myself as an integral part of the Internal Affairs team, I was stunned to see it functioning without me. Although I had the most experience there, they'd just made other arrangements while I was away on the task force. I'd worked hard to make myself essential, but management didn't seem to give a hoot. This was perhaps the rudest awakening I'd ever had in DPD.

Older and wiser, I drove back to DFW and worked on my cases. Instinctively, though, my thoughts turned to Leslie and Sarah. My vague future prospects weren't inspiring, and I doubted I could do well at any job if my heart wasn't in it. But I wanted my kids to have the best of everything, including the finest education available. So I resolved to keep an eagle eye out for promising new professional opportunities.

PART FOUR

A NEW PROFESSION

"To achieve things never before accomplished,
we must employ methods never before attempted."
— *Sir Francis Bacon*

"The person who says it cannot be done should
not interrupt the person who is doing it."
— *Chinese proverb*

CHAPTER 18

RISK AND REWARD

The DFW task force's fight against fraud was going great guns, and I was making good progress on several investigations. But as the week wore on after my sobering visit back to Internal Affairs, I realized I'd lost some of my enthusiasm. It wasn't that the work no longer appealed to me; I was eager as ever to put crooks behind bars. Yet I felt like a foot soldier overseas who learns the generals back in the States remember his mission but not his name.

The notion of DPD solidarity—spanning the ranks from chief to street cops—had always bucked me up, even if it had been challenged by one or two dispiriting incidents during my fifteen-year tenure. Now, though, I saw what my fellow officers and I had always been in top management's eyes—badge numbers. DPD's mission to protect and serve the people of Dallas came first, of course, and individual officers' careers were of secondary importance. I had no

265

problem with that. But I was disappointed that no one had even bothered to tell me I'd be involuntarily transferred out of Internal Affairs when the DFW task force pulled up stakes. Instead, I'd found out purely by chance that my hard work and achievements had earned me a coach ticket to parts unknown. Maybe my next assignment would be important and fulfilling; maybe it wouldn't. With a family to support and ambitions to satisfy, I wasn't happy about my uncertain future.

Another World Beckons

"JD!" a fellow investigator called out to me as I returned to my desk with a sandwich one afternoon at DFW. "Some guy just called you. Here's his name and number."

I looked at the message slip. *Joe Wells. Austin.* My mind flew back three years to 1983, when I first heard of him.

> The Assistant Attorney General of Texas had called Joe in to investigate a fire in the Capitol Building in Austin. A front-page story in the *Dallas Morning News* told how the blaze had broken out there late the previous night. The state maintained two small residences—one for the governor and another for his lieutenant—on an upper floor for their intermittent use. Sometimes, when the apartments were unoccupied, relatives and others spent the night there.
>
> On this occasion, the lieutenant governor's daughter and her male guest were asleep when the fire started. Thick smoke spread rapidly throughout the apartment.

In the resulting panic and confusion, the daughter escaped unharmed, but the young man suffocated. No one else was injured. The AAG immediately directed the state fire marshal to assist Joe in any way possible. And as Joe's investigation evolved, the local newspapers and television ran one story after another about him and the case.

With all this attention, Joe popped up on a lot of people's radar, including that of billionaire Ross Perot, who I later learned closely followed Joe's work on the case. Ultimately, the fire marshal was unable to determine what had caused the fire. And Joe, working on the scant evidence available, noted that the dead man was a smoker and might have fallen asleep with a lit cigarette. But the state's top law enforcement official, the attorney general, somehow concluded that faulty wiring in the apartment's television had ignited the blaze. Attempts to reproduce that supposed event failed, but that didn't dissuade the AG, who launched a state lawsuit against the TV's manufacturer.

There Joe's involvement ended and a product liability battle began. That killed my interest in the case—but not in Joe and his work. The idea of being an independent, dedicated investigator greatly appealed to me. So I carefully clipped out that first *Morning News* story about Joe and tucked it into my wallet for future reference.

Several months later, my wallet had grown so full of various scraps of paper—little of it cash—that I had to empty it. In doing so, I came across something I'd lost track of: the article about Joe Wells. A quick re-reading of it brought back thoughts I'd been avoiding. Joe's work still captured my imagination and highlighted my uneasiness about what awaited me after DFW.

At that point, I'd just passed my fifteenth anniversary with DPD and had loved every minute of at least ten of those years. When I moved to Internal Affairs, however, I gradually began to regard my work as a job, rather than a privilege as I'd felt on street patrol. Like Jill Muncy, I'd have done the work for free if I didn't have a family to support. The Peter Pan lyrics I sang with my little daughters came to mind: "I'll never grow up! Not me!" But at this point in my career, I knew it was time to "grow up." My DPD salary was just enough to get by on and probably wouldn't rise much higher. And now that I'd remarried, five people depended on me. Not least, I yearned to keep growing professionally and achieve what I felt I was capable of.

So I decided to give Wells a call and introduce myself. Who knew what it might lead to? At the very least, it would be interesting to speak with someone with his background, which I'd learned from the *Morning News* included high-profile work in the FBI. The next day I tracked down his Austin phone number and found him in. Graciously, he spared me a few minutes. I mentioned that in addition to my fifteen years with DPD, I'd earned a degree in accounting. Joe replied that he'd gotten into the FBI by virtue of being a CPA, which the Bureau needed to help investigate financial crime. But, he said, he'd encountered few state or local police officers with a degree in the field.

Sensing an opening, I said I was in Austin often and wondered if I could stop by his office to talk. Joe said yes, but made one thing clear up front: His startup consisted of only one person—him. He wouldn't hire anyone until he had more clients. I said I understood, and asked if he were ever in on a Saturday.

"Almost always," he replied, and gave me his address. A few days later, we met for the first time. His office was so small it reminded me of the joke that you had to step outside to change your mind.

Quickly I posed the question most important to me. "Is the fraud investigation market big enough to make a steady living from it?"

"I'm betting yes," Joe said. "But we'll see." He told me about a mini-refrigerator rental business he'd once had on the side. It was working out fine until a large competitor entered the market, forcing Joe to sell his operation at a loss. His ambition was still bold, he said, but now it was better informed. "I understand the investigation business," he added. "I didn't really know much about renting mini-fridges."

I liked what I was hearing. Perhaps it showed, because Joe reiterated what he'd told me over the phone about not hiring yet. Still, he encouraged me to stay in touch. I said I would and left with a better sense of what the future might hold.

"JD! Hand over that sandwich if you ain't gonna eat it," my partner said. Abruptly, my thoughts returned from 1983 to the here and now—DFW in 1986.

"Get your own," I growled, smiling. My ham on rye had gotten a little soggy, but I bit into it with gusto. Suddenly I was famished.

On the Same Wavelength

Next morning, I reached Joe before I left for work. I later learned that like me, he's always been an early riser. So we had time for a quick, mutually informative conversation. Business was booming, he said, thanks to a long-term consulting contract he'd inked with Ross Perot, who'd followed Joe's work on the Capitol fire and needed seasoned hands to perform a variety of investigations for his company, Electronic Data Services (EDS). To handle this workload, Joe was looking for someone whose knowledge, skills, and experience would complement his. As a federal investigator, Joe knew the ins and outs of interstate crime and commerce and the federal legal system. What he needed, he said, was an investigator who knew a lot about big-state, big-city crime, legal systems, and government.

"Makes sense," I said.

"What are you working on these days?"

"Been out at DFW on an anti-fraud task force for almost a year now." I spoke briefly about the variety and extent of high-dollar fraud we'd uncovered and the array of personnel we'd filed charges against. "Fraudsters think nothing of plundering their company and government. I just couldn't make sense of their attitude until I read a book by a Dr. Cressey, who's formulated what he calls the 'fraud triangle.' Once I read that and understood rationalization, I knew just how to approach fraudsters in an interview. Now I get most of them to either confess or inadvertently reveal a cover-up, proving intent."

"I'm glad to hear that," Joe said. "You know, I met Cressey not long ago."

"Really? Aside from a professor at UT-Dallas, no one I know has even heard of him."

"Good thing we have UT. I found his book in the UT-Austin library!" We had a good laugh about that, and marveled at the coincidence. Joe went on to explain that he'd sought out Cressey much the same as I'd contacted Joe. "Last time we spoke, you sounded interested in my line of work. Is that still true?"

I said it was.

"Good," Joe said. "When can we discuss this further?"

"I have to head out to DFW now. How about another in-person talk this Saturday?"

"I'll be here," Joe replied, and gave me the address of his new office.

I hung up, hoping it was at least a little bigger than the last one. That night, I told Gloria about my conversation with Joe.

"You might have to make a big decision sometime soon," she said.

I nodded in agreement; Gloria was right.

271

Decision Time

The following Saturday, I drove down to Austin. From the look of the building to which Joe had relocated, his business was on the uptick. Inside, he welcomed me and introduced me to his first employee, Kathie Lawrence, his office manager and former FBI colleague. The new space, mostly unoccupied, could comfortably accommodate a staff of five to six. Wells & Associates was clearly in expansion mode, but Joe was low-key about it all.

More and more he struck me as someone I could enjoy working with, and I sensed the feeling was mutual. It remained to be seen, though, whether we could come to mutually acceptable terms. As Joe described the scope and variety of situations EDS wanted his help on, I gained confidence in the firm's current revenue and potential growth. I listened attentively for signs of what that might mean for me.

One assignment seemed to stand out: investigating an EDS competitor that Perot was suing because, he believed, it had employed unfair business practices to win away from EDS a lucrative data processing contract awarded by the State of Massachusetts. The work required weekly commutes between Austin and Boston, as well as travel all over the country to interview key witnesses and informants whose testimony could help EDS win the contract or substantial damages in court.

"What do you think?"

"It sounds demanding, but interesting. I've always liked a challenge," I answered honestly.

"We're both aware of the financial and career risks involved in leaving civil service to join a startup," Joe said. "I faced them when I left the FBI and launched this practice. You'd be my first professional employee. I can't offer the job security and benefits you have now, and this isn't a 9-to-5, weekday-only position. You'd have to respond whenever and wherever clients require services."

"I understand. What are you offering?"

"Responsibility, challenging casework, and a small bump up in compensation. I hope we can work something out."

"All right," I said. "I'll think it over, discuss it with my family, and let you know."

"Thanks for coming in again."

We shook hands, and I headed home with a lot to consider. On the drive back to Mesquite, I remembered the fascination I'd felt when reading about Joe's investigation of the Capitol fire. Now, three years later, I was more skilled but less satisfied. It seemed unlikely that my current and upcoming situations at DPD would offer the career advancement opportunities I wanted. Eyes on the road but mind partly elsewhere, I wondered whether I had what it would take to do better in another organization. My thoughts drifted to my mother and sisters, gutsy achievers all. And Daddy, despite his illness, had made his mark in the world. The massive structures he'd help build would stand tall well after his time ended.

Something occurred to me that I already knew: My family is a remarkable group of people with the guts to take a risk and the determination to make it pay off. Of course, a little bit of luck never hurt, and I hoped I was due for some. In any case, if a career change didn't work, I'd find another way to move ahead. That's what we do in my family; my kids have that fire in them too. As I peeled off I-30 and onto I-20 for Mesquite, I smiled at the memory of my first two-year stay in Austin with Daddy. We accomplished a lot together and I learned so many new and interesting things along the way. Maybe something like that would happen again, this time with my wife and kids.

Going for It

Gloria was as excited as I was in telling her about the opportunity Joe and I had discussed. While it was weaker on job security and major benefits than what I had at DPD, it offered a small raise and room to grow. The next morning, I called Joe, finalized the numbers with him, and agreed to start in two weeks. Then Gloria and I worked on the logistics of relocating our family to a good school district and comfortable home in Austin. That night, I sat down with the kids to share the news of our upcoming move. While they were sorry to leave their friends and the drill team, they were eager for adventure. In the morning, I stopped by the kids' school and informed their teachers of our plans.

With that underway, I broke the news to my colleagues at DFW and formally submitted two weeks' notice of my intent to resign from the Dallas Police Department. That hurt, but I knew in my mind, heart, and gut it was for the best. I spent my remaining time at DFW updating the documentation on each of my pending investigations and briefly reviewing it with those task force members who would assume my workload.

On my last day as a Dallas police officer, I stopped by the chief's office downtown to see a number of longtime friends. One, my former supervisor, Sgt. Sam Johnson, was particularly glad I'd come in. I greatly admired and respected Sam and his professionalism. Seeing me making the rounds, he walked over to wish me well. In doing so, he humbled me by saying I was the best investigator he'd ever seen.

"When I assigned a case to you, I knew it was in good hands and that you'd find out exactly what happened."

"Sam," I said and paused, at a loss for words. "That means so much to me. I know how high your standards are." We shook hands as I waved to everyone and promised to come back often. I always have…and always will.

D-Day

My first day as a civilian again, I rented a U-Haul trailer that Gloria, the kids, and I all pitched in to pack. Dead tired that night, we went to bed early and were on the road not long after dawn Sunday. After arriving in Austin, we spent the rest of the day unpacking, arranging, and rearranging.

Monday morning I sprang out of bed, wolfed down breakfast, and headed over to Wells & Associates. I feared I might arrive before anyone else, but Joe was way ahead of me. Still, I was ready for anything—or so I thought. The surprise must have shown on my face when Joe asked whether I had a passport. With no idea what he had in mind, I said I did but never had an opportunity to use it.

"The time has come," Joe said with a smile. "Pack your bags. We're going to London."

Business and Pleasure

Two days later, we flew across the Atlantic on behalf of a New York attorney who'd engaged Joe to do opposition research on a courtroom adversary. It was my first trip to Europe, a journey I hadn't expected to take anytime soon, if ever. Life was simpler then, and so was travel. You didn't, for example, have to present double ID to get on a plane. And that made it possible for me to fly from Texas to England without realizing I didn't have my wallet.

I first noticed it was missing upon arrival at Heathrow and assumed I'd lost it en route. We checked into the posh Dorchester Hotel, paid for by our client, who doubtless passed the cost on to his client. There the desk clerk handed me a message from Kathie Lawrence. Apparently, I'd left the wallet at DPD on my last day, and one of my friends had tracked down Wells & Associates and called to let me know he had it. Amazed I hadn't noticed it earlier, I realized what a frenetic pace I'd kept for the last few days.

After settling into my room, I called DPD; it was mid-afternoon in Dallas. I got ahold of the officer who'd called Austin—John T. Williams, another sergeant I was tight with.

"John T.," I said. "It's JD. People say you stole my wallet."

"Oh, that's rich," he replied. "Who'd want it? Nothing but trash inside."

"No need to embellish. I won't press charges. Seriously, thanks for finding it. I'll be in next week to pick it up."

"No sweat. How're things at the new place?"

"Not bad. I'm on my first assignment—in London."

"London? What London is that?"

"London, England."

"Ratley, you're the worst liar. You can't even *spell* London."

"I'm serious. We're doing research for a court case."

"You better research the art of lying, because you don't know the first thing about telling a good one."

"I'd love to continue, John T., but I'll have to rob a bank if this call goes on any longer. Thanks again."

"Anytime, JD. See you next week."

I didn't blame John T. If he'd called me with that story, I wouldn't have believed him either. Back then, the idea of traveling to Europe without being in the military was far-fetched for people like us. I finished unpacking and sat down to review the file on our assignment.

Then I got some sleep. Now *that's* a lie.

Unlike me, Joe had already been to and thoroughly explored London while he was in the Navy. But it being my first trip there, I spent virtually every minute of down-time seeing and learning as much as I could about one of the world's greatest cities. I figured I'd catch up on sleep when we got home. During the day, Joe and I worked hard, but as soon as work ended, he'd go his way and I mine, taking double-decker buses and the Underground and walking all over. Many of the interesting places were closed in the evening, but I enjoyed walking past Big Ben and along the Thames Embankment. Part of the fun was meeting Londoners, who got a kick out of coming across a real live Texan. The minute I'd open my mouth, they'd ask where I was from. When I fudged slightly and told them I was from Dallas, not Marshall, several actually asked if I knew J.R. Ewing. At first I didn't know what to say. They didn't seem to realize he was just a character on TV. And even if he did exist, what were the odds a guy like me would know an oil baron? After a while, though, I couldn't resist the temptation to put them on. "Oh, yeah," I said. "He lives right down the road from me. My ranch is pretty big, but his is huge." Those who asked seemed satisfied with that answer, and there was good will all around. I quickly developed a real affection for London and its people.

On the job, Joe did all the talking with everyone we interviewed; I took notes. After four days, we'd obtained all the information our client had asked for. By then, my energy was wavering, but my interest wasn't. The assignment was instructive, and every night I stayed out late sightseeing.

A Touchy Matter

My official title at Wells & Associates was *fraud investigator*, and at the time I was the firm's only professional besides Joe. Since founding the firm in 1982, Joe had taken on all the work he could. He managed this by tapping an informal country-wide network of law enforcement professionals he'd worked with in one capacity or another. By engaging them as independent contractors on an as-needed basis, he minimized expenses and maximized client service. When I came on board, I worked as a private investigator under Joe's supervision. In Texas, the supervising investigator has to be fully licensed, and Joe was.

The first assignment I handled alone was part of the work Wells & Associates was doing for EDS. Joe dealt directly with EDS General Counsel Claude Chappelear in Boston. He'd identify the people and issues Perot wanted investigated. Joe and I would then fly or drive wherever necessary, get the intel, and bring it back to Chappelear. On this assignment, Joe and I both went to Boston, but I alone drove to Hyannis, a charming Cape Cod village eighty miles southeast.

My task was mostly straightforward, but had a wrinkle. One of the people Perot believed had helped cheat him out of that big data processing contract with Massachusetts was the former lover of a woman married to a dentist in Hyannis. It was up to me to find out what—if anything—her old boyfriend might have told her about his work on the disputed contract. As it turned out, she was the dental hygienist in her husband's practice.

I drove up, walked in, showed the receptionist my card, and asked to see Ms. So-and-so. When I learned she was out to lunch, I snatched up my card and said, "I'll come back later. Thank you very much." I didn't want the target to know who I was until we were face-to-face. The element of surprise always helps when you want to see someone who probably doesn't want to see you. No sooner did I reach the parking lot than I heard the office screen door bang open and a deep voice yell, "Hey, you! Wait a minute!"

Behind me and closing fast was a top-heavy guy dressed like a dentist, but bigger than any I'd ever seen. By now, he was closer to me than I was to my rental car. I stopped, turned, and played it cool.

"Are you talking to me?"

"Damn right!" he yelled. "I own this practice. The woman you asked for is my wife. What do you want with her?"

I put on my best glad-to-meet-you look. "Oh, I see. I'm a private investigator looking into a legal matter involving data processing services." If that didn't sound unrelated to adultery, nothing did. If this guy knew about his wife's affair, I didn't want to re-light his fuse. I named the man EDS wanted information on.

"So what's the connection with my wife?"

"Well, a couple of weeks ago, I saw your wife's name on some documents related to the contract this man worked on. I hoped she might be able to discuss them with me. The legal matter I mentioned has nothing to do with her. I just thought she might know something about the man I'm investigating."

"She knows him, all right," the dentist said. "They had an affair."

I put on yet another face. "I am so sorry. I had no idea. I apologize for bringing back that memory."

Not happy, but a bit less angry, he said she'd be back soon and would answer my questions. We waited inside. A few minutes later, she arrived.

"This man wants to talk to you about that guy you were seeing. Sit down and answer his questions."

And she did just that, her hands folded neatly in her lap. I kept it as brief as possible, obtained the information I needed and got the hell out of there. I thought the receptionist should abandon ship too; there was going to be one big argument in that little office.

Driving back, I reflected on how naked I felt unarmed and in danger of being assaulted. Carrying a gun is a big responsibility, though, and I was relieved that as a civilian, I no longer had to. For the first time in ages, if trouble started, I could run. A cop can't. You've got to stay there and face it. That dentist was big and mean, but he would've had to run long and hard to catch me. I'm not the least bit ashamed to say it: A good run is always better than a bad stand.

Florida Dreaming

Another time, Joe and I had to perform a couple of unannounced interviews in quick succession. The first was on the Sunshine State's west coast, the second on its east. We flew into Florida on a small regional airline still running—believe it or not—DC-3s. With so few left, even back then, it was a great experience to ride in a fifty-year-old aircraft.

Because our first job went faster than expected, we reconsidered our plan to also fly to the east coast. This time, our ride would've been in a recent-model airliner—a comparative bore after that Douglas classic. So we rented a Dodge convertible and hopped onto Alligator Alley, a hundred-mile-long straightaway from Naples to Fort Lauderdale. The Alley bisects Big Cypress National Preserve, which borders Everglades National Park. With few curves to negotiate, traffic speeds along quickly, resulting in frequent collisions with wildlife from the surrounding wilderness. As the road's name indicates, alligators abound in that area. But the Florida panther, already an endangered species, was the more frequent roadkill because of its habit of crossing the highway with no regard for passing cars. Numerous signs warned drivers to proceed with caution because only 37 panthers were left. And just as I took my foot off the gas to slow down, one of the big cats sprinted past our radiator grill. I guesstimated it at eight feet long; we missed it by inches. That panther was gone before I could even move a foot toward the brake pedal. Fortunately, that was our only close call, and we arrived without further incident at our hotel on the Atlantic Intracoastal Waterway on Florida's east coast. At dinner that night, I mentioned to someone sitting at the next table that I was an amateur scuba diver. He said not to miss Ginnie Springs, a great freshwater dive site just south of Jacksonville. But that was 300 miles north of where we were, and there wasn't enough slack in our schedule, so I filed that tip away for another day.

That day came sooner than I would've guessed. Maybe a month after Joe and I returned to Austin, Daddy called me up one Saturday evening from Dallas, where he spent most of his time.

"Boy," he said, "I want to see someone in Orlando about a job out there. Why don't you drive up here and pick me up? We'll go together."

"I can't do that, Daddy! I'll be at work all week. Besides, why not fly? I'll get the tickets."

"No, no. I hate flying. I'll work out something else. Bye."

Gloria was sitting nearby. "What happened?"

I told her, making Daddy's proposal seem outlandish. "Thousand-mile drive, one way."

"And he won't budge on flying?"

"No. The whole idea is ridiculous. I just can't do it."

"If you don't go, you'll regret it one day." She was right again, of course.

I called Daddy. "When do you want to leave?"

"Four."

"All right. I'll pack." I got to Dallas at one a.m. and dozed on his couch for three hours. Then he shook me awake. "Come on, boy, let's go."

And with that, we were on our way. About nine o'clock I called Joe to break the news. He was really good about it, and told me to enjoy the time with Daddy. With that off my mind, I concentrated on driving, and we stopped for the night somewhere in Mississippi—the halfway point. After dinner, we were just about to fall asleep in our motel room, when Ginnie Springs came to mind. I told Daddy about it, and he said he'd like that, but wouldn't join me in the water. Two days later, I rented scuba gear and had a wonderful time diving in Ginnie Springs' crystal-clear waters while Daddy watched from the bank of the Santa Fe River. We talked, we laughed, we cut up. We had the best time. Daddy didn't get that job after all. But we had so much fun, he didn't seem to mind.

On the way back we stopped again in Mississippi and then he came to my home in Austin. Daddy's grandkids really enjoyed getting to know him, which pleased him no end. He had faults, but many fine and positive traits as well, and I was so glad we were able to take this road trip together. I owe that good fortune entirely to Gloria.

Do It Right or Get Out

I put my interviewing skill to good use on a case one of EDS's in-house investigators had badly mishandled. A young kid working his way through college was on the night shift in an EDS computing laboratory. One morning after he'd gone home to get some sleep before classes, the lab's day shift discovered that some equipment and cash were missing. They notified Security and pointed out that the kid was the last employee to leave. Security collared the young man when he came back to work later that day. The EDS investigator assigned to the case confined him in a conference room and applied the third degree. But the kid denied everything.

The investigator wasn't having any of it. "I know you're lying," he said. "You left last; you're the only one who could've done it. If you don't come clean, I'll make sure you go to prison."

That crude tactic failed miserably. The young man repeated his denial and stormed out to get a lawyer. Stymied, the investigator notified his superiors, who called Wells & Associates.

"This has gotten out of hand," the security director told Joe. "We need your help."

Joe filled me in on the case and asked me to handle it. By now, the kid's lawyer had contacted EDS, and I got them to give me his number. Quickly, I reached him by phone.

"I don't like the way the investigation has been handled so far," I said.

"My client denies everything," the attorney replied. "I wouldn't take the case if I didn't believe him. In fact, I'm doing it *pro bono*."

"If he's innocent and willing to talk with me, I'll do all I can to prove it."

The attorney took my number and said he'd encourage the young man to call me.

An hour later, my phone rang. "I didn't do it," were the first words out of his mouth.

"Tell me each and every thing you did that night," I said, and he did. "Did you lock up when you left?"

"No, I didn't."

"So, you just walked out and left everything wide open?"

"I had to," he said. "The cleaning crew was there."

I asked him to describe every crew member he could remember was there that night. Then I called EDS Security and asked who they'd interviewed from the cleaning crew.

"No one."

"Why not?"

"No need. We had a prime suspect."

That was all I needed to hear. Upon further investigation, it became clear there was a more likely suspect—one of the cleaning crew. When confronted, he confessed, and EDS ended its investigation of the young college man. In my view, the investigator who interviewed him should've been dismissed. Every suspect deserves the best fraud examination possible. There's always a chance he didn't do it. I proved this suspect didn't. Despite the good outcome, I was angry that a fellow professional hadn't bothered to find out how he could do a better job. You *have* to try to improve yourself. Anyone who doesn't believe that should find another profession. In ours, what we do and don't do profoundly affects people's lives.

Over time, I had many opportunities to observe Joe's interviewing technique. Like I had in DPD, he'd refined it during his years in the FBI. What particularly appealed to me was that when he wasn't sure whether a suspect was guilty, he admitted it—and didn't let it hinder the interview or his honest search for the truth. A good example was the way he handled a case in which an EDS employee had sent anonymous, handwritten threats to the company president. After studying the wording of the letters, Joe and I compiled a list of several hundred suspects. Joe then had a handwriting expert examine the handwriting on their employment applications. He identified four potential matches to the letters.

That was as far as analysis could take us. Any further progress would have to come from interviewing the suspects, of whom none was more likely guilty than the others. Accepting this ambiguity without resorting to pressure tactics, Joe randomly picked one suspect and asked him to handwrite what Joe read from a copy of one of the letters. Almost immediately, the suspect confessed, convinced that Joe had proof of his guilt. That was the beauty of this technique: When you don't know who's guilty, simply set the stage for the culprit to confess. Of course, it was just luck that the first suspect turned out to be the guilty party and confessed. But if Joe had used the same technique on all four suspects, the culprit would have confessed anyway, regardless of the interview sequence.

The Turning Point

After Joe got an embezzler to confess that he'd fraudulently altered EDS's payroll system, he had a great idea—make an anti-fraud training video about it. In Joe's vision, the embezzler would, from jail, tell EDS employee viewers how his scheme had ended his marriage, ruined his life, and betrayed the employer who'd treated him well. When Joe proposed it to EDS, they promptly put their audio-visual team at Joe's service. The big question, though, was whether the embezzler would participate. But Joe's psychological assessment of him was right on target, and the "star" of the show agreed to tell his story in the hope it would dissuade others from making the same mistakes he had. At least ten thousand EDS employees saw Joe's video and gave it high marks.

Alongside this encouraging news, we also saw how weak and ineffective corporate fraud detection and prevention programs were, if they existed at all. Too often, business leaders simply ignored their fraud exposures. Losses didn't come out of their pockets, and boards and shareholders seldom heard anything about fraud.

These factors put in sharp relief what Joe called the "litigation pie." He explained that most of his firm's income came from assignments doled out by corporate counsels and law firms. They paid investigators as little as possible for as much as they could get out of them. Wells & Associates had nevertheless profited handsomely, but Joe also had tired of civil cases—the firm's bread and butter. Like me, he'd enjoyed criminal work most, but realized those days were over for him. I knew the same was true for me.

Still, Joe wanted to help improve fraud prevention and detection, and so did I. His video showed that employees needed and wanted anti-fraud training. But we, the professionals, also needed to refine and improve our methods. That's why Joe and I had sought guidance. Fortunately, we both found it in Dr. Cressey's works. Joe, going further, had established a relationship with Cressey, whose theories and insights were constantly evolving to keep pace with the spread of white-collar crime. In 1986, Joe accompanied Cressey to Australia, where he had a series of speaking engagements. Two weeks later Joe returned, greatly inspired by Cressey's insights into the causes of—and most effective responses to—financial crime.

Tragically, Cressey died in 1987 at only 67 years of age. Joe felt indebted to him, and precisely conveyed to me the essence of Cressey's thinking: It was time someone found a way to bridge the skill gap between cops, who knew how to investigate but didn't understand finance, and accountants and auditors who understood finance but didn't know how to investigate. As long as that skill gap persisted, fraudsters would continue to wreak havoc. Some would be caught, many would not. And seldom would losses be even partially recouped. Joe, perhaps better than anyone, thoroughly understood this challenge. In my view, if someone came up with a solution, it would be Joe Wells.

CHAPTER 19

CLOSING THE SKILL GAP

In 1988, I was well into my second year at Wells & Associates. By then, Joe and I routinely split the firm's caseload between us. Because high-profile clients sometimes insisted on personal attention from the firm's founder, Joe handled those assignments. I was in charge of investigations—particularly of internal frauds and conflicts of interest—and litigation support.

To ensure we each knew the latest developments on every case, we got in the habit of having our morning coffee together on the front porch of a repurposed property Joe had recently bought on the edge of downtown Austin. A three-story Victorian built in 1925 as a residence, it remained largely unoccupied even after Joe transferred the firm's offices there. Still, he didn't rent out any of it, and later, as our business and staff multiplied, space became scarce.

Joe christened our new home *The Gregor Building* in honor of Jerry Gregor, his father-in-law, a decorated World War II veteran he greatly admired. Little did we realize that one day it would be world headquarters of the professional association we were about to establish.

The Gregor faces east, uphill toward the Governor's Mansion and State Capitol, several blocks away. One morning, sitting on its porch and enjoying the relative cool before the sun rose high and heat built up, we were trading status reports, discussing new clients, and daydreaming about taking time off.

Joe, changing the subject, said, "I can't believe it's almost a year since Don Cressey passed away."

"I know," I replied. "And the skill gap between investigators and auditors is as big as ever."

"There's only one thing to do, then."

"What's that?"

"Close it ourselves," Joe said. "There might not be enough people like us—skilled in both the financial and investigative aspects of fraud-fighting—but there must be a good number. Still, there isn't a single organization through which we can share knowledge and gain visibility. Other professions have their associations; why don't we start our own—for professional fraud fighters?"

"My God," I said. "What an idea! We've got to do it." Now that Joe had identified the need, the whole concept seemed obvious. Hindsight, after all, is flawless.

Two Cowboys

Joe concluded that *fraud examiner* was the most accurate job title for people in our line of work. His research indicated there was no evidence that these two *ordinary* words—*fraud* and *examiner*—had ever been used together. So we broke new ground, combining them to form the name of our *extraordinary* profession.

Because Joe had already created anti-fraud training videos that clients' employees had greatly benefited from, he wanted to do more than start a professional association. He wanted our organization to offer certification in the skills needed to be an effective fraud examiner. But he viewed that as only one-half of a complete offering.

To help members get ready for an assessment of their proficiency, Joe also aimed to provide exceptional anti-fraud training. Accordingly, he researched state laws and regulations governing educational organizations, and we began designing training programs that would fully comply with them. He studied other professional associations' structures, bylaws, and codes of conduct, and identified several prominent fraud professionals and educators who might be willing to serve on our board of regents. While Joe was busy with that, I drew up a membership application form and sent it to 400 investigators and auditors, and we eagerly waited to see whether our market analysis was on target.

Meanwhile, we formulated guiding principles for our fledgling association. First, we wouldn't provide any products or services that weren't the best available. Second, in support of that approach, we decided to put our money where our mouths were. Anyone who wasn't completely satisfied would get a full refund. We also settled on a name for our organization—the National Association of Certified Fraud Examiners. Thus, the CFE credential was born, at least in theory.

Not much later, Joe called me at home early one morning, burning up the line with the good news that sixteen people had applied to become CFEs. We were thrilled, and hardly had time to evaluate and respond to those first applications before an avalanche of others followed them. In June, we issued a press release announcing the formation of the National Association of Certified Fraud Examiners and an interim board of regents. As applications poured in, we saw that many were from abroad. At first, we wondered whether our programs would be helpful to fraud examiners in, for example, Indonesia. But the more we communicated with applicants from all over the world, the clearer it became that fraudsters perpetrate the same schemes—and victimized companies need the same help—everywhere. So, in recognition of the global interest in our organization, we changed its name from the NACFE to simply the ACFE.

Things were going even better than we'd dared to hope, just the opposite of what virtually everyone we knew had predicted. In fact, if Joe and I had listened to our friends and associates, there never would've been an ACFE. Not one of them thought anyone would be interested in what we were offering. But we never saw it that way. If the initial response from our target market had been weak, we wouldn't have lost faith. We just would have made adjustments again and again until we achieved our goals. It simply never occurred to us that the ACFE wouldn't come to life and flourish. We knew from Day One, sitting on the porch of the Gregor Building, that the world needed dedicated, multi-skilled fraud fighters who, in turn, deserved a professional association of their own.

Once it became clear the ACFE was here to stay, some of the same people who'd earlier scorned our idea now said they'd proposed it before we had. The truth, however, is that we at first were known as "two cowboys who don't know what they're doing." Ironically, that was partly true; we weren't sure exactly *how* we'd achieve our objective. But we were positive we had the *right* objective, and that of course made all the difference. Joe and I were determined to do whatever it took to make the ACFE the best anti-fraud association in the world. We put all our efforts, every penny, everything we had, into making it work.

Joe, with my input, devised our strategy, while I, with his guidance, designed implementation tactics. We've always been big on planning and follow-through. Joe sums it up in a neat little saying: *Plan your work; work your plan.* Easy to say, but not easy to do if you don't believe in preparation, commitment, and accountability.

The Value of Membership

One of my earliest roles in the ACFE was to be the contact person for members and those considering becoming a member. I spent virtually all my time on the phone, averaging more than a hundred calls each day. In those pre-Internet, pre-email days, it was the primary platform for business communication. While it could be wearisome to spend that much time on the phone, it was inspiring to speak directly with fraud fighters from all over the world who wanted to excel in their profession. One member said to me, "Until you established the ACFE, when my children asked what I did for a living, I didn't know what to say. Now I can tell them and everyone else that I'm a fraud examiner. That matters to me and to them."

Another member called for help with a case involving official corruption, here in Austin. A service firm under contract with the municipal government was approached by a city inspector, whose brother had just been released from prison. The inspector demanded that the contractor hire his brother. When the contractor refused, the inspector fraudulently failed the contractor on its next two inspections. Admitting defeat, the contractor hired him.

Almost predictably, the inspector insisted that the contractor falsely document a long employment history and high salary for his brother, who wanted to obtain a car loan. Again, the contractor complied. Matters came to a head, however, when the contractor caught the man stealing and fired him. More failed inspections swiftly followed, leading the contractor to complain to the city auditor and the police department. Both wanted to help, but didn't know of any laws or regulations that would support filing charges against the inspector. The contractor then turned to an investigator who'd joined the ACFE, and she called me for guidance.

"This *must* be illegal," she said, exasperated. "How could it not be?"

I knew just how to help—via the state penal code. "It definitely is against the law," I reassured her. "Tell the police to look in the

290

penal code section on public corruption. There's a subsection on official oppression, abusing a government position for personal gain. They can cite it when filing charges against that crooked inspector."

The CFE looked it up and called me back the next day. "That section is tailor-made to charge that guy! I showed it to the police, and they were amazed. They said it was a great law, but that they'd never heard of it before. And they are filing charges. Thank you so much!"

"Glad I was able to help," I said, and rang off. It was sad that the police couldn't tell there'd been a criminal violation. Plus, they'd shown no interest in becoming more familiar with the penal code. You can't properly investigate an alleged crime if you don't know the law governing it. While the ACFE member hadn't known the relevant citation, she'd done the next best thing by searching for the answers her client needed. I figured she'd now make a point of studying the penal code and any other legal or regulatory provisions related to fraud. That's how I became an effective fraud examiner, and that member would have to do the same. But now, she and every other member had a professional association to turn to. The ACFE was there to help develop the knowledge and skills necessary for success.

Fulfilling Commitments

The ACFE held its first big training event in 1989. Before that, the only significant thing we'd hosted was a two-day seminar. But we knew it only partially met our members' educational needs. Joe had the foresight and wisdom to envision a larger, more responsive gathering—a four-and-a-half-day event we called the *Fraud Symposium*.

Just as they'd done when we proposed establishing the ACFE, several naysayers thought the idea was impractical. "People can't be away from work that long," they said. "Two days is the most they'll go for."

But Joe had two responses the skeptics couldn't refute. First, he said, four-and-a-half days are barely enough for an introduction to fraud examination. Two days are simply not enough. Second, Joe believed that if the symposium agenda fully addressed attendees' interests, they'd devote a week to learning what they needed to know. So he got to work on an agenda, and I helped him. At the same time, we rapidly added staff to keep pace with the needs of our steadily surging membership. The phone calls and mail were overwhelming.

Another warning the doubters gave us was that we would collapse under the strain of standing and teaching all day for nearly a full workweek. That one they got almost right. We didn't collapse, but we both got sick and had to tough it out until the Symposium was over. Our day would start at 6:00, making sure that the continental breakfast and all the classrooms were ready for prime time. Then we'd teach all day, and host an evening social event of one kind or another. It would be midnight before we'd get to bed. Five hours later, we'd get up and do it again. Late in the week, Joe and I were talking about how tired we were.

"Like my granddad told me," I said. "You can get used to just about anything except a good hanging." We got a wry laugh out of that—grim humor with a Texas twist—and went off to teach the next sessions. One thing I learned—and Joe taught me a lot of it— is that you can accomplish nearly anything if you put the necessary time, effort, and money into it. We did.

As Joe predicted, the Symposium was a huge success. It gave members a comprehensive overview of the fraud examination field and the various skills they'd have to develop to succeed in it. In fact, that first Symposium was so well-received that we began offering it twice a year. One of the most beneficial things we did was insert session evaluation forms in each Symposium attendee's package of handouts. They turned out to be a goldmine of valuable feedback on how to make our sessions more useful and informative. We were so eager to read what people had to say that Joe and I nearly got into a fistfight over who'd get to read the evaluations first. And from that point on, we always sought member comments on each training session.

On and Off the Road

In keeping with my official title of program director, I oversaw all aspects of the ACFE's training and education programs. I'd hold that post for many years to come. It involved a lot of travel, far and wide, to teach fraud examiners what they needed to know. Most of what I taught was how to interview—the backbone of investigation.

That's what brought me to Traverse City, a small town in northern Michigan, in October 1992. I had just dismissed my class for lunch, and stopped by the hotel's front desk to check for messages. One surprised me; it was from the ACFE and recapped a message to me from an old-time friend of Daddy's. *Urgent*, it said, with a Dallas number. I hurried back up to my room, fearing the worst.

A couple of minutes later, he told me how Daddy had succumbed to a sudden heart attack. Alone at his little home, he'd gotten severe chest pains and called his friend for help. The friend came immediately, but it was too late. He'd found my business card in Daddy's wallet. I told him how grateful I was for what he'd done. After putting the phone back in its cradle, I sat down in disbelief. Daddy had been around, bigger than life, for all 42 years of my existence. It was unthinkable that he was gone—and far too soon, at only 62. He'd been barely out of boyhood himself when he became my father.

I had to teach two sessions that afternoon, and the first was due to start in twenty minutes. Well, I thought, if Daddy were here, he'd tell me to go on out there and do my job. And that's what I did, on the road, far from home.

*****

It had occurred to me more than once, especially while traveling, that the ACFE had to improve its distance-learning capabilities. Even in those pre-Internet days, there was an alternative to offering training in person, especially for small groups of people in distant locations, which was an increasingly uneconomical proposition. And so, sometime in the mid-1990s at an ACFE staff meeting, I proposed that we offer the ACFE's exam preparation course on DVD. Everybody there embraced my proposal, which when implemented met members' needs for many years until so-called webinars made distance learning fully interactive and even more economical. Joe and I enthusiastically supported the ACFE's adoption of these and other new communication technologies. They certainly enabled us to help our members share and develop important skills, including the one I consider essential to effective fraud investigation.

The Art of the Interview

I've studied every kind of interview theory there is, spoken with countless experts on the subject, and read hundreds of books about it. After gleaning their key insights, I've tweaked and tailored them to fit my own needs and circumstances. No single style or method works for every investigator and situation. Each of us, through a combination of study and experience, has to develop our own personal interview style. Mine has evolved gradually, and serves me well. I continually refine it as necessary.

One of the fundamental interviewing principles I learned from Gus Rose is to always be courteous. It fits right into my plan of action when I begin an admission-seeking interview. Everyone's seen television shows where the interviewers are rude and abrupt;

that's what a suspect expects. But I throw him off balance when I treat him with respect.

To prepare, I will have already done research and perhaps identified a lie the suspect has told me or someone else earlier. The pace and flow of the interview will determine whether I point it out now or later on. Whenever I do, though, I'll merely ask about the inconsistency; I won't use the word *lie*. That would be confronting the suspect, challenging him—not what I want to do.

Instead, I want to make it easy for him to talk to me. So I ask open-ended questions that get him to do most of the talking. I don't learn anything when I'm speaking, only when he is.

I begin with unthreatening queries. "Where'd you grow up?"

If, for example, he says Atlanta, I ask, "Was that the place on Peachtree?"

Then, "Where'd you work before you came here?"

If he says IBM, I ask, "When you were IT director, right?" I seldom do that more than twice.

If the suspect asks where I got that information, I tell him I'm sorry but I'm not at liberty to discuss my investigative techniques. And I keep right on questioning him about his background, making him wonder what I do and don't know. People see fictional investigators on TV pull up all sorts of information online, including the color of the suspect's mother's hair. I can't do that, of course, but most suspects don't know it.

To get all the information that really is available, I go over the suspect's resume and all his performance evaluations. And I scour the Web—his Facebook page, LinkedIn, everything I can find on him. That gives me the answers to roughly half the questions I ask him. And it enables me to just sit there, listening to the suspect, waiting for him to tell me something I know isn't true. If he does, I don't challenge him just yet. I simply note that he's begun to lie, and I wait to see what other, more significant matters he might try to deceive me on.

One sign that we live in an "information age" is the prevalence of *open records* laws that guarantee public access to government-maintained data. Every state has its own such law, and their provisions vary from one jurisdiction to another; the same is true in other countries. These legal frameworks make background searches relatively easy and inexpensive. That's how organizations as diverse as the *National Enquirer* scandal sheet and private investigation firms make their money.

An astonishing variety of information is available from government databases—driving records, including arrests for DUI and other violations; information on professional licensing, censures, or disbarments; educational records; places of employment; business and residential addresses; and much more. If a suspect has been divorced, a search will identify the ex-spouse, who just might tell me where all the bumps and blemishes are. If a suspect has or had a bank loan, I'll visit the secretary of state's office and see what he used for collateral; it might be a fraudulently obtained asset. I also can find out how much that suspect borrowed and how quickly he's paying it back, which can shed light on a hidden revenue stream. To conduct a background search, I either visit the county courthouse or go online, where numerous companies compete to email me scads of useful intelligence that same day for as little as fifty dollars. I don't even have to leave my office.

Armed with what my search turned up earlier, I can unsettle the suspect by showing how much I know about him. As the suspect tries to evade questions that make him uncomfortable, I pay close attention to see what makes him sweat. After that first 15 minutes, I've got a pretty good sense of what, if anything, he's trying to hide.

When a suspect does lie, he'll usually do it indirectly, by omitting incriminating details rather than directly making a false statement. Say, for example, that I ask the suspect to tell me what he did and who he spoke with at work on a certain morning. He might reply that a colleague stopped by at 9:00, that they had coffee, talked for a while, and at noon, went their separate ways. It's improbable, though, that they did so for three solid hours.

So I'll say, "Tell me more about what you did that morning."

If the suspect says, "Well, what exactly do you want to know?" *Everything*, I reply.

"Where do you want me to start?" *At the beginning.*

At this stage, I phrase my reply as a command: *Tell me about this.*

Then I virtually shut up, saying as little as possible. The more the suspect talks, the greater the chance he'll make a mistake. So I sit there silently staring at him until he says something. And if I'm tempted to speak, I ask myself whether I'm sure it's worth interrupting that tense silence. Many times, the answer is no. So I mostly keep my mouth shut and wait for the suspect to feel the pressure and reveal something.

"Talk to me," I eventually say. "I've got to tell management something, and you have two choices. I can go back in there and tell them you're not cooperating. Or I can tell them your version of how this happened." Then I make eye contact and say, "I'll do anything I can to help you, but if you don't talk to me, there's nothing I can do." Again, I shut up and wait for the suspect to succumb to the pressure and say something.

I don't necessarily have to get him to admit intentional fraud. If I got him to admit hiding his acts from auditors or other employees, that would show intent and be enough to file charges. Likewise, lying to me or others would be a sign of intent. Often, the suspect will continue to deny awareness or intent. But if I persist, implying I know everything and that further denial is self-defeating, the suspect will gradually admit at least some responsibility. I keep the pressure on, asking even more penetrating questions. Eventually, the suspect will see that there's enough solid evidence against him.

At that point, cooperating is clearly the smart choice, and the suspect usually will confess. If he still doesn't, I'll interview other people and examine relevant documentation to see whether the suspect lied. I'll get the truth one way or another.

The Joy of Sharing

I'm so fortunate to have had the opportunity to teach interview techniques all over the world. After all these years, I still get excited when I get emails or phone calls from members who attended my classes. One I received not long ago is a good example.

A retired police officer in Louisiana wrote me, saying he'd just begun a new career as a fraud investigator. A local bank hired him, he studied for and passed the CFE Exam, and then he attended one of my interview seminars. Two months later, the bank discovered that one of its employees had embezzled a large sum. The evidence was overwhelming, but the employee denied everything when management confronted her. Unable to get a confession, management was about to simply fire the employee, absorb the loss, and go back to business as usual. But then they remembered they now had a CFE on staff, and asked him to interview the embezzler. They made it clear to the CFE, though, that calling him in was strictly pro forma, to fend off criticism from the board of directors. They certainly didn't expect the CFE to do any better than they had.

"I approached her just as you outlined in class," the CFE wrote in his email to me. "I couldn't believe it when she confessed."

I knew just how that CFE felt; I'd had the same thrill when I got my first confession after attending Gus Rose's class. To top it off, the embezzler signed a restitution agreement. Needless to say, the bank's managers were dumbfounded.

"Everybody in the bank thinks I'm a hero," the CFE wrote me, "and it's all because of your class at the ACFE." I was as happy as he and his colleagues were. Helping people fight fraud has motivated me from the beginning, and it always will. That's how CFEs achieve great things—we work together.

CHAPTER 20

NATIONAL CRISIS

B y the mid-1990s, the ACFE and its members had done more to fight fraud than any private organization in history. But no single entity or profession could win the war singlehandedly. Government and business would have to pay more attention and pitch in. To attract that support, though, our profession needed an authoritative voice it didn't yet have. Joe saw that need and knew how to meet it. He called our management and research teams together and told us we were going to produce the largest-ever privately funded study of fraud. And in 1996, we met our objective by publishing the ACFE's first *Report to the Nation on Occupational Fraud and Abuse* (RTTN). Based on data from more than 2,600 CFEs nationwide, it analyzed cases from the preceding ten years.

By comprehensively identifying and analyzing fraud's cost, victims, perpetrators, and methods, the report firmly established the

ACFE as the nation's foremost professional authority in this critical field. Among other findings, it noted that losses from frauds by managers and executives were 16 times greater than those by rank-and-file employees. With this and other fraud trends so clearly identified, the opportunity for mitigation had never been better. Unfortunately, the support we hoped the report would bring was slow to emerge; government and corporate America remained mostly passive. Meanwhile, as the second millennium ended and the third began, the ACFE and its members kept on fighting fraud, raising awareness, and promoting anti-fraud legislation. Sometimes, though, the most far-reaching solutions emerge in the midst of crisis.

In the greatest disaster to strike America in sixty years, terrorists took the lives of 3,000 innocent civilians on September 11, 2001. Following this unprecedented tragedy, strengthening homeland security became the nation's top priority. But meeting that goal would be difficult if the economy faltered. And the economy was soon threatened, when massive financial statement frauds by top executives brought down several of America's biggest companies. These schemes were exactly what our *Report to the Nation* had warned of. One aspect of the crisis was particularly harmful and unnerving: Certain watchdogs in government and industry colluded with the fraudsters.

The best way to understand the challenge the ACFE and its members faced in 2001 is to review what preceded the crooked executives' frauds and made them possible. After the stagflation of the 1970s and early 1980s, America tried to revive its economy by reducing government's influence over business and the capital markets. On the plus side, tax rates dropped and, gradually, so did inflation. But reduced oversight caused serious problems. Nearly half of the nation's savings and loan associations, for example, failed as a result of their reckless, unregulated lending practices. One of them, the Lincoln Savings and Loan Association, went under in 1989, costing the federal government billions and leaving tens of thousands of investors with worthless corporate bonds they'd bought through Lincoln. Its infamous chairman, Charles Keating, went to prison after pleading guilty to wire and bankruptcy fraud.

Encircled by Corruption

Lax regulation allowed Keating's fraud to swell to gigantic proportions. But three years earlier, Lincoln's auditor, Arthur Andersen LLP, had refused to approve the S&L's misleading financial statements, which concealed huge loan losses. Because Lincoln wouldn't reveal its true financial status, Andersen did the right thing: it dropped Lincoln as a client. Andersen's commitment to trustworthy audits ultimately weakened, though, when a new generation of top managers moved into the accounting firm's C-suite. For them, the prospect of selling their audit clients lucrative technological advisory services was irresistible. By the mid-1990s, Andersen's consultants were bringing in twice as much revenue as its auditors. And that put enormous pressure on the auditors to ensure their clients were happy. From then on, if clients wanted quick audits with few questions about their accounting, Andersen complied. No one objected.

In one telling incident, another Andersen client, Waste Management, Inc., overstated its profits by $1.7 billion. Not wanting to jeopardize the $20 million consulting fee it earned advising Waste Management on technology, Andersen signed off on the falsified financial statements. The SEC managed to detect the fraud, but fined Andersen a mere $7 million. Still ahead by at least $13 million on the engagement, Andersen saw the penalty as simply a cost of doing business. For auditors and everyone who depended on them, this was an ominous sign of even greater problems to come.

Fraud had been brewing elsewhere as well. Earlier in the 1990s, a clever McKinsey and Company management consultant named

Jeffrey Skilling jumped ship to work for Enron Corp., a client of both his firm and Arthur Andersen. Skilling's influence soon transformed Enron from a gas pipeline company into an energy trader. To support its innovative strategy, Enron courted the right government officials. In 1992, it persuaded the chairwoman of the federal Commodity Futures Trading Commission to exempt Enron from compliance with regulations governing energy futures trading contracts. Within two months of granting Enron that exemption, the chairwoman resigned from her government post and joined Enron's board of directors, serving—of all places—on its audit committee.

This, along with the arrival and rapid expansion of the World Wide Web, set the stage for Enron to implement Skilling's brainchild: a proprietary electronic trading platform called Enron Online, or EOL. By 1999, Enron's annual revenue from EOL had passed $90 billion. Continuing its successful lobbying efforts, Enron gained the support of a lame-duck U.S. senator—the husband of the former CFTC chairwoman. In 2000, before leaving office, the senator shepherded into effect a federal law that further deregulated energy trading. The following year, in the first quarter alone, Enron took in $48 billion through EOL by manipulating the now mostly unregulated energy market.

Because it was legal to charge more in California for electricity that came from other states, Enron used EOL to make it look as if the energy Enron sold there had been *transported into* California when it actually had *originated in* California. This scheme, which earned Enron billions in illicit profits, came to be known as *megawatt laundering*. Desperate to contain its soaring energy costs, California's government had no choice but to impose several dozen blackouts on San Francisco and other cities. Where were the auditors while Enron was perpetrating this outrageous fraud? Everywhere, but they did nothing to stop it. Enron's external auditor, Andersen, had helpfully agreed to perform Enron's internal audits as well, effectively auditing itself. In this way, a full circle of fraud-sters—Enron, its auditors, a regulator and a legislator—enriched themselves by violating the public trust.

Enron's ability to manipulate the energy markets came to an abrupt end in mid-2001, however, when the federal government imposed price controls. As a result, California's energy prices quickly fell back to their normal levels. And Enron's revenue plum-meted, driving its share price down from ninety dollars to mere pennies. Skilling resigned and Enron folded in December; at that time, it was the biggest bankruptcy in U.S. history. If there was any question whether Enron's board shared the responsibility, a clear answer came when big investors won a civil judgment against the bankrupt company and its directors. Ten Enron board members, including the former CFTC chairwoman, had to pay—out of their own pockets—$13 million in compensation to the victims. Enron's insurer paid $155 million more.

Somehow, government still didn't believe tighter regulation was necessary. The SEC's new chairman, Harvey Pitt, a former corporate defense attorney, promised on his appointment in 2001 to make the SEC a "kinder, gentler" regulator.

That approach didn't work out well. Only eight months after Enron's record failure, WorldCom, another corporate giant, went down in an even bigger bankruptcy. Both collapses resulted from years of rampant but mostly undetected false accounting by top management. A few weeks later, the two companies' auditor, Ar-thur Andersen, having participated in both frauds, surrendered its CPA license, effectively ending its existence.

Many people suffered greatly because of these three failures. In only nine months, 130,000 blameless employees lost their jobs and most if not all of their retirement savings. Later, Skilling and other architects of Enron's scheme went to jail, as did fraudsters at WorldCom and other big companies who'd faked their num-bers. But imprisoning those executives didn't undo the great harm they'd done. Ultimately, these preventable tragedies occurred because government and industry had long failed to rein in corporate fraud.

The F-Word

On a smaller scale, Joe and I encountered the same stick-your-head-in-the-sand denial time and again at numerous Wells & Associates clients. Sometimes when we caught a fraudster, the company didn't even want us to write up our findings in a report. Its leaders simply wanted to fire the perpetrator and move on, never to speak of the incident again—especially not to the police or district attorney. For those managers, fraud was a four-letter word. The faster and more quietly you put a scheme behind you, they reasoned, the faster things would return to "normal." Later, after we founded the ACFE, some members told us their employers too held that belief. I even heard from one member who said he wasn't allowed to display his CFE certificate on his office wall. "My bosses said it would make employees think the company suspected them of theft," he told me.

The way we at the ACFE saw it, no one had looked closely enough at the various kinds of people who committed fraud and at how they went about it. The best way to do that was to classify perpetrators, their schemes, and victims and use the findings to devise proactive training and countermeasures. The ACFE took the lead in that effort by issuing its initial RTTN.

Nevertheless, throughout the 1990s fraud prevention remained a difficult service for our members to sell. Few business leaders were willing to spend money on anything that didn't boost revenue. Their investors, clients, and employees paid the price, as fraud losses rose to 5 percent of U.S. GDP. Yet not until the Sarbanes-Oxley Act became law on July 31, 2002, was there any meaningful attempt to mitigate the corporate fraud the ACFE and its members had been fighting and calling attention to for years. Now CEOs and CFOs had to sign off on their companies' financial statements as well as develop and maintain robust internal controls over financial reporting. For executives determined to fight fraud, the ACFE and its members continued offering guidance and support. But those managers still eager to cook the books found the kitchen had gotten hot.

Seizing the Opportunity

Finally, our profession had gotten what it sought. Government was pushing industry to actively mitigate corporate fraud. To make the most of this opportunity, CFEs knew they had to keep pace with fraudsters' inevitable attempts to defeat the latest internal controls and audit techniques. The ACFE community, which had grown substantially over the preceding decade, played a central role in this effort. By offering extensive training and a variety of collegial forums for sharing anti-fraud insights and techniques, the Association helped ensure its members were fully prepared to detect and prevent whatever new schemes fraudsters devised. Still, we were missing a key ally in our war against fraud.

Regulators, fraud examiners, and senior executives knew their roles and how to perform them. But many rank-and-file corporate employees in a position to detect and prevent fraud were an untapped resource. Some, if better informed about anti-fraud work and training, might choose to obtain professional certification, especially if their employers supported such efforts. In fact, a growing number of companies wanted fraud awareness training for their staffs and were using the CFE credential as a preferred criterion when hiring. It was clear that a closer relationship between the ACFE and large organizations would help them. We got right to work on strengthening that bond.

Extending Our Community

To achieve this goal, we needed to inform companies and their employees that CFEs' mission was to join hands with them in fighting fraud, not to conduct witch hunts. We wanted a CFE credential on the wall to be a symbol of partnership, not oppression. The name we chose for this arm of our community—*The ACFE Corporate Alliance*—reflected that approach. We explained that member organizations not only better protected themselves against the latest forms of fraud, but also avoided regulators' penalties for inadvertent noncompliance with strict new requirements. Another tangible benefit of membership in the Alliance, we noted, was setting an anti-fraud tone at the top of the organization. This gave employees, investors, and business partners greater confidence in the company's commitment to fighting fraud. Corporations, seeing the value in Alliance membership, responded enthusiastically to our offer.

We focused additional outreach efforts on the law enforcement and government sectors. While these were agencies not businesses, their anti-fraud training needs were well served by the same collaborative approach we offered the corporate sector. The FBI, SEC, and Drug Enforcement Agency were among those who accepted our offer of membership in the group we called *The ACFE Law Enforcement and Government Alliance.*

We also wanted to make the benefits of our community available to students who were interested in a career as a fraud examiner. We therefore extended our offer to institutions of higher learning by means of our *ACFE Anti-Fraud Education Partnership.* Through membership in it, universities and colleges have access to the materials, tools, and resources they need to establish world-class anti-fraud courses and programs.

CFE in Action

Training and education can greatly improve your ability and career prospects. But you've got to do more than take the first steps in that direction. You have to keep at it, always moving forward and becoming more proficient. I was raised that way—to be persistent, especially when a lot is at stake. So when I see people strive to achieve something important against great odds, I can't help but admire them—whether they win or lose.

Harry Markopolos, CFE, is famous for being the first person to identify Bernie Madoff's investment firm as a Ponzi scheme. But Harry wasn't always well known, and he didn't become a CFE until far into his career as a financial analyst.

Based on analysis he'd begun in 1999, Harry concluded early on that Madoff's returns were mathematically impossible in the absence of fraud. For the next eight years, he continued scrutinizing Madoff's numbers. During that period, he contacted the SEC four times about Madoff's scheme. But each time, the SEC deemed his analysis inconclusive. Yes, it was unlikely that a former NASDAQ chairman would set up a Ponzi scheme, but that's exactly what Madoff, fine pedigree and all, had done. And federal prosecutors refused to believe it.

Many people in Harry's shoes would have given up. He'd accomplished a lot, detecting the biggest fraud in U.S. history, but no one would listen. Yet, instead of sitting back and relying on his existing skills, Harry's response was to expand them by becoming a CFE. It paid off.

After a year of steep declines in the housing and equity markets, cash flow—the lifeblood of all Ponzi schemes—had slowed to a trickle at Madoff Securities. Late in 2008, Madoff saw it was all over and that he'd soon be indicted for stealing $65 billion from his investors. So he turned himself in to the FBI and confessed to the massive fraud Harry had been blowing the whistle on for the past eight years. But Harry's extensive forensic labors had not gone to waste. At Madoff's trial, prosecutors were able to cite the 30 red flags of fraud at Madoff Securities that Harry had identified in his submissions to the SEC. The fraudulent intent that Harry's evidence documented helped earn Madoff a 150-year sentence.

Proud to have a person of Harry's caliber in our ranks, the ACFE named him 2009's CFE of the Year. No one exemplifies the CFE spirit better than Harry Markopolos does. Our ongoing commitment is to give all our members the tools, resources, and community they need to follow Harry's example. The rest is up to each individual. And having met tens of thousands of our members, I know that's just what they want. We pull out all the stops to see that they get it.

Ensuring Excellence

Since 1989, right up to this very day, Joe and I read each attendee evaluation of every seminar and conference we offer. The first thing we look for is the answer to one of our standard questions: *What did you like least about this event?* We want to know how members think we can do better. The answers to that and other questions have greatly helped us improve our training and all member services. Joe and I meet with our Events staff on a regular basis to talk about member feedback and how to improve our future offerings.

Members who attend an ACFE event invest two things—money and time. From Day One, our policy has been to issue full refunds to any members who aren't completely satisfied. What we can't give back, though, is perhaps more precious—their time. We want our members to be glad they came and eager to get back to work and apply their new skills.

Clearly, exceptional training is impossible without exceptional teachers. We've assembled a faculty of roughly 30 outstanding hands-on specialists who teach our recurring classes. Each of them is active in our profession, performing fraud examinations for clients and employers. Every other year we bring them to Austin for refresher training in our instruction methods and requirements. In addition to teaching our courses, they speak at our conferences. For many of the training events and other gatherings we host around the world, we also engage local anti-fraud specialists well versed in regulatory and legal requirements peculiar to their jurisdictions. To ensure that attendees experience uniformly high-quality instruction at these events, we've developed written guidelines for all our speakers and instructors. We've refined this approach over the past quarter-century, and constantly strive to make it even better.

Ensuring excellence in these events requires complete candor with instructors about their effectiveness, as measured by attendees. Sometimes being honest about poor performance is tough. One time I had to fire an instructor because attendees had given him low scores in their evaluations. He deserved the truth, and I gave it to him.

"Our members aren't satisfied with your performance," I said. "I can't ignore what they're telling us. I'm terminating your engagement with us as of today." The man was stunned; I felt for him.

"I can't be that bad," he replied, naming another association, which he said had asked him to teach at its events.

"I wish you the very best of luck with them," I replied, and said goodbye.

If only it weren't necessary to have conversations like that; but it is. Our duty is to meet or exceed attendees' expectations in their first ACFE event and to repeat that performance in every other one they attend. Joe and I have always believed that the best way to satisfy members is to listen to what they tell you *and act on it*.

Like our faculty and other instructors, I too have to perform well. When speaking abroad, for example, I continually educate myself about the fight against fraud in other countries and regions.

The ACFE's research staff is enormously helpful in that respect. What varies most isn't the kind of scheme or target; it's how the authorities deal with them. In the United Kingdom, for instance, the law governing investigative interviews differs from that in the United States. There, interviews must be recorded; most everywhere in the U.S., recording is optional. But through ACFE research and meetings with CFEs in Australia, China, Greece, Russia, and many other countries, I've learned that fraudsters steal much the same way they do in America. Likewise, I've found that in interviews most suspects communicate—intentionally or inadvertently—in the same predictable ways, regardless of their culture. This enables me to teach interviewing techniques I know will work with any suspect or witness, anywhere. We aim to meet the needs of our members, no matter where they are.

To help make that happen, I do a lot more than teach. As president, I oversee ACFE operations and meet regularly with each of our departmental directors to review their progress. I don't pretend to know their jobs better or even half as well as they do. They're specialists in their respective fields; I'm not. But it's my responsibility to make sure that every ACFE department is in sync, on time, and on target. If it weren't, members would suffer the consequences, and I won't let that happen.

Fortunately, I've got wonderful colleagues. Every ACFE staff member is a top-of-the-line, trained professional, committed to excellence. Building our team was a learning experience for Joe and me. But after some initial missteps, we put our recruitment and retention policies in proper order. As a result, our current roster is outstanding. In fact, one of my most important tasks is staying out of their way. So I focus on strategy and empower them to implement it.

"What'll you be doing five years from now?" I sometimes ask our employees. If they don't know, I urge them to give it some thought and come up with a plan. Otherwise, expect to be doing the same thing as now. Maybe that's fun, but growth and variety keep things fresh and interesting. It goes without saying that education is a key part of any good career plan. Accordingly, the ACFE's incentive program pays our employees' college tuition if they maintain at least a B average. Bottom line: if they have goals, I help them get there. It's a privilege to participate in someone's progress toward a better life. That's my definition of true wealth.

The Wrong Way...and the Right Way

Recently, one of the top people at a competing association called me. I recognized his name, but we'd never met. He wanted my advice on a problem.

"Glad to help if I can," I said. "What's the situation?"

"Well," he told me, "a large number of our members work for the same company, which pays their dues. As you might expect, their renewal dates are all over the calendar, and the company wants us to bill it for everybody at once. I thought you might have the same problem. Any suggestions?"

I told him we'd faced that issue and had our IT staff modify the system.

"You reprogrammed your billing module?"

"That's right. It was well worth the effort to meet our members' needs."

"I don't know," he said.

"Tell you what. I'll send you the names and phone numbers of our IT staff. They'll explain everything and answer any questions you have."

"Sounds like a lot of work."

"It's not. But even if it were, that's what we're here for." I put the phone down and shook my head. That man saw this situation as a problem; to me it was an opportunity. When it came up at the ACFE, we welcomed the challenge to serve our members better.

We were pleased with the outcome, and so were they. As promised, I sent the guy our IT staff's contact information. A few weeks later I checked around to see if he'd called, but no, we never heard from him again. He just wasn't willing to spend time and money on what his members needed.

It's a whole different situation at the ACFE. As I've said, we're always asking members how well we meet their needs. Case in point: A CPA/CFE wrote me to say how happy he was with our service. I took his message to the staff Christmas party, and read it out for all to hear. The member, who'd just been certified, wanted us to know how much he appreciated the Association's support throughout the entire process, from studying for the exam, to taking and passing it, and satisfying other certification requirements. Along the way, he'd had questions and needed more information on various matters. At each point, he said, the Association had responded quickly and thoroughly. Several ACFE departments had shepherded him through the whole thing—most of it online—and he also praised their coordinated efforts and systems. "Thank you to the ACFE," he concluded, "for doing such a wonderful job."

I looked up and saw smiling faces all around me. "IT, Certification, and Membership worked in perfect cohesion to bring this CFE on board," I said. "Well done. Let's keep it up." My little speech wasn't necessary, of course. Everyone's already performing at 110 percent. The important thing was for my ACFE colleagues to hear how much they helped that member. It's good to know what we're doing just right.

On the Go

I admire our members. They're not satisfied with reliving one year of experience over and over. Instead, they look for ways to improve and learn new skills. And I understand where they're coming from; I've been there. Some were given a white-collar crime case

313

to investigate and had no idea where to start or what to do. When I landed in that situation back in the early 1980s, there was no ACFE to turn to. I had to find the information I needed and stitch it together. But Gus Rose's four-hour interviewing class showed me what was possible, and I took it from there, bit by bit.

Finding good training used to be hard. That led Joe and me to establish the ACFE. We want our members to spend their time learning, not searching. When I teach a class, my last slide lists my email address, phone number, LinkedIn, and Twitter accounts. I encourage attendees to stay in touch and continue our conversation. And they do; I routinely take calls from and exchange email with our members.

Few things please me more than giving out members' names when companies call me looking for CFEs. Perhaps the only thing I like as much is getting out among our members. We all have two big things in common—our profession and our community—and I consider them my friends. Sometimes we meet when they visit Austin or attend a conference. But I spend a great part of my time traveling to meet them on their home ground. I was on the road 220 days last year and had to send my passport back in to get more pages added to it. You name a country, I've been there, meeting with members, spreading the word. I've logged three million miles on American Airlines alone. It's the most convenient airline to fly out of Austin. When I die and go on to the hereafter, I'll have to change planes in Dallas.

Over the years, my trips abroad have become more frequent to keep up with the increasing number of ACFE chapters around the world—180 at last count. Reflecting that growth, the RTTN has for some time encompassed far more than the United States. We acknowledged that in 2010 by changing its title to the *Report to the Nations on Occupational Fraud and Abuse*.

Fraud is, of course, still a serious problem, but awareness is greater than ever and our profession's unique ability to fight it is widely recognized and sought. According to the latest *Report to the Nations*, the typical fraud scheme lasts 18 months before being discovered. But if the victim organization has a CFE on staff, the median duration is only one year. Rarely does a profession make so big a difference. We all can take great pride in that.

PART FIVE

ALWAYS LEARNING

"If you don't know where you're going, you won't know when you get there." — Yogi Berra

CHAPTER 21

HEART AND MIND

I've been very fortunate, with a loving family, enduring friendships, and a fulfilling career. Some of that came about because I happened to be in the right place at the right time. But the majority of it I actively sought, driven by an eagerness to learn and an appetite for adventure. One of the most important things I've learned is how much we all can achieve if we set our minds to it.

By 2003, our children had graduated from college and moved out on their own. Suddenly Gloria and I had spare time, and I began looking for something interesting to do, just for fun. My search led me to a nearby flight school, where I got my first taste of flying's pleasures and challenges. Soon I'd earned a single-engine pilot's license, obtained certification to fly by instruments through clouds and after dark and, together with a friend, bought a 1971 Cherokee 235. For eleven years, it served me well on flights around the Southwest with Gloria and, on one occasion, to Florida with Joe.

But the Cherokee experience was a spartan one, and as I gained flying time and knowledge, a more advanced single-engine make and model caught my eye—the Cirrus SR22. Faster and air-conditioned—the latter a big advantage in torrid Texas—it was more fun to operate. Gloria liked it too; so I traded up in 2014, knowing I'd get to enjoy her company on more flights. It didn't hurt that the Cirrus came with a built-in airframe parachute system that safely floats the entire plane to the ground in the event of sudden pilot disability or major equipment failure. Such problems occur far more often than most people realize. The former CEO of Walmart was glad to be flying an SR22 when he deployed its parachute after losing engine oil pressure at 10,000 feet over Arkansas in 2015. Two passengers were with him when the plane gently came to rest on a five-lane road, only to be struck by a pickup truck. Still, no one suffered more than minor injuries. Cirrus's parachute system has performed equally well in hundreds of similar situations. It's a great thing when you can safely rely on a product or service and the people behind it.

My Dream Come True

One day, two years after buying my Cirrus, I was high over the Caribbean with Gloria. We'd just left U.S. airspace and were headed for Cuba, a destination we'd long been interested in. After a decades-long American embargo, diplomatic relations had thawed and we were taking advantage of a reduction in travel restrictions. Our airspeed was 180 knots—a little over 200 miles an hour. Glancing to my right, I exchanged grins with Gloria; she was as eager as I was. Intermittently visible through breaks in cloud cover, the sea lay not quite two miles below us, blue-green, placid, glistening in dappled sunlight.

About 20 minutes after taking off from Key West, Florida, on our 40-minute flight, I'd contacted Havana Approach, the outermost layer of Cuba's air traffic control system. Approach was about to hand me off to my next contact, the control tower at Jose Marti International Airport, slightly west of the capital.

"November five six three Delta Tango," Approach said, addressing me by my plane's call sign. "Expect VOR and runway one-seven. Maintain niner thousand until established on ILS localizer." That told me what navigation systems to use as I neared Cuba, the appropriate altitude, and exactly where I'd land.

I acknowledged those instructions. My approach was complete; now it was time to contact the airport. "Marti Tower," I said. "November five six three Delta Tango, checking in at niner thousand. Inbound, north of runway one-seven."

The tower repeated my call sign and said, "Cleared to land. Runway one-seven." I began our descent, and at 3,000 feet, we broke through to bright sunshine. I near shouted, "I can't believe we're about to land in Cuba!"

"You've done it!" Gloria said, taking in the view as we passed over the coastline. "This is amazing!" Beneath us sprawled a verdant landscape and, on our left, Havana. Straight ahead in the near distance, our designated runway came into view.

A few minutes later, my wheels touched the ground and the tower said, "Welcome to Cuba."

"It's my pleasure to be here," I replied, and taxied toward the terminal. We were thrilled, but the fun was just beginning.

Mine wasn't the first Cirrus to land at Marti that day. In fact, my plane was one of a small fleet that flew down together. I and the other flyers belong to an affinity group—the Cirrus Owners and Pilots Association. Together we'd arranged our trip to Cuba, one of many flights we've taken together. While we plan all our group travels carefully, this journey required much more advance work than usual.

First, like travelers from any other country, we had to get visas from the Cuban authorities. Then, because of ongoing U.S.

restrictions, we needed special travel permits from our own State Department. And, finally, since we arrived in private planes rather than on commercial airliners, we also needed authorization to land our aircraft on Cuban soil. That took time, as did our preparation of an itinerary that complied with State Department regulations.

In the very first stage of our journey, I flew the Cirrus to Miami Executive Airport, with Gloria as my only passenger. There, I and the rest of the group had dinner the night before departure and reviewed our flight plan. The next morning, we and our passengers—all told, there were 31 of us—left Miami; every plane but mine flew directly to Havana. I took a detour because one pilot, a friend of mine, couldn't get insurance coverage for flying his plane to Cuba. The rest of us had been able to add foreign travel riders to our policies, but his insurer wouldn't do it. So I told him he could make the last leg of the trip with Gloria and me. First he and I flew our planes to Key West, where he secured his. Then he climbed in with us; my plane can seat four. Soon afterward, we touched down at Marti and joined the other 14 Cirrus aircraft already on the ground.

You couldn't imagine a more cordial welcome. Smiling Cuban customs officials said they'd never seen anything like our little squadron. They asked our permission to take dozens of photos of us and our planes; we gladly obliged and also took shots of us together. After passing through customs, we boarded a touring coach along with two English-speaking guides we'd engaged in advance. For the next four days, our group explored the capital's grand architecture. El Morro, a giant stone fortress that has watched over Havana's harbor for nearly five centuries, is but one example. Throughout it all, Cuba's rhythmic music and savory cuisine kept us energized.

Our itinerary for each day followed State Department regulations, which allow American citizens to visit Cuba for academic programs, professional research, journalism, sport competitions, and certain other purposes, but not for tourism alone. So we visited cultural institutions, including schools and museums, as well as farms and even private homes, where we were received with great courtesy and hospitality. This helped us understand Cuban culture and daily life far better than we otherwise would have. Tourists—most are from Canada or Europe—typically spend all their time at resorts, where they learn little about how the average Cuban lives. The government does all it can to minimize people's social interactions with foreign visitors.

One day, Gloria and I hired a taxi to sightsee apart from the group. Our driver, Jesus, was the third-generation owner of a 1958 Edsel sedan. Jesus's grandfather had bought the Edsel new and drove it until he retired, when he passed it on to Jesus's father. And when his dad got too old to drive, Jesus got behind the wheel, beginning the Edsel's third generation of service to the family and its customers.

Because of the embargo, spare parts for American cars have long been hard to come by on the island. So Cubans routinely take components from all kinds of broken-down vehicles to rejuvenate others that chug along far beyond their normal life cycle. When the engine in Jesus's car died, he replaced it with one from a 1957 Chevy whose body he'd stripped of useful parts. We even saw old cars powered by engines cannibalized from decrepit farm tractors. Yet under a corrupt government, such creativity earns Cubans only a fraction of what it would elsewhere. Although their classic autos would sell for as much as six figures in the U.S., most Cubans can barely afford to put a good meal on the table. The authorities reserve the best domestic produce for themselves and foreign visitors; the vast majority of Cubans get a small portion of what's left.

Even when the Cuban government provides an essential public service, it does so grudgingly. For instance, communities receive electricity and other utilities at no charge. Yet while power is free, there's little of it; only low-watt light bulbs are permitted. I was told that each night the police patrol neighborhoods, on the lookout for brightly lit homes. When they find one, they force their way inside and break all its "illegal" bulbs. For many people, that's a serious expense.

On a more positive note, we capped off our stay in Cuba with a brief visit to Varadero, a pleasant seaside town about eight miles east of the capital. Far too soon, we felt, our stay was ending. Everyone in our group left Cuba greatly impressed with its natural beauty and dynamic people. Their good nature and grit made me realize how fortunate I am to live in a country where I can fulfill my personal dreams and professional ambitions.

Thirst for Know-How

I'm not happy unless I'm learning something new, and my interests vary widely. Whether working in wood or stained glass, playing music or sports, I enjoy getting absorbed in anything interesting and challenging. When Daddy came with me while I went scuba diving at Ginnie Springs, Florida, I'd already been at it for several years. I eventually earned certification as an advanced diver, and Gloria too grew to love the sport. For ten years, she and I dove in many parts of the world—Honduras, the Virgin and Cayman Islands, and Australia's Great Barrier Reef—bringing our own fins, regulators, and masks, and renting oxygen tanks wherever we dove. It was thrilling.

While I'm a competent guitar player, I'd rather listen to my favorite performers, especially Johnny Rivers, who's still touring and has a loyal following. Over the years, I'd heard rumors that he'd lost his spark and was in decline. One day I decided to look into it myself. With a little luck on the Web, I found his agent's name and phone number and gave him a call. He told me Rivers' next gig was in Salt Lake City. When I said my wife and I would fly there from Austin if he'd take my payment over the phone for two front-row seats, he kindly agreed. What luck; it turned out to be a rocking good show.

Opening for Rivers was another classic group, the Kingsmen, playing their signature piece, "Louie, Louie," which has mesmerized fans for decades. As usual, lead singer Jack Ely intentionally slurred the lyrics over an irresistible electric piano and bass line—*bom-bom-bom...bom-bom, bom-bom-bom...bom-bom*—that roused the crowd into a shoulder- and hip-shaking frenzy. When Rivers came on, everyone jumped up in anticipation. And he did not disappoint, playing "Seventh Son," "Secret Agent Man," "Mountain of Love," "Midnight Special," and other hits. It was just wonderful; that man was nowhere near done bringing crowds to their feet.

After the show, one of the police officers in the security detail let me send a note backstage to Rivers. In it, I asked if he'd be kind enough to spare me one of his guitar picks. Class act that he is, Rivers sent out two picks and an autographed photo. I didn't think the night could end on a finer note, but I was wrong. As Gloria and I made our way out of the arena, we saw a group of men standing off to the side. One of them was Jack Ely; we walked over to him.

After chatting for a good half hour about music and touring, we thanked him and shook hands, impressed by his gracious modesty. He wasn't a top-ranked star, but over the years, millions had seen or heard him perform. People in the public eye that long sometimes take their agents' press releases a bit too seriously. But not Jack Ely, a famous yet down-to-earth gentleman. A while after we spoke, I heard he'd died at age 71. I'm glad I got the chance to speak with him; it was a real pleasure.

A Man's Got to Know His Limitations

Sometimes I go on long motorcycle rides with old friends; it's a great way to relax. But on a trip last year, I came across some people with mischief on their minds. I was on my way to join several of my former partners from Dallas Police Department street patrol. Our ultimate destination was Caddo Lake, about 20 miles northeast of my birthplace, Marshall. The only natural lake in Texas—the rest were created by dams—it's just beautiful, surrounded by magnificent bald cypresses and gently sloping hills.

Most of my pals still live near Dallas, west of the lake; I had to ride northeast from Austin. We agreed to meet on the way, at a town called Tyler, then head for Caddo. I had more ground to cover than they did, so I left home the day before. My plan was to spend the night in Tyler and meet them when they arrived there the following day. I'd never been to Tyler before, and cruised into town just as darkness fell. After checking my bike's GPS for a hotel, I saw I was near one in a nondescript neighborhood. Across the street was all I wanted besides a clean bed: a Denny's Restaurant and a Dairy Queen ice cream parlor. I parked and checked in.

At Denny's, I didn't linger over my burger and went next door for dessert. Inside, three men in their thirties were sitting on a bench, not eating, just loitering it seemed. I ordered a vanilla cup with chocolate syrup. When I turned from the service counter and went to sit down, I saw they'd left. The ice cream was good; in minutes I was done and out the door. They were waiting for me.

The sun hadn't been down long, but it was chilly. In a hip holster under my windbreaker was a Sig Sauer .45-caliber P220. In my wallet was a concealed handgun permit.

The three fanned out in front of me.

"Hey, man," the one in the middle said. "I need some money."

"Hey, man, I can't help you," I told him. I tried to walk around him, but he moved to block me.

"Hey, man, I'm serious!"

"Hey, man, I'm serious too. I can't help you."

This time he bopped me in the chest. "I need some money!"

I put the Sig in his face. "You touch me again, I'll make a hole between your eyes."

He backed right off. "Man, I'm just kidding!"

"I'm not," I said. He and his pals scrammed.

Back in my room, I quickly fell asleep. The following day, I met my buddies and toured Caddo and the surrounding countryside. Later in the week, we went our separate ways, looking forward to the next ride. Longtime friends are one of life's great pleasures.

First and Foremost

Nothing's more important to me than my family. Every major holiday, Gloria and I get together with our kids and their families and have a wonderful time. We love and care for one another and enjoy each other's company.

And Momma loves us all; we treasure her. She's a force to be reckoned with, but still can laugh at herself. Never short of advice for others, she was once photographed in mid-delivery to some poor soul, probably me. Her hand is raised, forefinger extended in admonishment. I didn't take the photo, and don't remember who did. But I wasn't about to let that beauty disappear into a photo album. I had it framed and gave it to her for Christmas. On the matte border, I inscribed a selection of helpful pointers she's given me. ~ *You need to quit being so moody* ~ *You need to keep short hair* ~ *You need to be more polite* ~ I would've listed my other needs, but the border wasn't big enough. Momma was a good sport about it and nodded at me with a wry smile. My teasing in no way weakened her conviction that I do—and always will—need her advice. I have to admit it, though; she might be on to something there.

On my fiftieth birthday, I got a tattoo on my right shoulder: the Texas and American flags crossed, with an outline of Texas in the middle. Ten years later, I got one on the other shoulder: a star with flames rising from it. I'd never thought to tell Momma. One time she visited while I was doing some yard work, wearing a sleeveless shirt. She saw one tattoo, gasped, saw the other, and nearly passed out.

"What on Earth were you thinking?" she cried, hands to her face in dismay. I just got on with my work.

My sister Patty's a high-school principal. She was about to re-tire, but the board of education offered her a whopping raise to stay on and straighten out troubled schools. She agreed, but not because of the money; she just loves making an important contri-bution. My younger sister, Debra, is in banking, a vice president of mortgage lending. Competitors try to lure her away, but like me, she's happy right where she is.

My younger daughter, Sarah, is a senior program analyst at CapGemini, a global management consultancy. Her older sister, Leslie, is director of events at the ACFE. She started with us at the tender age of nine, doing simple clerical tasks and learning a little about business. Right after high school, she announced her first career goal: becoming an NFL cheerleader. I supported her in that ambition, but honestly thought the odds against it were overwhelming. At that time, the Houston Oilers were recruiting, so she focused on them. The competition was for six slots, and a lot of young women were expected to apply. But Leslie was clear-eyed and determined. She hired a coach and rehearsed for weeks, perfecting her dance routine. On the day of the tryouts, three hun-dred women showed up. It was truly daunting, but Leslie was ready and at her best. The Oilers picked her and five others—a stunning victory for her. I was so proud.

As she and I knew all along, the job was difficult and paid next to nothing. But it was a once-in-a-lifetime opportunity, and Leslie enjoyed it to the fullest. After one exciting season, though, she called it quits and went to college. Having achieved her first career goal, she was ready for the next one. Four years later, business degree in hand, Leslie had to decide where she wanted to work. Knowledge of the ACFE's important work—coupled with posi-tive memories of her very first work experience—led her back to the Association, where she's been happy and productive ever since.

Family and Community

The ACFE is my second family; that's how much the Association and its mission mean to me. That commitment, shared by all my colleagues, is why members can rely on us. Together we form a global family—a community—of fraud fighters.

Years ago, Joe and I started a revolution in fraud detection and prevention, and we're not done yet. Standing on the shoulders of giants—Cressey, Sutherland, Rose—we expanded and refined their insights, often by trial and error with our ACFE colleagues. We will not allow the practical benefits of that hard-earned experience to be lost. To that end, Joe and I developed an executive leadership team and succession plan through which the ACFE will continue to expand the common body of knowledge and serve our growing community. In this way, up-and-coming anti-fraud professionals will benefit from our experience without repeating our mistakes. Joe and I understand how highly our members value this practical legacy. Their skill and diligence will carry it into the future.

They've got a solid foundation to build on. With more than 80,000 members in 180 countries, the ACFE is well versed in every aspect of anti-fraud work. We've always aimed to be the world's *best* anti-fraud association. To earn that distinction, we've become the world's foremost provider of anti-fraud instruction and intelligence. Our courses, research, conferences, distance learning, and online community are peerless. The present and the future belong to today's up-and-coming generation of fraud fighters. We're helping them make their way forward to meet society's needs.

Closing Thoughts

I was grateful to receive the ACFE's 2005 Cressey Award for a lifetime of achievement in fraud detection and deterrence. I was ACFE Program Director until 2006, when I became president; in

2010, I also became CEO. I was honored to be among *Security Magazine's* Most Influential Security Executives in 2010, and in 2012, 2013, and 2014 to be among *Accounting Today's* 100 Most Influential People in Accounting. I have taught a master's-level course in fraud examination at UT-Austin's McCombs School of Business. Many people are impressed by all that and by my co-founding the ACFE. But I'm happy for them to know me as the man I've always been: Jim from Marshall, Texas.

Throughout the years, three principles in particular have guided me. First, I take responsibility for everything I do. People often judge themselves by their intentions, as if meaning well is as good as doing well. But those depending on you don't care about intentions. They want results.

Second, my life has largely been what I've made of it. If I hadn't taken the reins, planned my future, and made the most of opportunities, I wouldn't be where I am today.

Third, Momma taught me to set my sights on a goal and never give up. And Coach Hartzel instilled in me the belief that it didn't matter how many times I got knocked down. What matters, he said, is how many times I got up and went at it again. These people shaped my thinking; for them, failure was not an option and it isn't for me.

You might remember how in Chapter 9 I described my early childhood and said I was completely happy. Six decades later, I still am. Sure, there've been rough patches along the way. But such things have tended to work themselves out. After all, life's an adventure and challenges keep things interesting.

Abe Lincoln expressed my view best when he said, "You're as happy as you make up your mind to be." It's always worked for me.

POST-SCRIPT

Well, I've been thinking 'bout
All the places we've surfed and danced and
All the faces we've missed, so let's get
Back together and do it again

"Do It Again," The Beach Boys, 1968

ACKNOWLEDGMENTS

Throughout my lifetime, I've had a number of people who supported me and helped me reach the level I am at today, most notably Dr. Joseph T. Wells. I've been fortunate to have so many others who shined the light on the right path and I could not list them all here. To those fine folks, thank you for everything. And last, I'd like to thank Bob Tie for his help with this book.

The adventure continues.

—Jim

INDEX

INDEX

337

INDEX

INDEX

Made in the USA
Coppell, TX
16 January 2024

27737299R00193